Test Yourself

Electronic Devices and Circuits

Eric Donkor, Ph.D.
Electrical and Systems Engineering
University of Connecticut
Storrs, CT

Shakib M. Saria, Ph.D.
Electrical and Systems Engineering
University of Connecticut
Storrs, CT

Contributing Editors

Thomas Hall, M.S.
Northwestern State University of Louisiana
Natchitoches, LA

Nadipuram R. Prasad, Ph.D.
Electrical and Computer Engineering Department
New Mexico State University
Las Cruces, NM

Robert E. Pursley III, M.S.

NTC

NTC LEARNINGWORKS
NTC/Contemporary Publishing Group

Library of Congress Cataloging-in-Publication Data

Electronic devices and circuits / Eric Donkor, Shakib M. Saria ;
contributing editors, Thomas Hall . . . [et al.].
p. cm. — (Test yourself)
ISBN 0-8442-2355-7
1. Electronic circuits—Examinations, questions, etc.
2. Electronic circuits—Examinations—Study guides. 3. Electronic
apparatus and appliances—Examinations, questions, etc.
4. Electronic apparatus and appliances—Examinations—Study guides.
I. Donkor, Eric. II. Saria, Shakib M. III Series: Test yourself
(Lincolnwood, Ill.)
TK7863.E44 1997
621.3815′076—dc21 97-13865
CIP

A *Test Yourself Books, Inc.* **Project**

Published by NTC LearningWorks
A division of NTC/Contemporary Publishing Group, Inc.
4255 West Touhy Avenue, Lincolnwood (Chicago), Illinois 60646-1975 U.S.A.

Printed in the United States of America
International Standard Book Number: 0-8442-2355-7
18 17 16 15 14 13 12 11 10 9 8 7 6 5 4 3 2 1

Contents

Preface iv

How to Use This Book v

1. Diode Circuits 1
2. Bipolar Junction Transistor Biasing Circuits 16
3. Field Effect Transistor Biasing Circuits 30
4. BJT Single-Stage Amplifiers 42
5. FET Single-Stage Amplifiers 55
6. Compound Configurations 65
7. Power Amplifiers 97
8. Operational Amplifiers 116

Preface

This book is intended to be used as a supplementary text for courses in electronic devices and circuits. It illustrates and explains key concepts through problem solving. Each problem has been designed to emphasize an important aspect of the material, and to describe the techniques or methods for analyzing and designing electronic devices and circuits. Therefore, students are encouraged to work through as many problems as they are able in each chapter.

The topics covered include diodes, transistor-circuits (BJTs and FETs), and their applications. Also discussed are amplifier circuits, including single-stage, compound configuration, power, and operational amplifiers. Undergraduate students taking a course in electronic circuits will find this book very helpful in increasing their understanding of the subject matter and in preparing for examinations.

Eric Donkor, Ph.D.
Shakib M. Saria, Ph.D.

How to Use This Book

This "Test Yourself" book is part of a unique series designed to help you improve your test scores on almost any type of examination you will face. Too often, you will study for a test—quiz, midterm, or final—and come away with a score that is lower than anticipated. Why? Because there is no way for you to really know how much you understand a topic until you've taken a test. The *purpose* of the test, after all, is to measure your complete understanding of the material.

The "Test Yourself" series offers you a way to improve your scores and to actually test your knowledge at the time you use this book. Consider each chapter a diagnostic pretest in a specific topic. Answer the questions, check your answers, and then give yourself a grade. Then, and only then, will you know where your strengths and, more important, weaknesses are. Once these areas are identified, you can strategically focus your study on those topics that need additional work.

Each book in this series presents a specific subject in an organized manner, and although each "Test Yourself" chapter may not correspond to exactly the same chapter in your textbook, you should have little difficulty in locating the specific topic you are studying. Written by educators in the field, each book is designed to correspond, as much as possible, to the leading textbooks. This means that you can feel confident in using this book, and that regardless of your textbook, professor, or school, you will be much better prepared for anything you will encounter on your test.

Each chapter has four parts:

Brief Yourself. All chapters contain a brief overview of the topic that is intended to give you a more thorough understanding of the material with which you need to be familiar. Sometimes this information is presented at the beginning of the chapter, and sometimes it flows throughout the chapter, to review your understanding of various *units* within the chapter.

Test Yourself. Each chapter covers a specific topic corresponding to one that you will find in your textbook. Answer the questions, either on a separate page or directly in the book, if there is room.

Check Yourself. Check your answers. Every question is fully answered and explained. These answers will be the key to your increased understanding. If you answered the question incorrectly, read the explanations to *learn* and *understand* the material. You will note that at the end of every answer you will be referred to a specific subtopic within that chapter, so you can focus your studying and prepare more efficiently.

Grade Yourself. At the end of each chapter is a self-diagnostic key. By indicating on this form the numbers of those questions you answered incorrectly, you will have a clear picture of your weak areas.

There are no secrets to test success. Only good preparation can guarantee higher grades. By utilizing this "Test Yourself" book, you will have a better chance of improving your scores and understanding the subject more fully.

Diode Circuits

1

Brief Yourself

The diode is a two-terminal device that allows current to flow in only one direction, referred to as the forward direction. In the forward-bias direction, the current-voltage relationship obeys an exponential law. Only a small amount of current, called reverse saturation current, flows when the diode is reverse-biased. However, for large reverse-biased voltages around the breakdown voltage, the reverse current increases sharply for a small change in reverse-bias voltage. A diode can be designed to operate in any of those three regimes.

For the purpose of circuit analysis, the diode can be replaced with an equivalent circuit which consists of a series combination of a resistor, a built-in voltage, and a switch. The switch is taken to be "ON" if the diode is forward-biased and the applied bias exceeds the built-in voltage. Otherwise, the switch is "OFF." The resistance is determined relative to the operating point of the diode. The built-in voltage depends on the type of semiconductor (silicon, germanium, or gallium arsenide) used to fabricate the diode. Diodes are used in a variety of circuit applications. They are used in half-wave and full-wave rectifier circuits, clipper and clamper circuits, oscillator circuits, and voltage regulator circuits.

Test Yourself

1. The terminal characteristics of a silicon diode are shown in Fig. P1.1. Determine the forward resistance, R_F, and the dynamic resistance, r_{av}, of the diode at the Q-point.

2. The current of a silicon diode is 3mA at 0.7V, and 90mA at 0.8V. What is the saturation current, I_S, and operating temperature of the diode?

3. A 1 kΩ resistor is connected to the positive terminal of a 10-volt d.c. supply. A parallel combination of a Si-diode and a Ge-diode is connected between the other end of the resistor and the negative terminal of the battery so that

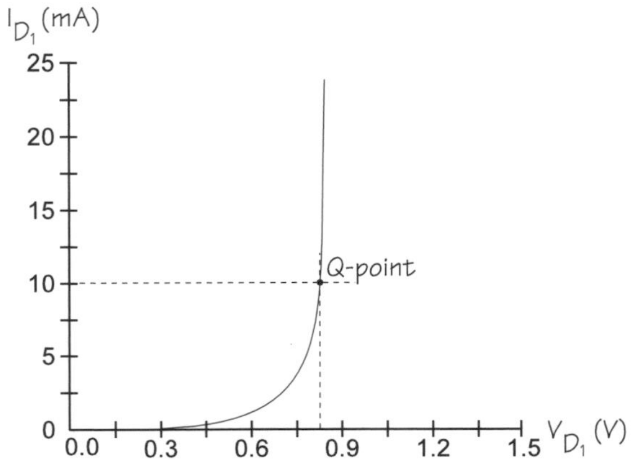

Fig. P1.1

both diodes are forward-biased, as shown in Fig. P1.3. The built-in voltages of the Si-diode and Ge-diode are 0.7V and 0.3V, respectively. What is the voltage measured across each diode?

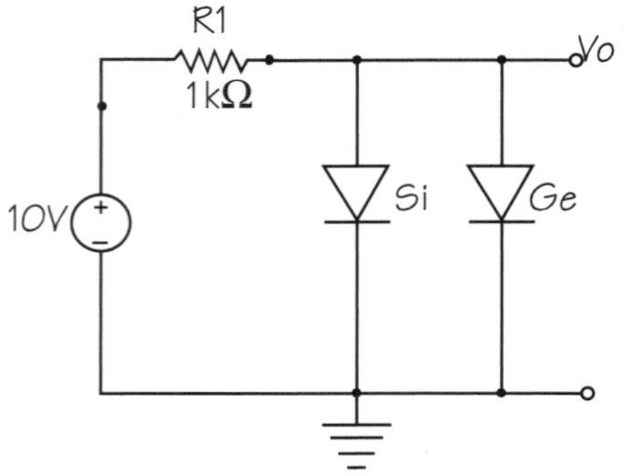

Fig. P1.3

4. The circuit of Fig. P1.4 is designed using identical silicon diodes, with built-in voltage of 0.7V and forward resistance of 10 ohms. Calculate V_0 and the current through each diode.

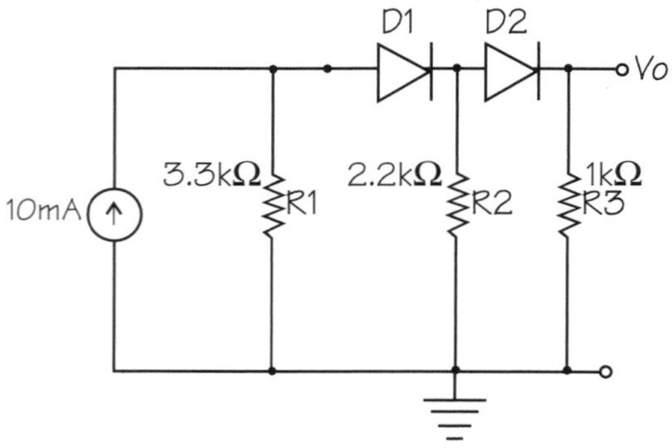

Fig. P1.4

5. Repeat problem 4, with the diodes replaced by Ge-diodes with built-in voltage of 0.3V and forward resistance of 3 ohms.

6. The circuit of Fig. P1.6 is designed with Si diodes with built-in voltage of 0.7V and forward resistance of 4 ohms. Determine the current through the 2.2 kΩ resistor.

7. Determine the average d.c. voltage delivered across the 1 kΩ-load resistor in the full-wave rectifying circuit of Fig. P1.7. Assume the diodes to be ideal.

8. Determine the average d.c. voltage delivered across the 1 kΩ-load resistor in the full-wave rectifying circuit of Fig. P1.7. Assume the

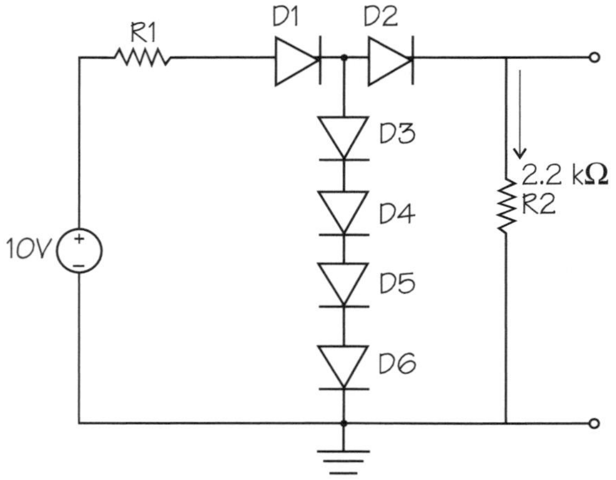

Fig. P1.6

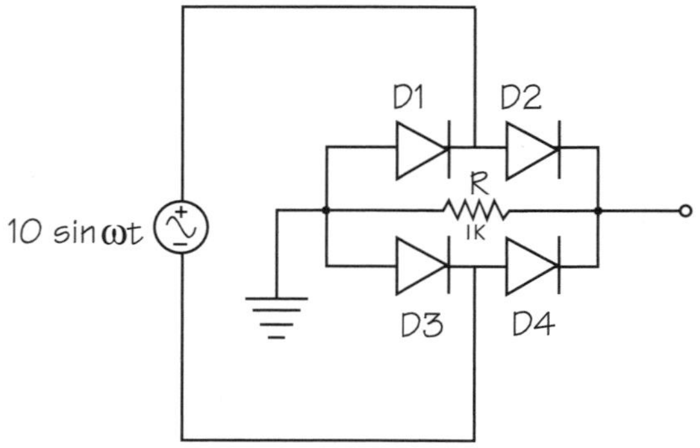

Fig. P1.7

diodes to have a forward resistance, $R_F = 0$, and built-in voltage, $V_{bi} = 0.7V$.

9. Repeat problem 7 if the input signal is replaced by a square wave with peak-to-peak voltage of 10V.

10. Repeat problem 8 if the input signal is replaced by a square wave with a peak-to-peak voltage of 10V.

11. A full-wave rectifying circuit, such as shown in Fig. P1.7, is designed with ideal diodes and has as its input voltage a triangular wave-form defined by:

$$V(t) = \begin{cases} \dfrac{40t}{T}, & 0 \le t \le \dfrac{T}{4} \\ 20\left(1 - \dfrac{2t}{T}\right), & \dfrac{T}{4} \le t \le \dfrac{3T}{4} \\ 40\left(\dfrac{t}{T} - 1\right), & \dfrac{3T}{4} \le t \le T \end{cases}$$

Calculate the average d.c. voltage across the load resistor.

12. Repeat problem 11 for a saw-tooth input signal defined by:

$$V(t) = \begin{cases} \dfrac{20t}{T}, & 0 \le t \le \dfrac{T}{2} \\ 20\left(\dfrac{t}{T} - 1\right), & \dfrac{T}{2} \le t \le T \end{cases}$$

13. Repeat problem 7, if the diodes are replaced by Si-diodes with forward resistance of 10 ohms and built-in voltage of 0.7 volts. Also calculate the peak-inverse voltage (PIV) of the diodes.

14. A half-wave rectifying circuit has an average d.c voltage of 10 volts across a load resistance of 2.2 kΩ. The input signal is a sinusoid with frequency 60 Hz. Determine the peak-to-peak voltage of the input signal. Take the diode to be ideal.

15. Sketch the output waveform of the circuit in Fig. P1.15, as a function of time, and determine the average d.c. voltage across the load resistor, R_3. Take the diodes to be ideal.

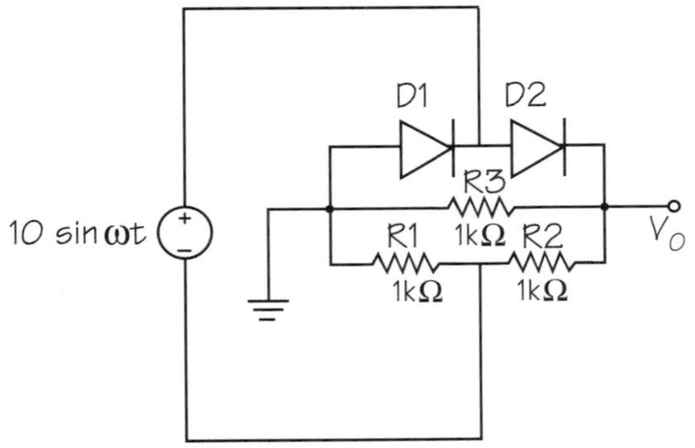

Fig. P1.15

16. Sketch the output waveform of the circuit in Fig. P1.15, as a function of time, and determine the average d.c. voltage across the load resistor, R_3. The diodes have forward resistance of 3 ohms and built-in voltage of 0.6V.

17. Sketch the output waveform of the circuit in Fig. P1.17, as a function of time, and determine the average d.c. voltage across the load resistor, R_3. Assume ideal diodes.

18. Sketch the output waveform of the circuit in Fig. P1.18, as a function of time, and determine the average d.c. voltage across the load resistor, R_3. Take the forward resistance of the diode to be 0 and the built-in voltage as 0.6V.

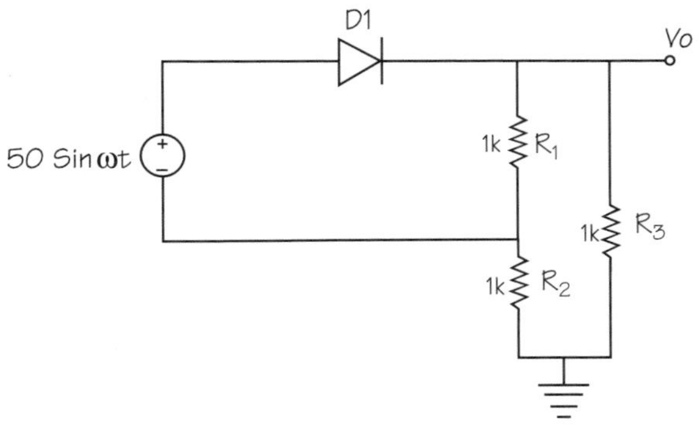

Fig. P1.17

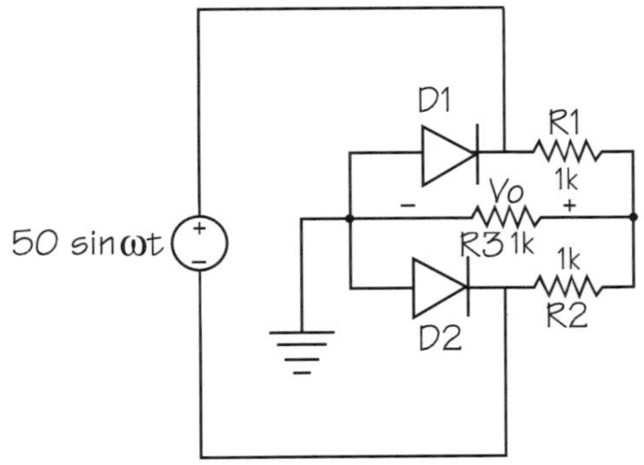

Fig. P1.18

19. Repeat problem 17, if the diode has a forward resistance of 10 ohms and 0 built-in voltage.

20. Repeat problem 18, if the diodes are ideal.

21. Determine the voltage, V_0, and the current through each diode in the circuit of Fig. P1.21. Take $R_F = 0$ and $V_{bi} = 0.7V$ for each diode.

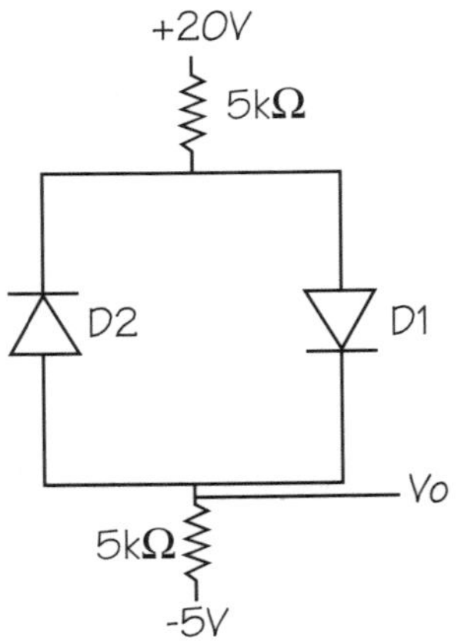

Fig. P1.21

22. Determine the voltage, V_0, and the current through each diode in the circuit of Fig. P1.22. Take $R_F = 0$ and $V_{bi} = 0.7V$ for each diode.

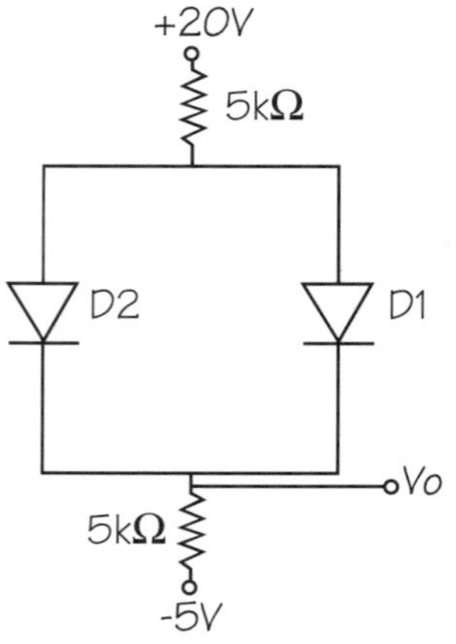

Fig. P1.22

23. Fig. P1.23b is a graphical solution of the circuit in Fig. P1.23a. Label the load line, and determine: a) the diode current, I_D; b) the forward resistance of the diode; c) the load resistance, R_L; d) the output voltage, V_L.

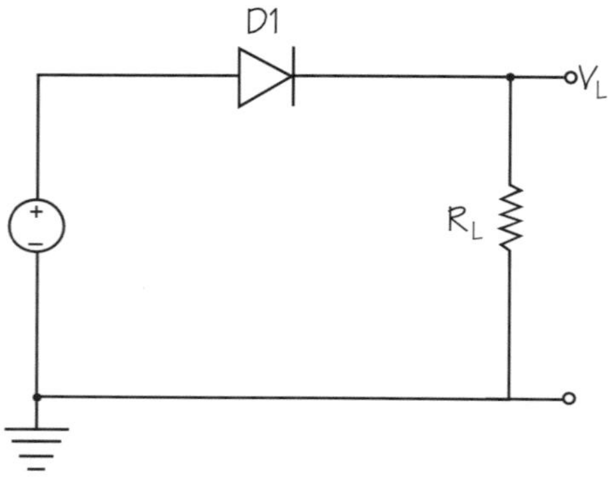

Fig. P1.23a

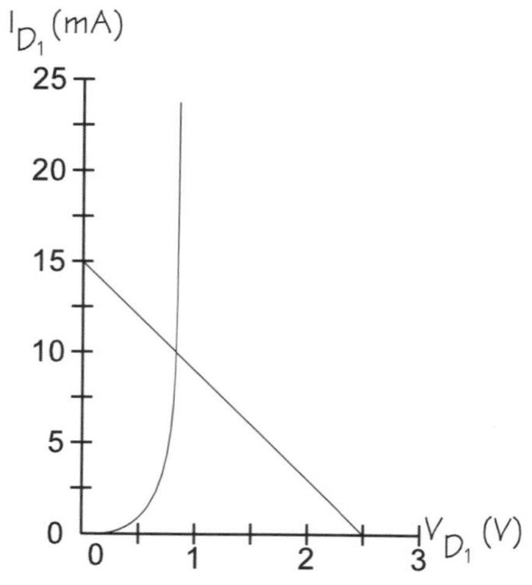

Fig. P1.23b

24. Fig. P1.24b is a graphical solution to the circuit of Fig. P1.24a. Label the load line, and determine: a) the diode current, I_D; b) the load resistance, R_L; c) the output voltage, V_L.

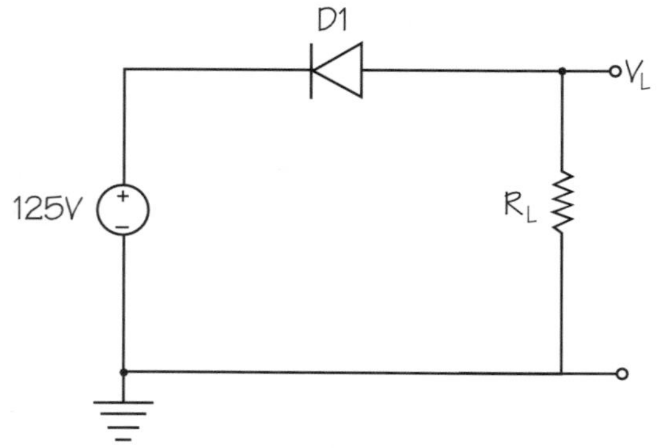

Fig. P1.24a

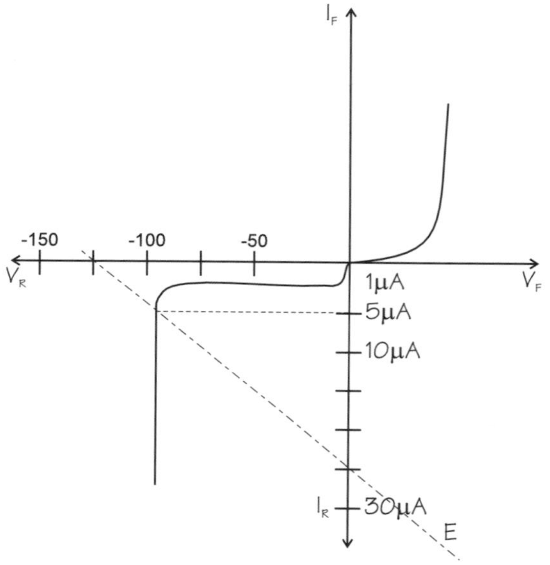

Fig. P1.24b

25. Identify the circuit of Fig. P1.25 and sketch, on the same graph, input and output voltages as functions of time. Take the diodes to be ideal.

26. Identify the circuit of Fig. P1.26 and sketch, on the same graph, the input and output voltages as functions of time. Take the diodes to be ideal.

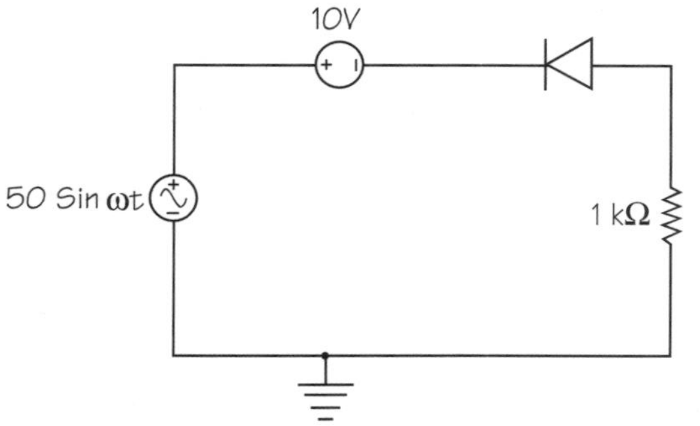

Fig. P1.25

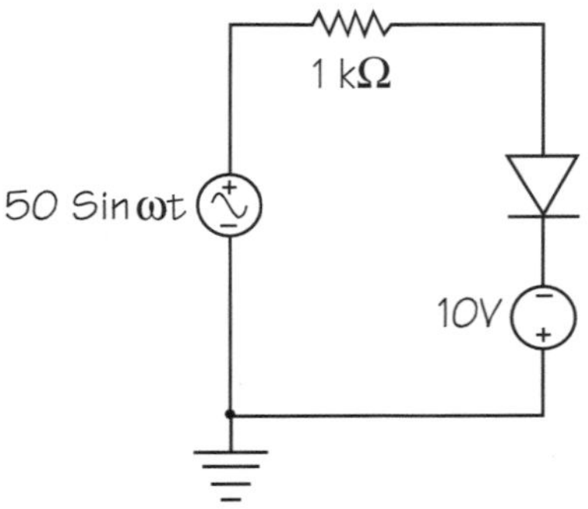

Fig. P1.26

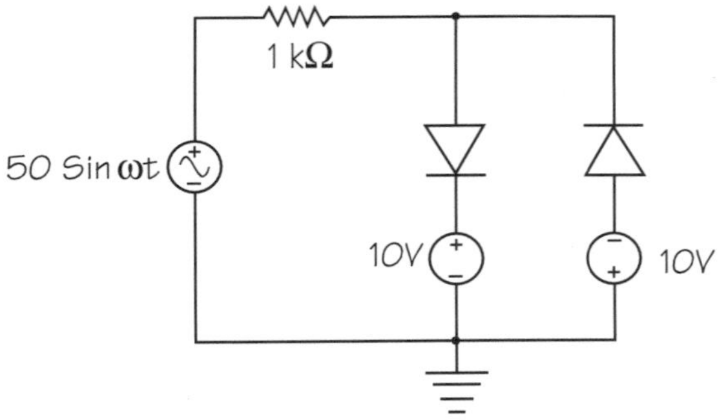

Fig. P1.27

27. Identify the circuit of Fig. P1.27 and sketch, on the same graph, the input and output voltages as functions of time. Take the diodes to be ideal.

28. Identify the circuit of Fig. P1.28 and sketch, on the same graph, the input and output voltages as functions of time. Take the diodes to be ideal.

29. Design, using ideal diodes, a clamper circuit that can provide a +2 V clamped level to a square wave input signal having peak-to-peak voltage of 10 volts and a frequency of $\omega = 10$ rad/sec. Explain the choice of component values. Calculate and compare the voltage swing of the input and clamped signals.

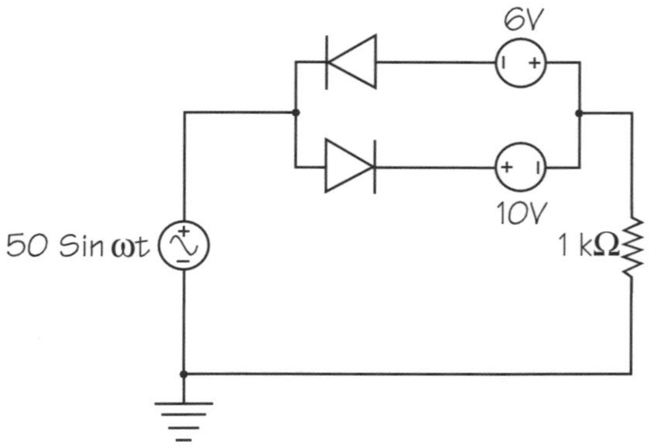

Fig. P1.28

30. A zener diode is used in a voltage-regulator circuit. The diode has a reverse breakdown voltage, $V_Z = 6.1$ V, and a current rating of 500 mA. Calculate the power dissipated by the diode, and the resistance of the zener diode at 500mA.

31. A circuit consists of a series connection of a 15-volt d.c. supply, a resistor, R = 10 ohms, and a zener diode. The reverse breakdown voltage of the zener is 8.2 V, and has a power rating of 6 W. A load resistor, $R_L = 100$ ohms, is connected parallel with the zener. Determine the voltage across the load, and the diode current.

32. The fixed-load resistor in the circuit of problem 31 is replaced by a variable resistor. Find the range of R_L that will maintain an output-regulated voltage of 8.2 V if the diode resistance is 100 ohms.

33. Fig. P1.33b is a graphical solution to the circuit of Fig P1.33a. Determine the tunnel-diode resistance at the Q-point, and the values of R_1 and R_2.

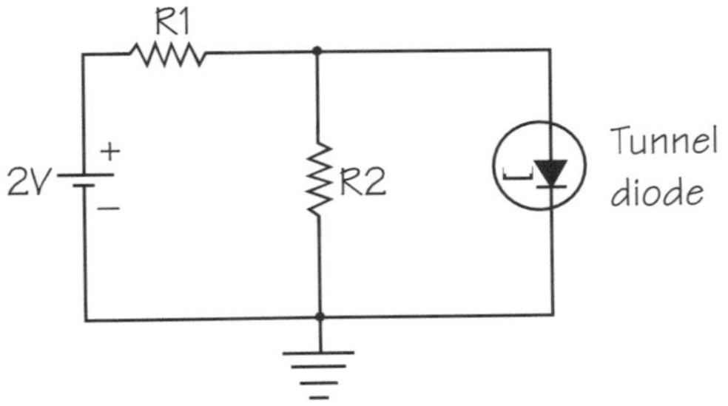

Fig. P1.33a

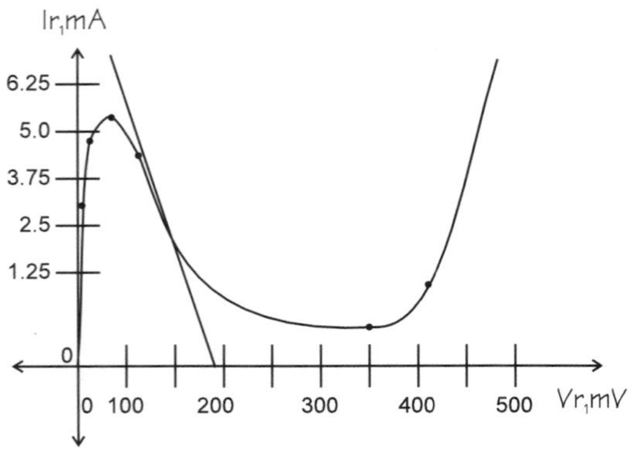

Fig. P1.33b

34. Fig. P1.34 shows a series circuit of 20V d.c. supply, a current-limiting resistor, R_S, and a zener diode with $V_z = 10$ V. The switch, S, connects the load resistor parallel with the diode at position 1 but disconnects the load resistor from the circuit at position 2. The power dissipated by the zener is 50mW and 500mW when the load resistor is respectively connected and disconnected from the circuit. Determine R_s and R_L.

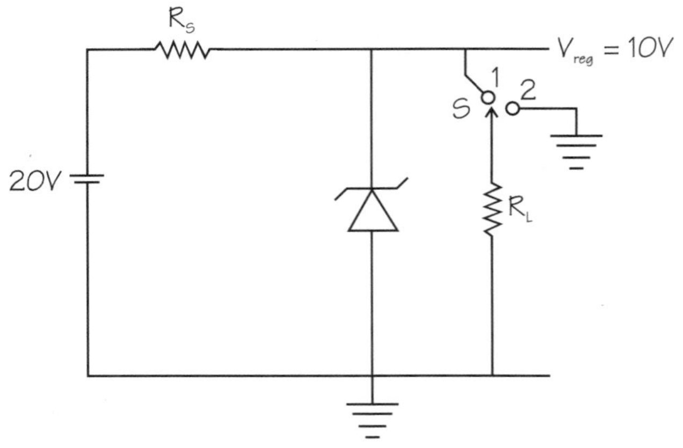

Fig. P1.34

35. A 6.1V zener diode has a maximum junction temperature $T_j = 200^o$ C, and a thermal resistance of $\theta_R = 10^o$ C/W. It is supplied with a heat sink of thermal resistance $\theta_{RS} = 15^o$ C/W. If the ambient temperature $T_A = 35^o$ C, what is the maximum allowable zener current?

36. A 10-V zener diode used in a voltage-regulator circuit is specified to operate in the current range $5mA \leq I_z \leq 50mA$, and has diode resistance of 3 ohms. What is the percent regulation of the circuit?

Check Yourself

1. Determine the voltage, V_Q, and current, I_Q, at the Q-point. The forward resistance, R_F, and the dynamic resistance, r_{av}, are:

$$R_F = \frac{V_Q}{I_Q} = \frac{.8V}{10mA} = 80\Omega; \qquad r_{av} = \frac{26mV}{I_Q(mA)} = 2.6\Omega$$

(Diode characteristics)

2. The diode equation is $I_D = I_0[\exp(V_D/V_T) - 1]$; $V_T = KT/q$. Then:

$$\frac{I_D(90mA)}{I_D(3mA)} \cong \frac{I_0(e^{.8/V_T})}{I_0(e^{.7/V_T})} \Rightarrow V_T = .03 \Rightarrow T = 67°C$$

$$I_0 = \frac{90mA}{(e^{.8/.03} - 1)} = 2.36 \times 10^{-13}A$$

(Diode characteristics)

3. Since the Ge-diode has a smaller built-in voltage, it turns on before the Si-diode, resulting in an output voltage maintained at 0.3 V. This voltage is below the minimum value (of 0.7V) required to turn on the Si-diode. Thus, $V_0 = V_{Ge} = V_{SI} = 0.3$ V. **(Parallel diode circuits)**

4. A Thevenin's equivalent circuit for the 10mA source and the 3.3 kΩ resistor is:
$V_{TH} = IR = (3.3\ k\Omega)(10mA) = 33$ V; $R_{TH} = 3.3\ k\Omega$.

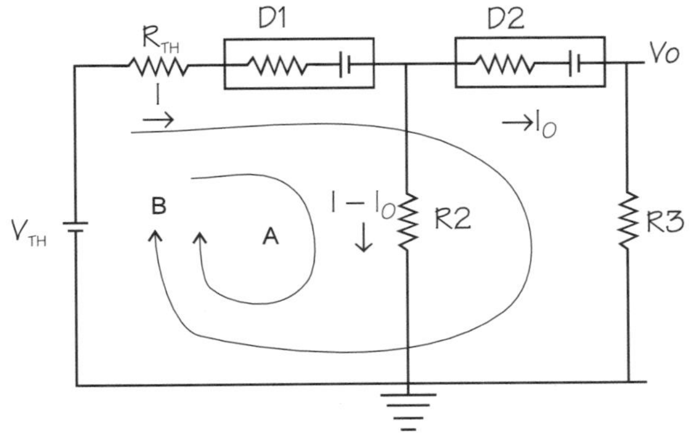

Fig. S1.4

Write KVL for any two circuit loops and solve the resulting simultaneous equation for I_0, and I.

KVL for loop A: $33V - 0.7V - (3.3\ k\Omega + 0.01\ k\Omega)I - 2.2\ k\Omega(I - I_0) = 0$
KVL for loop B: $33V - 1.4V - (3.3\ k\Omega + 0.01\ k\Omega)I - (0.01\ k\Omega + 1.1\ k\Omega)I_0 = 0$

Solution of the two simultaneous equations above gives $I_0 = 5.01mA$, $I = 7.86mA$.
Therefore, $I_{D1} = I = 5.23mA$; $I_{D2} = I - I_0 = 2.72$ mA and $V_0 = I_0R_3 = 5.23V$. **(Series diode circuits)**

5. $I_{D1} = 8.15$ mA; $I_{D2} = 5.51mA$. **(Series diode circuits)**

6. Replace the diodes in Fig. P6.1 by their equivalent circuit, as shown in the circuit of Fig. S1.6. Following a procedure as outlined for problem 4, determine the current, I_0, and the voltage required.

$I_0 = 1mA \qquad V_{2.2\ k\Omega} = (1mA)\ (2.2\ k\Omega) = 2.2$ V

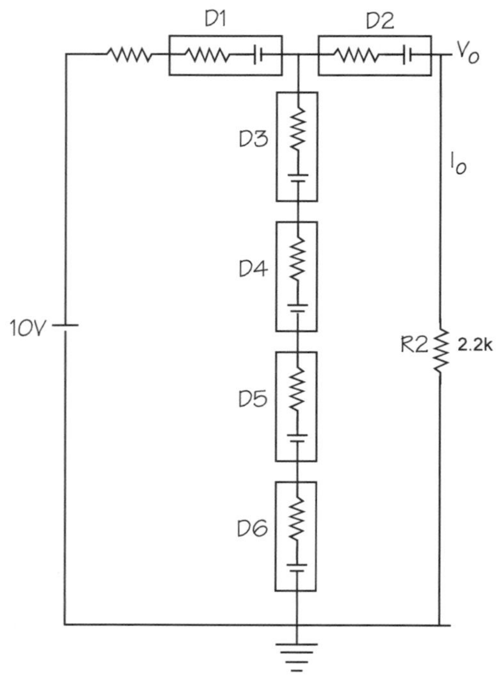

Fig. S1.6

(Series-parallel diode circuits)

7. The average d.c. voltage for a sinusoidal input signal, rectified by a full-wave rectifier circuit designed with ideal diodes is $V_{dc} = 0.636\ V_{max}$. For $V_{max} = 10V$, $V_{dc} = 0.636 \times 10\ V = 6.36\ V$.

   Note: If $V_{max} < V_{bi}$, $V_{dc} = 0\ V$. **(Rectifier circuits)**

8. The average d.c. voltage for a sinusoidal input signal, $V(t) = V_{max}\sin \omega t$, rectified by a full-wave rectifier circuit designed with ideal diodes with a given built-in voltage, V_{bi}, and forward resistance $R_F = 0$ is $V_{dc} = 0.636\ (V_{max} - 2V_{bi})$.

   $$V_{dc} = 0.636\ (V_{max} - 2V_{bi}) = 0.636 \times (10 - 2 \times 0.7)V = 5.47\ V.$$

   Note: If $V_{max} < 2V_{bi}$, $V_{dc} = 0\ V$. **(Rectifier circuits)**

9. The average d.c. voltage of a square-wave with a given peak-to-peak voltage rectified by a full-wave rectifier circuit using ideal diodes is $V_{dc} = V_{peak.}$ Therefore, $V_{dc} = 10\ V$. **(Rectifier circuits)**

10. The average d.c. voltage of a square-wave with a given peak-to-peak voltage rectified by a full-wave rectifier circuit using diodes with a given built-in voltage, V_{bi}, $R_F = 0$ is $V_{dc} = V_{peak}$, for $V_{peak} > V_{bi}$. Therefore, $V_{dc} = 10\ V$. **(Rectifier circuits)**

11. The average d.c. is, by definition,

   $$V_{dc} = \frac{1}{T}\int_0^T V_{out}(t)dt$$

   Lengthy algebra to evaluate the integral can be circumvented in this problem by recognizing that it is equivalent to finding the sum of the areas of the two (identical) triangles of the output waveform.

   $$V_{dc} = 2/T[(1/2)\text{base} \times \text{height}) = (1/T)[(T/2) \times 10)]\ V = 5\ V$$

   (Rectifier circuits)

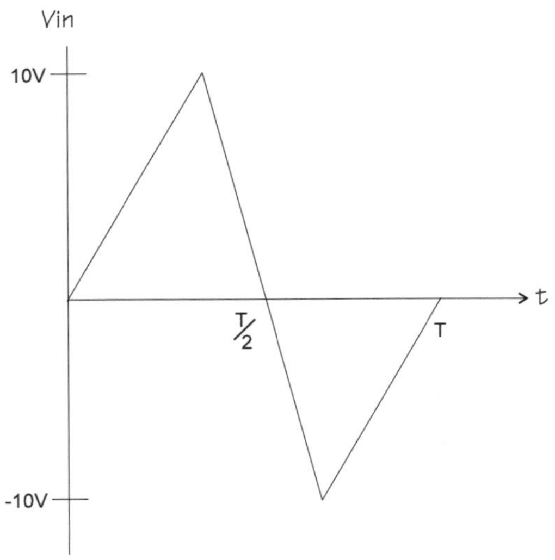

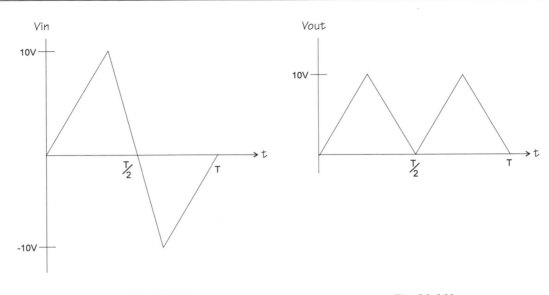

Fig. S1.11a

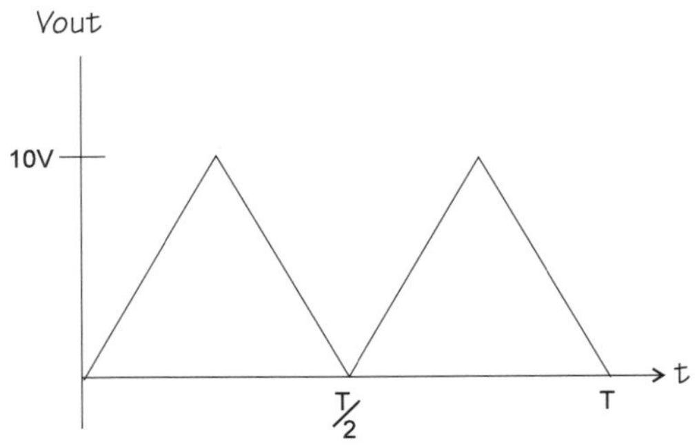

Fig S1.11b

12. $V_{dc} = 5$ V. **(Rectifier circuits)**

13. The average d.c. voltage is:

$$V_{dc} = \frac{2}{T}\int_{t_1}^{t_2} V_{out}(t)dt$$

Note that the integration should be evaluated over a full period. However, because of the symmetry of the output waveform of the positive and negative half-cycles; an identical result is obtained by doubling the integration over one-half cycle. Also notice that, in general, the respective times for the lower and upper limits are not equal to 0 and T_2. To calculate, say, t_1 (lower limit), write KVL for the equivalent circuit.

$0 = V_{in} - 2V_{bi} - V_{out}$. At t_1, $V_{out} = 0$ leading to:

$$1.4 = 10 \sin\frac{2\pi t_1}{T} \Rightarrow \frac{2\pi t_1}{T} = \frac{1.4}{10} \Rightarrow t_1 = \frac{T}{2\pi}\sin^{-1}(0.14).$$

From the symmetry of the problem we write:

$$t_2 = \frac{T}{2} - t_1$$

$$V_{dc} = \frac{2}{T}\int_{t_1}^{t_2} V_{out}(t)dt = \frac{2}{T}\int_{t_1}^{t_2} I_L dt = \frac{2}{T}\int_{t_1}^{t_2}\left(\frac{V_{in} - 2V_{bi}}{R_L + 2R_F}\right)R_L dt$$

The current expression was obtained from the equation for the KVL of the circuit where $V_{out} = I_L R_L$.

$$V_{dc} = \frac{2}{T}\int_{t_1}^{t_2}\left(\frac{1K}{1K + 2(0.01K)}\right)\left(10 \sin\frac{2\pi}{T}t - 1.4\right)dt$$

Evaluation of the integral with the appropriate limits gives:

$V_{dc} = 4.92V$; $PIV = 2V_{in}(max) = 2(10) = 20V$. **(Rectifier circuits)**

14. $V_{0-p} = 10/.318 = 31.4$ Volts; $V_{p-p} = 2 \times V_{0-p} = 62.8$ V. **(Rectifier circuits)**

15. $V_{dc} = (0.636)(25) = 15.9$ V. **(Rectifier circuits)**

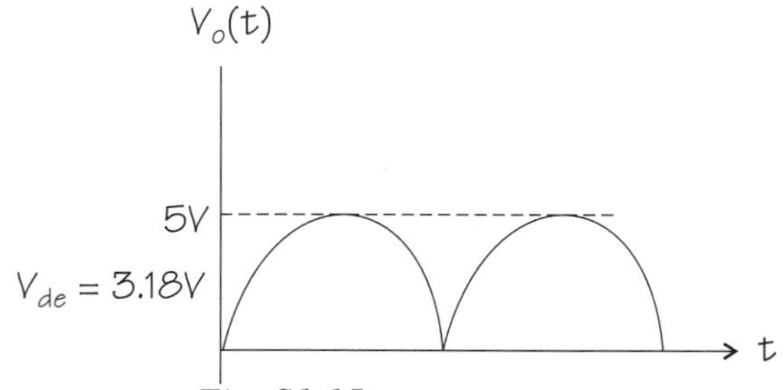

Fig. S1.15a

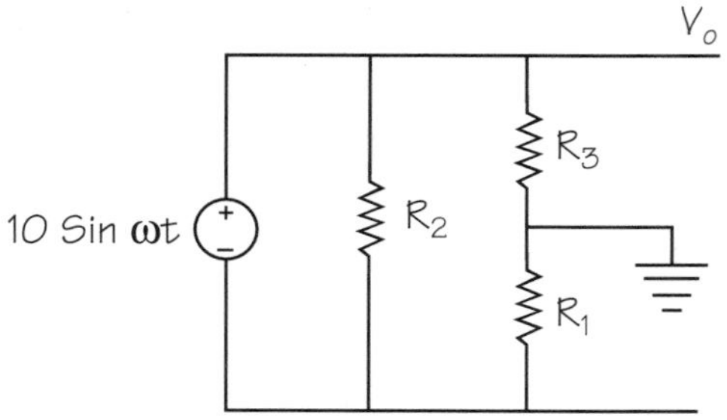

Fig. S1.15b

16. $V_{dc} = (1/2)(.636)(V_{max} - V_{bi}) = 15.7V$. **(Rectifier circuits)**

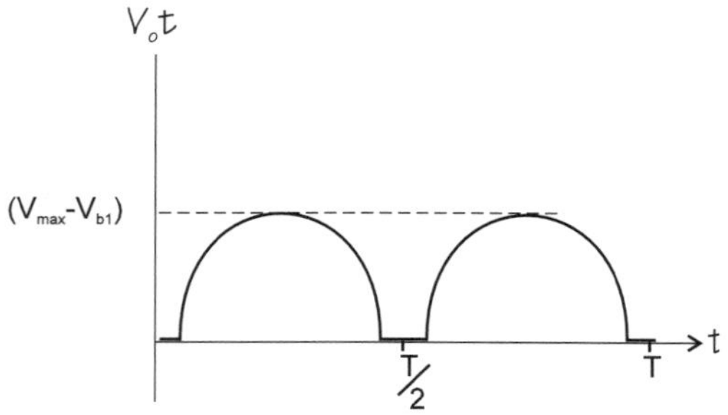

Fig. S1.16a

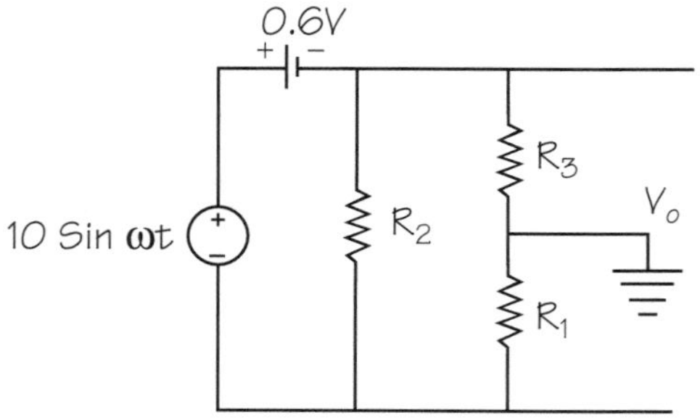

Fig. S1.16b

17. $V_{dc} = .318\,(25V) = 7.95V$. **(Rectifier circuits)**

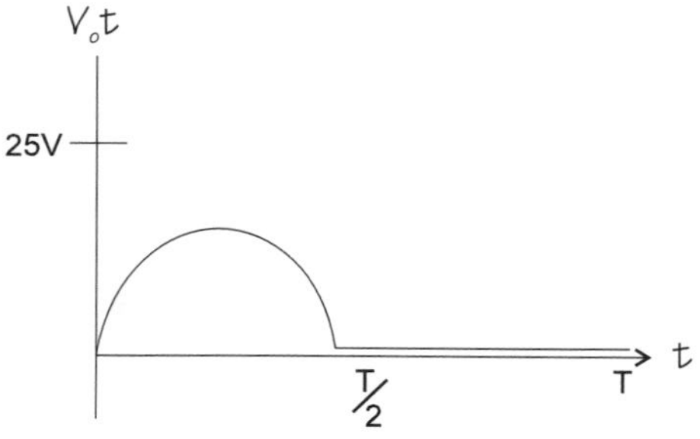

Fig. S1.17

18. $$V_{Lmax} = \frac{1k//1k}{1k//1k + 1k}(50 - V_{bi}) = \frac{1}{3}(50 - .6) = 16.47.$$
$$V_{dc} = 0.636V_{Lmax} = (0.636)16.47V = 10.47V.$$

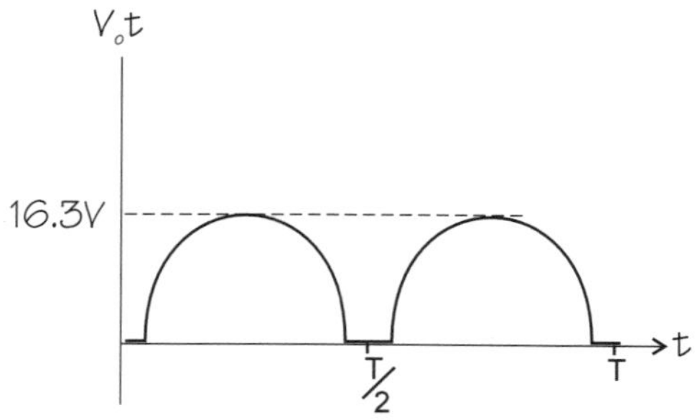

Fig. S18.1

(Rectifier circuits)

19. $$V_{dc} = \frac{1}{2}\frac{1K}{1K + 0.01K}(.318)(50) = 7.87V.$$ **(Rectifier circuits)**

20. $$V_{dc} = \frac{1K//1K}{1K + 1K//1K}(0.636)(50)V = 10.6V.$$ **(Rectifier circuits)**

21. Diode D1 is "ON" but D2 is "OFF."

$$I_{D2} = 0, \quad I_{D1} = \frac{20V + 5V - 0.7V}{5K + 5K} = 2.43mA$$

$V_0 = 25 - 0.7V - (2.43mA)(5K) = 12.15V.$ **(Parallel diode circuits)**

22. $$I_D = \frac{20V + 5V - 0.7V}{10K} = 2.43mA$$

$$I_{D1} = I_{D2} = \frac{1_D}{2} = 1.22mA.$$ **(Parallel diode circuits)**

23. a) $I_D = 10.9mA$

b) $R_F = \frac{.75V}{10.9mA} = 68.8\Omega$; c) $R_L = \frac{2.5V}{15mA} = 166.7\Omega$;

d) $V_L = I_L R_L = (166.7\Omega)(10.9mA) = 1.82V.$ **(Graphical method for diode circuits)**

24. a) $I_D = 5\mu A$ b) $R_L = 125V/5\mu A = 2.5\ M\Omega$; c) $V_L = I_L R_L = (5\mu A)(2.5\ M\Omega) = 12.5V$ **(Graphical method for diode circuits)**

25. a) Biased series clipper

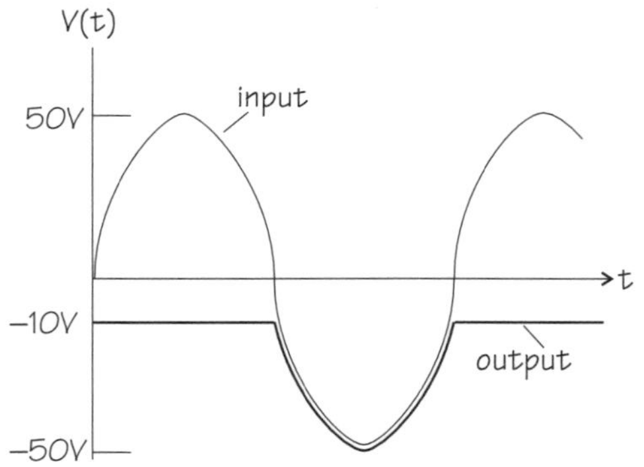

Fig. S1.25

(Biased series clipper)

26. a) Biased parallel clipper

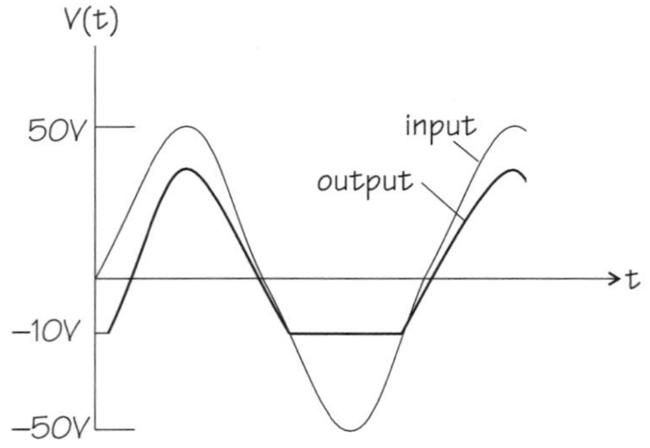

Fig. S1.26

(Biased parallel clipper)

27. a) Biased parallel clipper

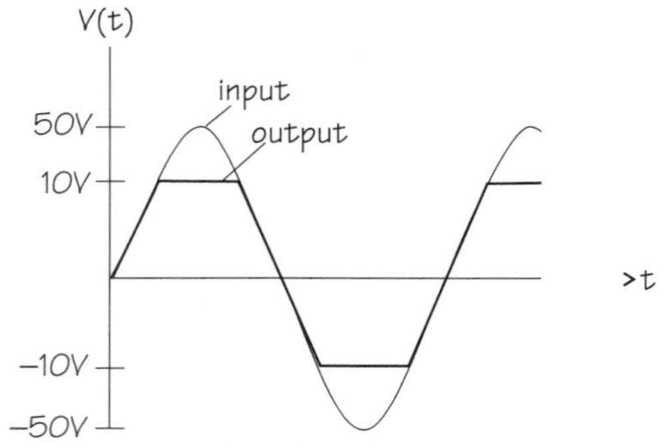

Fig. S1.27

(Biased parallel clipper)

28. a) Biased series clipper

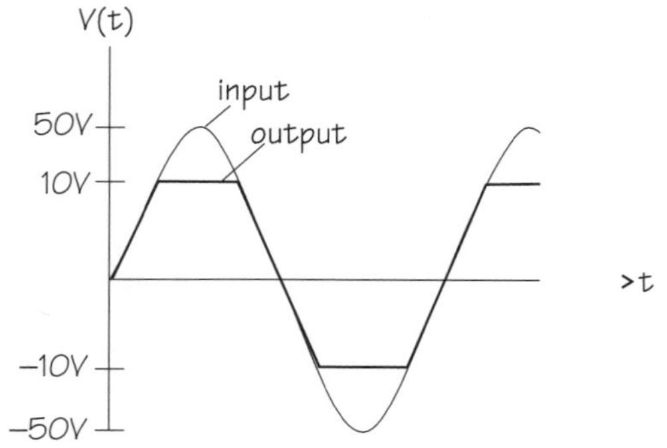

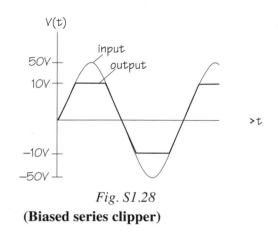

Fig. S1.28

(Biased series clipper)

29. The condition for the proper operation of a clamper circuit is that the discharge time of the capacitor should be far greater than the period of the input signal.

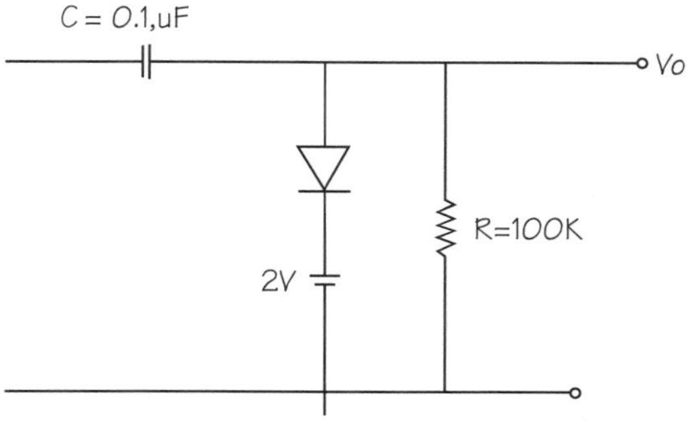

Fig. S1.29

$$T = \frac{2\pi}{\omega} = \frac{2\pi}{10kHz} = 0.6ms$$; choose t = 10ms and R = 100K. Then C = 0.1μF.

(Clamper circuit)

30. $P_Z = I_Z V_Z = (6.1V)(500mA) = 3.05$ W. **(Zener diode)**

31. a) $V_L = V_Z = 8.2V$; b) $I_Z = I - I_L = (15 - 8.2)/50 - 8.2/100 = 54$ mA. **(Zener diode)**

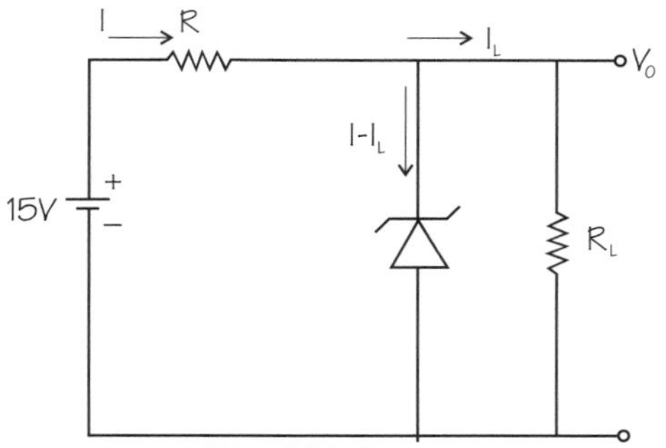

Fig. S31.1

(Zener diode)

32. $$R_{Lmin} = \frac{RV_z}{V_{in} - V_z} = \frac{10 \times 8.2}{15 - 8.2}\Omega = 12\ \Omega.$$

$$R_{Lmax} = \frac{V_L}{I_{Lmin}}$$, where $I_{Lmin} = I - I_{zmax}$; $I = \frac{V_{in} - V_z}{R} = \frac{15V - 8V}{10\Omega} = 680mA$.

$$I_{zmax} = \frac{P_z}{V_z} = \frac{6W}{8.2V} = 731.7mA;\ I_{Lmin} = 731.7mA - 680mA = 51.7mA;\ R_{Lmax} = \frac{8.2V}{51.7mA} = 159\Omega.$$

(Zener diode)

33. Draw a tangent line to the I-V characteristics at the operating point. The slope of this line gives the resistance of the diode, and it is given by:

$$r = \frac{225V - 0V}{0mA - 7mA} = -32\Omega,$$

Also, calculate the load resistance using the load line as $R_L = (175V\text{-}130V)/3.125$ mA = 14.4 ohms.

The Thevenin equivalent circuit of the input configuration is:

$E_T = I_F R_T + V_F = (3.13\text{mA})(14.4\Omega) + 130\text{mV} = 175\text{mV}.$

$R_T = 14.4\Omega = R_1//R_2;\ \ E_T = 175\text{mV} = \dfrac{R_2}{R_1 + R_2} V_{in}.$

Solve the simultaneous equation above involving R_1 and R_2 to get:

$R_1 = 164.5\Omega$, $R_2 = 15.8\Omega$. **(Tunnel diode)**

34. $P_z = 100\text{mW} = I_z V_z = \dfrac{V_{in} - V_Z}{R} V_z = 10\left(\dfrac{20\text{V} - 10\text{V}}{R}\right) \Rightarrow R = 1\Omega.$

$P_z = 50\text{mW} = V_z I_z = 10\text{V}(I - I_L) = 10\text{V}\left(\dfrac{20\text{V} - 10\text{V}}{1\Omega} - \dfrac{10}{R_L}\right); \Rightarrow R_L = 2\Omega.$

(Zener diode)

35. $P_j = \dfrac{T_j - T_A}{\theta_R + \theta_{RS}} = \dfrac{(200 - 35)°\text{C}}{(10 + 15)°\text{C/W}} = 6.6\text{W}.$ **(Zener diode)**

36. Percent regulation is given by $((V_{Zmax} - V_{zmin})/V_{Zmin}) \times 100\%$

$V_{Zmax} = V_{nom} + I_{Zmax} R_Z = 10\text{V} + (3\Omega)(50\text{mA}) = 11.5\text{V}$

$V_{Zmin} = V_{nom} + I_{Zmin} R_Z = 10\text{V} + (3\Omega)(5\text{mA}) = 10.2\text{V}$

% regulation = $((11.5\text{V} - 10.2\text{V})/10.2\text{V}) \times 100\% = 12.75\%$. **(Zener diode)**

Grade Yourself

Circle the numbers of the questions you missed. Then fill in the total incorrect for each topic. If you answered more than three questions incorrectly, you need to focus on that topic. If a topic has less than three questions and you had at least one wrong, we suggest you study that topic also. Read your textbook, a review book, or ask your teacher for help.

Subject: Diode Circuits

Topic	Question Numbers	Number Incorrect
Diode characteristics	1, 2	
Parallel diode circuits	3, 21, 22	
Series diode circuits	4, 5	
Series-parallel double circuits	6	
Rectifier circuits	7, 8, 9, 10, 11, 12, 13, 14, 15, 16, 17, 18, 19, 20	
Graphical method for diode circuits	23, 24	
Biased series clipper	25, 28	
Biased parallel clipper	26, 27	
Clamper circuit	29	
Zener diode	30, 31, 32, 33, 34, 35, 36	

Bipolar Junction Transistor Biasing Circuits

2

Brief Yourself

A BJT single-transistor circuit can be classified as common-base, common-emitter, or common-collector configuration. The current-voltage characteristics of a transistor are unique for these modes of operation. The analysis of any of these circuit configurations has dc and ac components. The dc circuit performance dependence on the transitor bias point, and the dc circuit network. Practical dc biasing circuits are classified into: a) fixed-biasing; b) voltage-divider biasing; c) voltage-feedback biasing; d) un-bypassed emitter-resistor biasing; e) bypassed emitter-resistor biasing; e) beta-independent biasing.

Analysis of BJT dc biasing circuits entails writing equations for the input and output circuits and solving for the desired circuit parameters. The current transfer relationship, such as $I_C = h_{fe}I_B$, for the common emitter configuration and the relationship between terminal currents, $I_E = I_B + I_C$, are used as necessary in analysing these circuits.

Test Yourself

1.

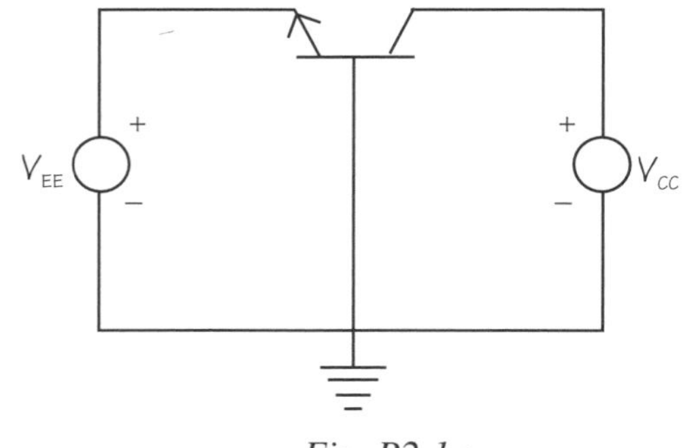

Fig. P2.1a

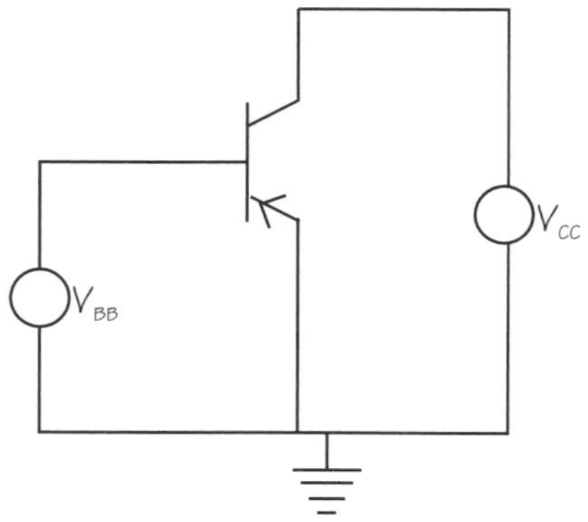

Fig. P2.1b

a) Explain why the circuit configurations in Fig. P2.1a, P2.1b, and P2.1c are referred to as common-base, common-emitter, and common-collector, respectively.

b) Identify the type of transistor in each circuit. Indicate, with arrows, the directions of the collector current, I_C, base current, I_B and emitter current, I_E.

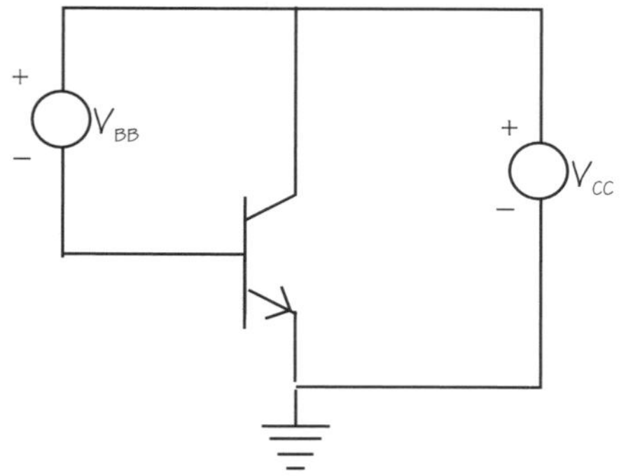

Fig. P2.1c

Input Bias	Output Bias	Mode of Operation
———	forward	inverse
reverse	reverse	
forward	———	saturation
forward	———	linear

Table 2.1

c) Complete the table T2.1 to illustrate the possible biasing scheme and the mode of operation for the transistor in the common-base configuration of Fig. P2.1a.

2. a) Show that the collector current, I_C, in a common-base configuration is related to the base current, I_B, and the collector-base saturation current, I_{CBO}, by:

$$I_C = \frac{\alpha}{1-\alpha} I_B - \frac{I_{CBO}}{1-\alpha}$$

where α is the CB current gain.

b) Deduce the following relationship between the CE current gain β and α,

$$\beta = \frac{\alpha}{1-\alpha}$$

3. Fig. P2.3b shows the output characteristics of the transistor and the load line of Fig. P2.3a. Determine:

a) the Q-point of the transistor.

b) α_{dc}, α_{ac}, β_{dc}, β_{ac}, namely the dc common-base, ac common-base, dc common-emitter and ac common-emitter current gain, respectively.

c) the dc power dissipated by the transistor.

4. A transistor with $\beta = 60$ is used to design the CE circuit shown in Fig. P2.4

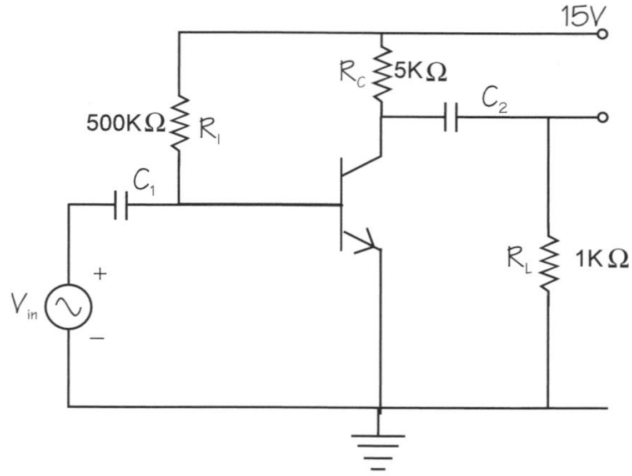

Fig. P2.3a

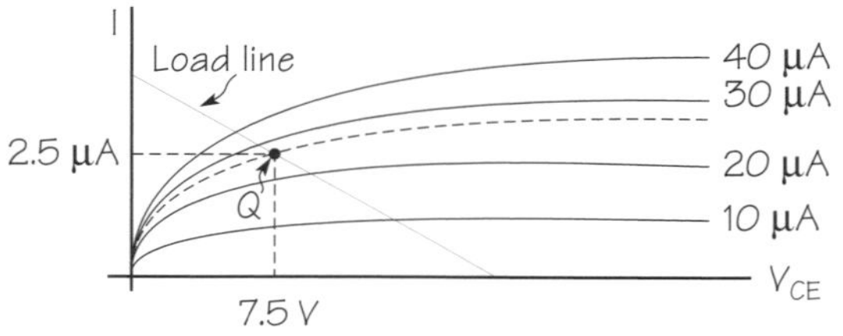

Fig. P2.3b

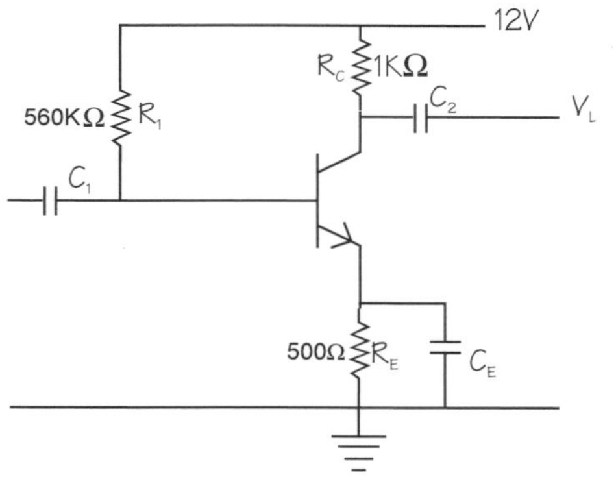

Fig. P2.4

a) Explain the function of the capacitors C_1, C_2, and C_E.

b) Calculate the collector saturation current.

c) Calculate the power dissipated by the transistor.

5. Calculate the maximum symmetrical ouput voltage swing, the a.c. power dissipation, the d.c. power dissipation, and the conversion efficiency of the circuit in Fig. P2.5.

6. The circuit of Fig. P2.6 shows a voltage-divider biasing scheme for a pnp transistor with $\beta = 110$. Switch S in position 1 shorts out

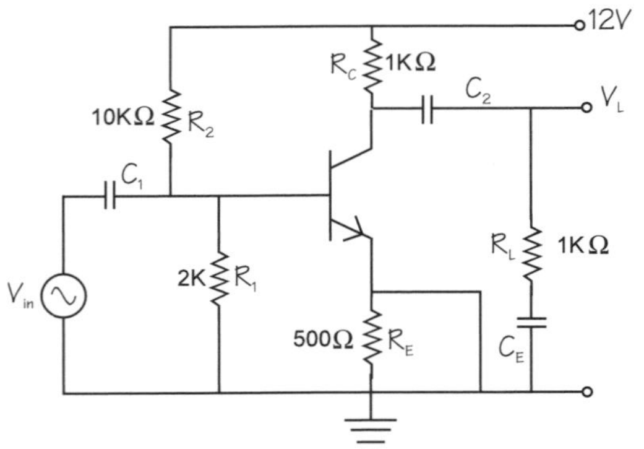

Fig. P2.5

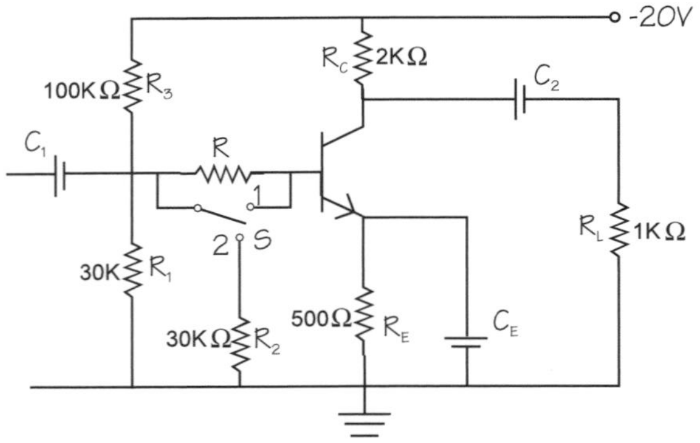

Fig. P2.6

resistor R, but when in position 2, it connects R_1 in parallel with R_2 and also maintains R in circuit. Find the value of R such that the power dissipated by the transistor with the switch in position 1 is half the value when the switch is in position 2.

7. For the circuit of Fig. P2.7 calculate:

   a) the resistance, R_{dc}, in the emitter-collector circuit for dc operation.

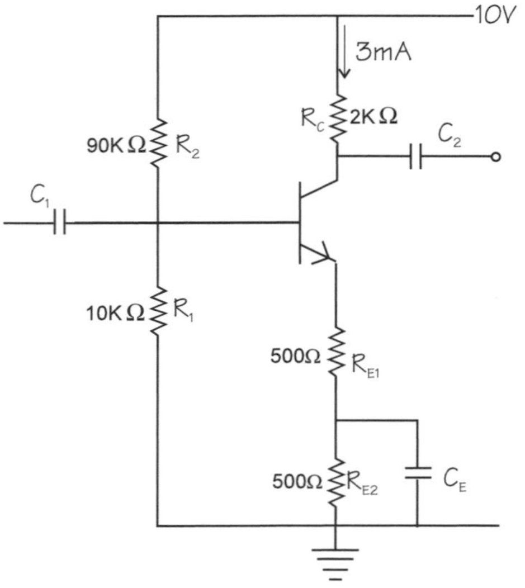

Fig. P2.7

   b) the resistance, R_{ac}, in the emitter-collector circuit for ac operation.

   c) the collector-emitter voltage, V_{CE}.

   d) the current gain.

8. Let the voltage and current of the Q-point for the transistor in Fig. P2.7 be V_{CEQ} and I_{CQ}, respectively. Show what the intercepts of the a.c. load line with the current and voltage axes are.

$$I'_C = \frac{V_{CEQ}}{R_{ac}} + I_{CQ}$$

$$V'_{CC} = V_{CEQ} + I_{CQ}R_{ac}$$

9. Find the coordinates of the Q-point and output voltage swing for the circuit of Fig. P2.9.

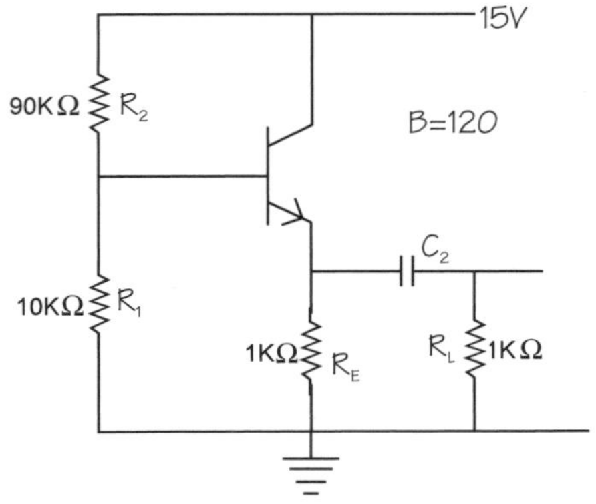

Fig. P2.9

10. a) Calculate the coordinates of the Q-point for the circuit of Fig. P2.10.

    b) What are the slopes of the a.c. and d.c. loadlines?

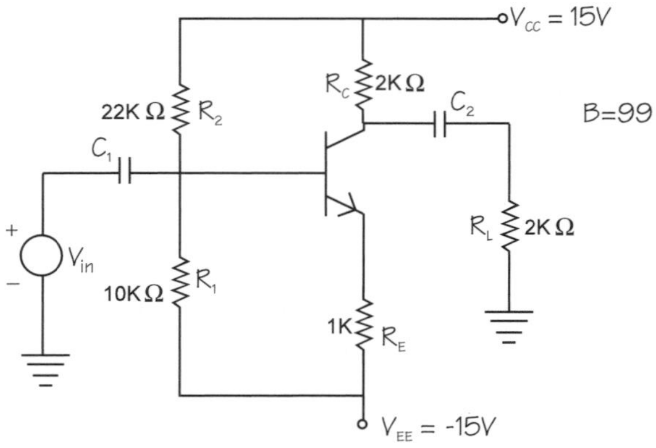

Fig. P2.10

11. The operating conditions of the transistor in Fig. P2.11a are given in Fig. P2.11b. Determine:

a) V_{CC}

b) R_B

c) R_C

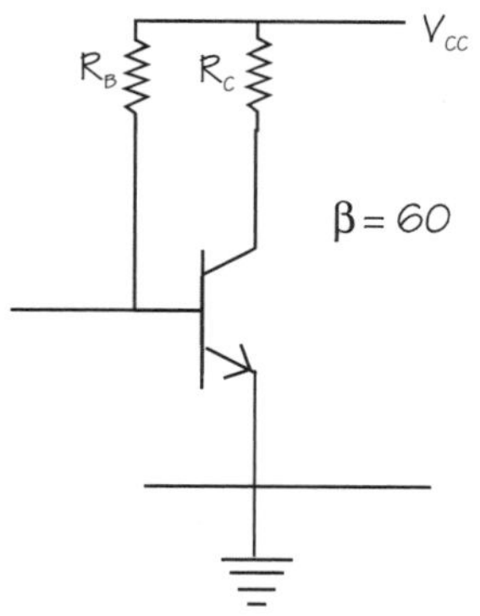

Fig. P2.11a

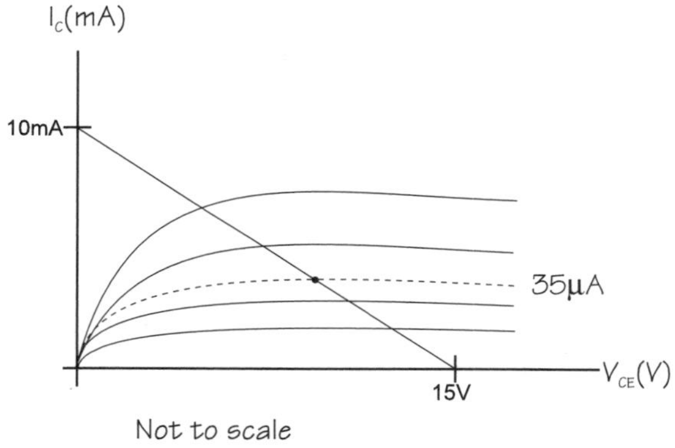

Fig. P2.11b

d) coordinates of the Q-point.

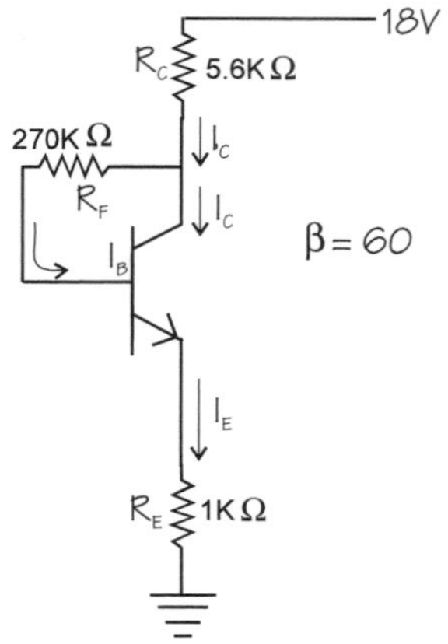

Fig. P2.12

12. Calculate the coordinates of the Q-point for the circuit of Fig. P2.12.

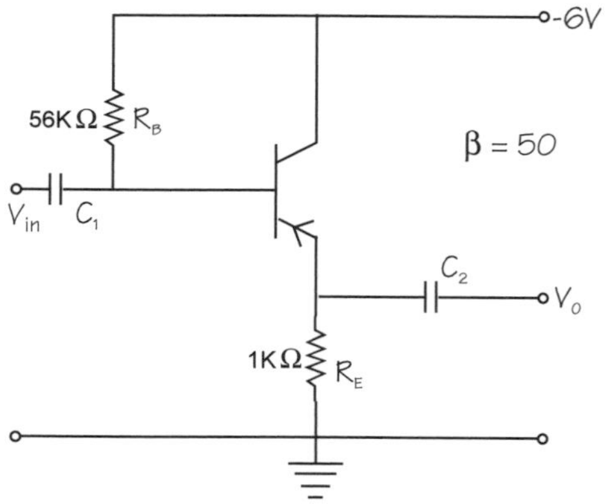

Fig. P2.13

13. Determine the Q-point for the circuit of Fig. P2.13.

14. a) Derive an express for I_C in terms of V_D, V_{EE}, R_1, R_2. R_E. Assume $I_B \cong 0$.

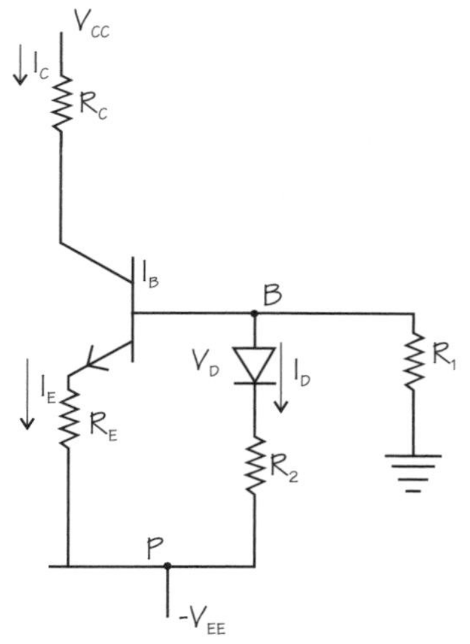

Fig. P2.14

b) Explain how the circuit may be used as a temperature compensator.

15. For the common-base circuit of Fig. P2.15 calculate:

    a) I_{BQ} b) V_{CEQ}

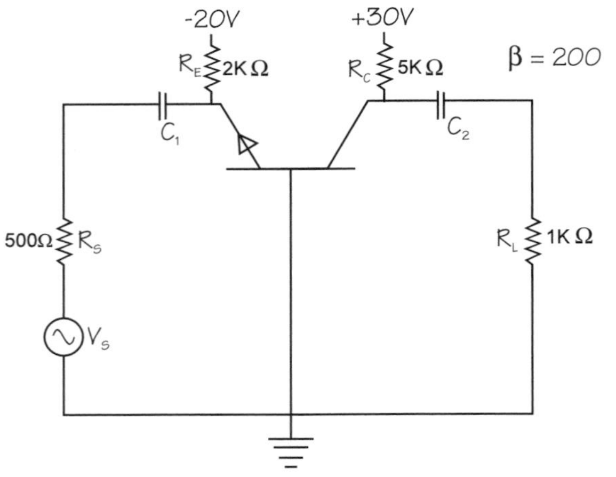

Fig. P2.15

16. Find the coordinates for the Q-point of each transistor in Fig. P2.16

17. Show that for the CE configuration of Fig. P2.16 small variations ΔV_{BE}, Δ_{ICBO}, $\Delta\beta$ and ΔV_{CC} in the base-emitter voltage, collector-base reverse saturation current,

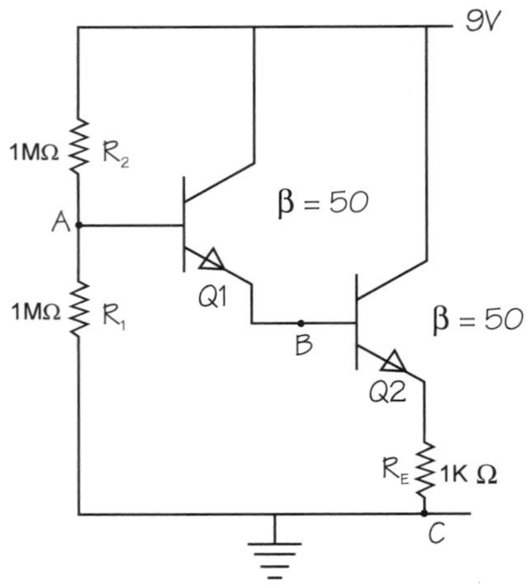

Fig. P2.16

current gain factor and the supply voltage respectively lead to a change in the collector current given by

$$\Delta I_{CQ} = \frac{-\Delta V_{BE}}{R_E + R_B/\beta} + \frac{\beta \Delta I_{CBO}}{1 + \beta R_E/R_\beta} + $$

$$+ \frac{R_B(V_{BB} - V_{BE})}{\beta^2 R_E{}^2} + \frac{\Delta V_C}{R_E + R_C}$$

where the parameters have their usual meaning. Assume $\beta >> 1$, $R_B >> R_E$.

Check Yourself

1. a) In the common-base circuit, the base terminal of the transistor is common to the input and output circuits (see Fig. S2.1a). In the common-emitter circuit, Fig. P2.16, the emitter terminal of the transistor is common to the input and output circuits (see Fig. S2.1b). In the common-collector circuit of Fig. P2.1c, the collector terminal of the transistor is common to the input and output circuits.

b)

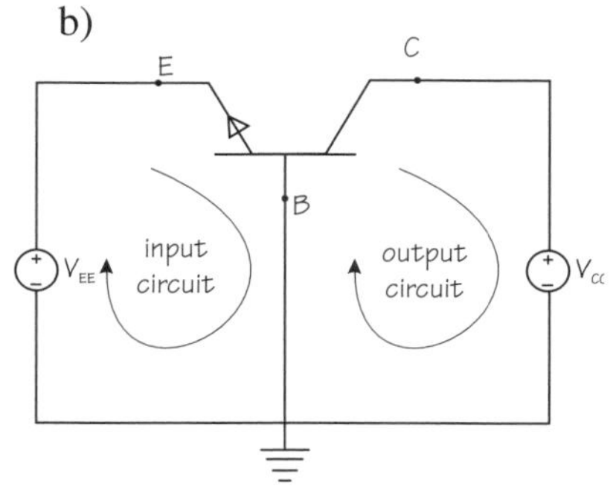

Fig. S2.1a

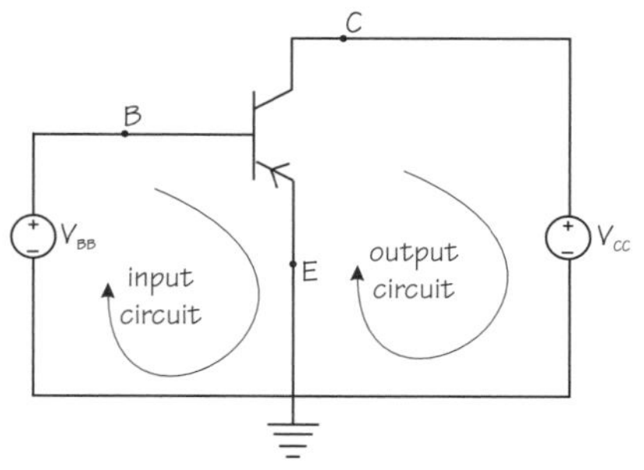

Fig. S2.1b

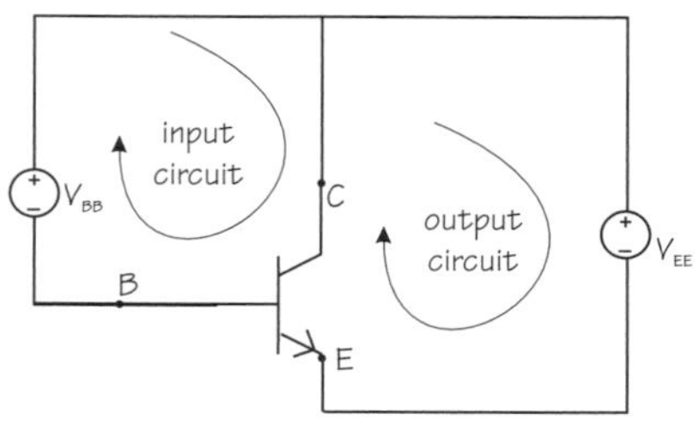

Fig. S2.1c

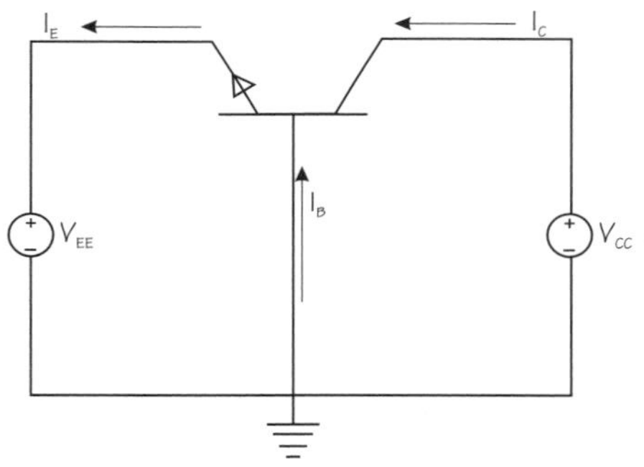

Fig. S2.1d

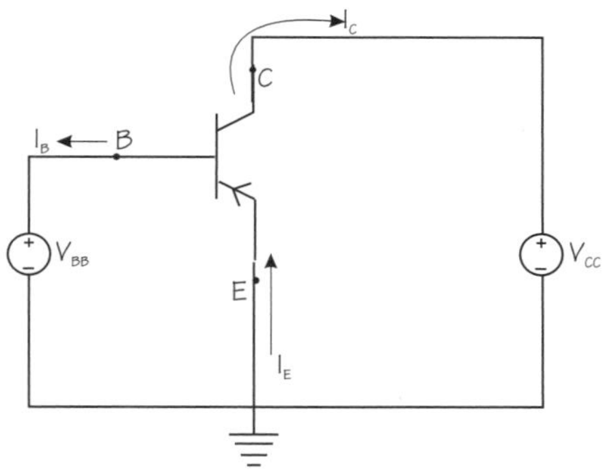

Fig. S2.1e

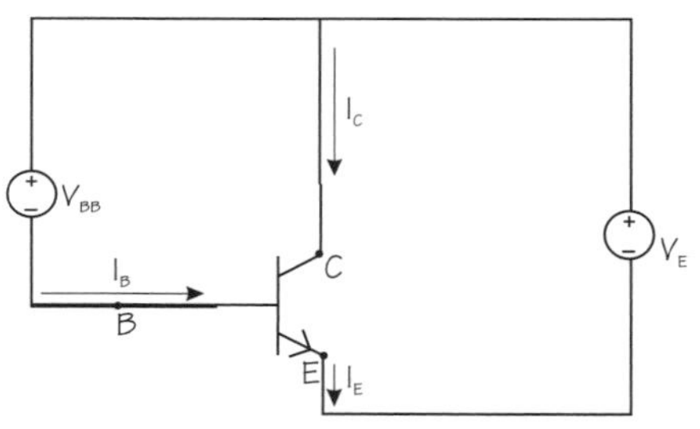

Fig. S2.1f

Input Bias	Output Bias	Mode of Operation
reverse	forward	inverse
reverse	reverse	cut-off
forward	forward	saturation
forward	reverse	linear

Table 2.1

(BJT configurations)

2.

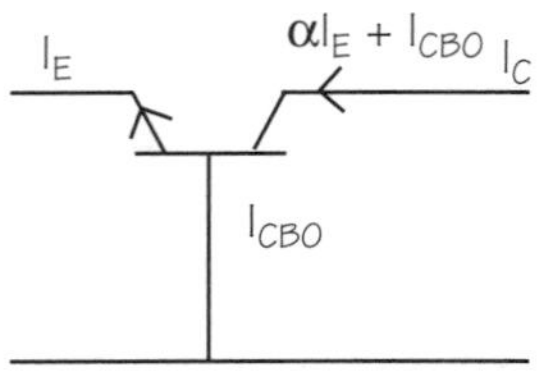

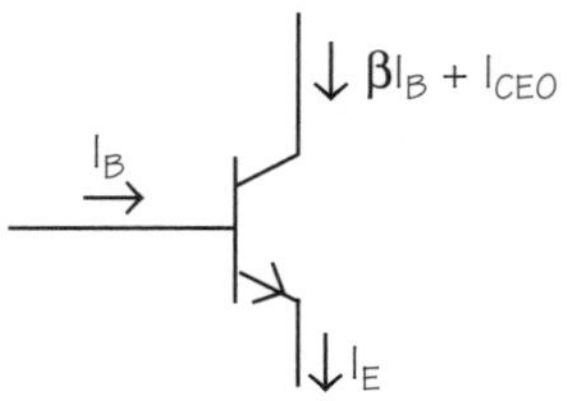

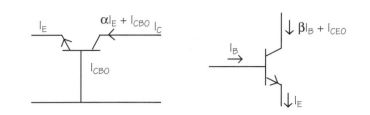

Fig. S2.2a *Fig. S2.2b*

a) From Fig. S2.2a:

$$I_C = \alpha I_E + I_{CBO}$$

but $I_E = I_C + I_B$

then $I_C = \alpha(I_C + I_B) + I_{CBO}$

or $I_C(1 - \alpha) = \alpha I_B + I_{CBO}$

$$I_C = \frac{\alpha}{1-\alpha} I_B + \frac{I_{CBO}}{1-\alpha}$$

b) From Fig. S2.2b:

$$I_C = \beta I_B + I_{CEO}$$

but $I_{CEO} = \dfrac{I_{CBO}}{1-\alpha}$

then $I_C = \beta I_B + \dfrac{I_{CBO}}{1-\alpha}$

Comparing with results from part (a) above, we can write:

$$\beta = \frac{\alpha}{1-\alpha}$$

(Common-base configurations)

3.

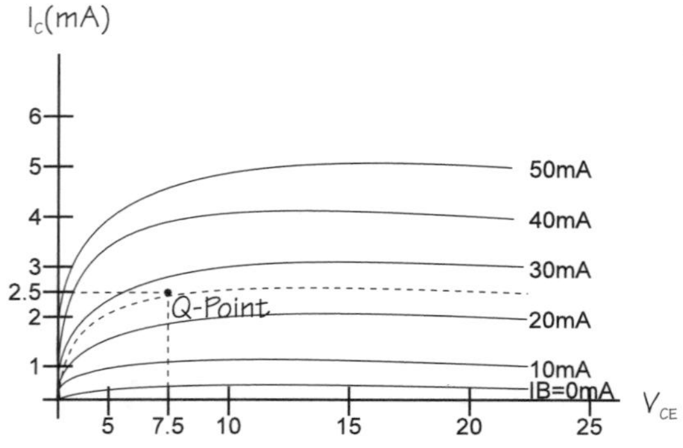

Fig. S2.3

a) the Q-points are:

$$I_{BQ} = 28.61\text{A}, \quad I_{CQ} = 2.5\text{mA}, \quad V_{CEQ} = 7.5\text{V}$$

b) $$I_B = \frac{V_{CC} - V_{BE}}{R_1} = \frac{15V - 0.7V}{500k} = 28.6\mu A$$

$$\beta_{dc} = \frac{I_{CQ}}{I_{BQ}} = \frac{2.5\text{ mA}}{28.6\mu A} = 87$$

$$\beta_{ac} = \left.\frac{\Delta I_c}{\Delta I_B}\right|_{V_{CEQ}} = \frac{2.5mA - 2.0mA}{28.6\mu A - 20\mu A} = 58$$

$$\alpha_{dc} = \frac{\beta_{dc}}{1 + \beta_{dc}} = \frac{87}{1 + 87} = \frac{87}{88} = .99$$

$$\alpha_{ac} = \frac{\beta_{ac}}{1 + \beta_{ac}} = \frac{58}{1 + 58} = \frac{58}{59} = .98$$

c) $$P_{dc} = V_{CEQ} I_{CQ} = 7.5V \times 2.5mA = 18.8mW$$

(Common-emitter biased)

4. a) C_1 and C_2 are coupling capacitors that couple ac signals in and out of the the circuit but block d.c. voltages, thereby maintaining a relatively fixed d.c. bias point of each transistor. C_E shorts out or bypasses the emitter resistor, R_E, during a.c. operation, thereby increasing the gain of the circuit.

b) $$I_{C(sat)} = \frac{V_{cc}}{R_C + R_E} = \frac{15V}{1k + 0.5k} = 10mA$$

$$I_B = \frac{V_{CC} - V_{BE}}{R_1 + (\beta + 1)R_E} = \frac{15V - 0.7V}{560k - (61)(.5k)} = 25\mu A$$

$$I_C = \beta I_B = 60 \times 25\mu A = 1.52mA$$

c) $$V_{CE} = V_{CC} - I_C(R_C + R_E) = 15V - 1.52mA\ (1.5k)$$

$$V_{CE} = 12.7V$$

$$P_{dc} = V_{CE} I_C = 12.7V \times 1.52mA = 19.3mW$$

(Common-emitter biased)

5. The Thevenin's equivalent voltage, V_{TH}, and resistance, R_{TH}, of the input circuit are:

$$V_{TH} = V_{BB} = \frac{R_1}{R_1 + R_2} V_{CC} = \frac{2k}{2k + 10k} \times 12V = 2V$$

$$R_{TH} = R_B = R_1 // R_2 = 10k//12k = 1.67k$$

$$I_B = \frac{V_{BB} - V_{BE}}{R_B + (\beta + 1)R_E} = \frac{2V - 0.7V}{1.67k + 101(.5k)} = 24.9\mu A$$

$$I_C = \beta I_B = 100 \times 24.9\mu A = 2.49mA$$

The symmetrical output voltage swing, V_{swing}, is:

$$V_{swing} = 2I_C(R_C // R_L) = 2 \times 2.49mA \times (1k\ //1k) = 2.49V$$

The a.c. power dissipation, P_{ac}, and the d.c. power dissipation, P_{dc}, are:

$$P_{ac} = \frac{1}{2} I_L{}^2 R_L = \frac{1}{2}\left(\frac{I_C}{2}\right)^2 R_L = \frac{1}{2}(2.49mA)^2 \times 1k = 0.78mW$$

$$P_{dc} = I_C V_{CC} + \frac{V_{CC}{}^2}{R_1 + R_2} = (2.49mA) \times 12V + \frac{(12V)^2}{2k + 10k} = 29.88mW + 12mW = 41.88mW$$

(Common-emitter biased)

6. a) With S in position 1:

$$V_{BB} = \frac{R_1}{R_1 + R_2}V_{CC} = \frac{30k}{100k + 30k}(-20)V = -2.3V$$

$$R_{BB} = R_1//R_3 = 30k//100k = 23k$$

KVL around input circuit gives:

$$-V_{BB} + V_{BE} + I_C R_E + \frac{I_C}{\beta}R_B = 0$$

$$I_C = \frac{V_{BB} - V_{BE}}{R_E + R_{BB/\beta}} = \frac{-2.3 - (-0.7V)}{.5k + \frac{23k}{100}} = -2.27mA$$

$$V_{CE} = -V_{CC} - (I_C)(R_C + R_E) = -20V - (-2.27mA)(2.5k) = -14.3V$$

$$P_{dc} = V_{CE} + I_C = (-2.27mA)(-14.3V) = 32.5mW$$

b) S in position 2:

$$R_{BB} = R_1//R_2//R_3 = 100k//15k = 13k$$

$$V_{BB} = \frac{R_1//R_2}{R_1//R_2 + R_3} \times V_{CC} = \frac{15k}{15k + 100k} \times (-20V) = -2.61V$$

$$I_C = \frac{-1.91}{\frac{R}{100} + 630}$$

$$V_{CE} = V_{CC} - I_C(R_C + R_E) = -20V + 2500I_C$$

$$P_{DC} = V_{CE} + I_C = (-20 + 2500I_C)I_C =$$

$$2500I_C^2 - 20I_C - 0.065 = 0$$

$$I_C = \frac{20 \pm \sqrt{20^2 - 4(2500)(-0.065)}}{2 \times 2500} = 1.1mA \text{ or } 9.1mA$$

Neglect I_C = 9.1 mA because it does not satisfy the circuit conditions. Thus:

$$I_C = \frac{-1.91}{\frac{R}{100} + 630} = -1.1 \quad \Rightarrow \quad R = 110.6k$$

(Common-emitter biased)

7. a) $R_{dc} = R_C + R_{E1} + R_{E2} = 2k + .5k\ .5k = 3k$

b) $R_{ac} = R_C//R_{E1} = 2k//.5k = 400($

c) $V_{CE} = V_{CC} - I_{CQ}(R_{dc}) = 10V - (3mA)(3k) = 1V$

d) $$V_{BB} = \frac{R_1}{R_2 + R_2} \cdot V_{CC} = \frac{10k}{10k + 90k} \times 10V = 1V$$

$$R_B = R_1//R_2 = 10k//90k = 9k$$

$$I_B = \frac{V_{BB} - V_{BE}}{R_{BB} + (\beta + 1)(R_{E1} + R_{E2})} = \frac{1 - 0.7}{9k + 100(1k)} = 2.75\mu A$$

$$\beta = \frac{I_C}{I_B} = \frac{3mA}{2.75\mu A} = 1090$$

(Common-emitter biased)

8.

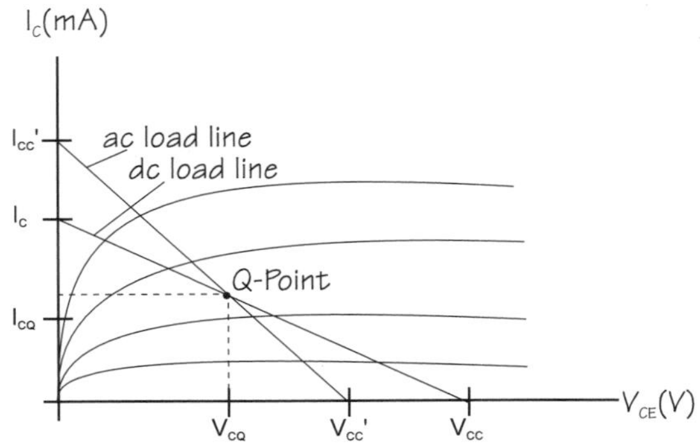

Equation of the a.c. loadline is:

$$\frac{I_C - I_{CA}}{I'_C - I_{CQ}} = \frac{V_{CE} - V_{CEQ}}{0 - V_{CEQ}}$$

$$I_C - I_{CQ} = \frac{I'_C - I_{CEQ}}{-V_{CEQ}}(V_{CE} - V_{CEQ})$$

Also $\dfrac{I'_C - I_{CEQ}}{-V_{CEQ}} = -\dfrac{I'_C}{V'_{CC}} \equiv$ slope of a.c. loadline

i.e. $I_C - I_{CQ} = \dfrac{-I'_C}{V'_{CC}}(V_{CE} - V_{CEQ}) = -\dfrac{1}{R_{ac}}(V_{CE} - V_{CEQ})$

for the I-intercept $V_{CE} = 0 \quad I = I'_C$

Therefore $I'_C = \dfrac{V_{CEQ}}{R_{ac}} + I_{CQ}$

for the V-intercept $V_{CE} = V'_{CC} I_C = 0$

$$V'_{CC} = V_{CEQ} + I_{CQ}R_{ac}$$

(Common-emitter biased)

9. $$V_{BB} = \frac{R_1}{R_1 + R_2} \cdot V_{CC} = \frac{10k}{10k + 90k} \cdot 15V = 1.5V$$

$$R_B = R_1 // R_2 = 10k//90k = 9k$$

$$I_B = \frac{V_{BB} - V_{BE}}{R_B + (\beta + 1)R_E} = \frac{1.5 - 0.7}{9k + 121(1k)} = 6.2\mu A$$

$$I_{CQ} = \beta I_B = 120 \cdot 6.5\mu A = .74mA$$

Maximum output voltage swing, V_{swing}, is:

$$V_{swing} = 2I_{CQ}(R_E//R_6) = 2 \cdot .74ma \cdot (.5k) = .74V$$

(Common-emitter biased)

10. $V_{TH} = R_B = 10k//22k = 6.9k$

$$V_{BB} = \frac{R_1}{R_1 + R_2} \cdot V_{CC} - V_{EE} = \frac{10k}{10k + 22k} \times (15V - 15V) = -10.3V$$

KVL around input circuit gives:

$$V_{BB} - I_B R_B - (\beta + 1)I_B R_E - V_{BE} - V_{EE} = 0$$
$$-10.3 - I_B(6.9k + 100k) - 0.7 + .5 = 0$$
$$I_B = \frac{15 - 10.3 - 0.7}{100k + 6.9k} = \frac{4}{106.9k} = 37.4\mu A$$
$$I_{CQ} = \beta I_B = 99 \cdot 37.4\mu A = 3.7mA$$
$$V_{CEQ} = V_{CC} + V_{EE} - I_C(R_E + R_6) = 15 - 15 - 3.7mA(3k) = -11V$$
$$R_{ac} = R_L//R_C + R_E = 2k//2k + 1k = 2k$$
$$\text{slope} = -\frac{1}{R_{ac}} = -\frac{1}{2k}$$

(Common-emitter biased)

11. The slope of the d.c. load line gives:

$$R = \left.\frac{V_{CC} = 15V}{I_C}\right|_{V_{CE=0}} = \frac{15V}{10mA} = 1.5k$$
$$I_B = 35\mu A = \frac{V_{CC} - V_{BE}}{R_B} = \frac{15 - 0.7}{R_B}$$
$$R_B = \frac{15 - 0.7}{35\mu A} = 409k$$
$$I_{CQ} = \beta I_B = 60 \cdot 35\mu a = 2.1mA$$
$$V_{CEQ} = V_{CC} - I_{CQ}R_C = 15V - (2.1mA)(1.5k) = 11.9V$$

(Common-emitter biased)

12. KVL around input circuit is:

$$18V - I'_C(5.6k) - I_B 270k - V_{BE} - I_E R_E = 0$$
$$I'_C \approx I_C = I_E$$

Then $I_{CA} = \dfrac{18 - 0.7V}{5.6k + \dfrac{270k}{\beta} + 1k} = \dfrac{17.3}{11.1k} = 1.56mA$

$$V_{CEQ} = 18 - I_C(R_C + R_E) = 18 - 1.56mA(6/6k) = 7.7V$$

(Common-emitter with feedback)

13. KVL around input circuit is:

$$-I_E R_E - V_{BE} - 56k\ I_B + V_{CC} = 0$$
$$-(\beta + 1)I_B(1K) + .7V - (56k)I_B - 6V = 0$$
$$I_B = \frac{-6 + 0.7}{56k + 51k} = \frac{-5.3}{107k} = -49.5\mu A$$
$$I_{CQ} = \beta I_B = -50 \cdot 49.5\mu a = -2.48mA$$
$$+ V_{CC} - V_{CEQ} - I_{CQ}R_E = 0$$
$$V_{CWQ} = -6 -(-2.48mA)(1k) = -3.52V$$

(Emitter follower bias)

14. a) $-V_{BE} - I_E R_E - V_{EE} = -V_D - I_D R_2 - V_{EE}$

$$V_{BE} + I_E R_E = V_D + I_D R_2$$

$$I_E = \frac{V_D - V_{BE} + I_D R_2}{R_E}$$

Also $V_{EE} - I_D(R_1 + R_2) - V_D = 0$

$$I_D = \frac{V_{EE} - V_D}{R_1 + R_2}$$

Substitute the expression for I_D in equation for I_E to get:

$$I_E = \frac{V_D - V_{BE} + \frac{R_2}{R_1 + R_2}(V_{EE} - V_D)}{R_E}$$

b) V_D and V_{BE} are diode voltages; thus, any temperature fluctuations in the base to emitter voltage, V_{BE}, of the transistor will be canceled or compensated for by the fluctuation in V_D.

(Common-emitter with temperature compensation)

15. a) $I_{EQ} = \frac{-V_{EE} - V_{BE}}{R_E} = \frac{20 - 0.7}{2k} = 6.65mA$

$$I_{BQ} = \frac{I_{EQ}}{\beta + 1} = \frac{6.65mA}{201} = 33\mu A$$

b) $V_{CC} - I_C R_C - V_{CEQ} - I_E R_E - V_{EE} = 0$

$$V_{CEQ} = 30 + 20 - 6.65mA(7k) = 3.8V$$

(Common-base bias)

16. The Thevenin's equivalent circuit of the input circuit of transistor Q1 gives:

$$V_{TH1} = V_{BB1} = \frac{R_1}{R_1 + R_2} \cdot 9V = \frac{1M}{1M + 1M} \cdot 9V = 4.5V$$

$$R_{TH1} = R_{B1} = R1//R_L = 1M//1M = 500k$$

KVL around ABCA gives:

$$V_{BB1} - V_{BE1} - V_{BE2} - I_E R_E - I_{B1} R_{B2} = 0$$

But $I_E = (\beta+1)[I_{B2}] = (\beta + 1)[(\beta + 1)I_{B1}] = (\beta + 1)^2 I_{B1}$

i.e. $I_{B1} = \frac{V_{BB1} - 0.7 - 0.7}{R_{B1} + (\beta + 1)^2 R_E} = \frac{4.5 - 1.4}{(51)^2 1k + 0.5k} = 1.2\mu A$

$$I_{EQ2} = (\beta+1)^2 I_{B1} = (51)^2 1.2(A = 3.1mA$$

$$V_{CEQ2} = V_{CC} - R_E I_{EQ2} = 9 - (3.1mA)(1k) = 5.9V$$

$$I_{CQ1} = \beta I_{B1} = 50 \cdot 1.2\mu A = 60\mu A$$

$$V_{CEQ1} = V_{CC} - V_{E1} = V_{CC} - V_{BE1} - I_E R_E = 9 - 0.7 - 3.1 = 5.2V$$

(Common-emitter biased)

17. Let the functional form of I_C be expressed as:

$$I_C = f(V_{BE}, I_{CBO}, (\beta, V_{CC})$$

Using partial differentiation, a change in I_C, ΔI_C, due to changes in the independent variables, is:

$$\Delta I_C = \frac{\partial I_{CQ}}{\partial V_{BE}} \Delta V_{BE} + \frac{\partial I_{CQ}}{\partial I_{CBO}} \Delta I_{CBO} + \frac{\partial I_{CQ}}{\partial \beta} \Delta \beta + \frac{\partial I_{CQ}}{\partial V_{CC}} \Delta V_{CC}$$

From the input circuit we get:

$$I_{CQ} = \frac{V_{BB} - V_{BE}}{R_E + \frac{R_B}{\beta}}$$

then $$\frac{\partial I_{CQ}}{\partial V_{BE}} = -\frac{1}{R_E + \frac{R_B}{\beta}}$$

Also $I_{CQ} = I'_{CQ} + I_{CBO}$

$$= ((I_{BQ} + I_{CBO}) + I_{CBO} = (I_{BQ} + ((+1))I_{CBO}$$

or $$I_{BQ} = \frac{I_{CQ}}{\beta} - \frac{\beta + 1}{\beta} I_{CBO}$$

But from the input circuit:

$$\begin{aligned} V_{BB} - V_{BE} &= I_{EQ}R_E + I_B R_B \\ &= (\beta + 1)I_{BQ}R_E + I_{BQ}R_B \\ &= \beta I_B R_E + I_{BQ}(R_E + R_B) \\ &= I_{CQ}R_E + I_{BQ}(R_E + R_B) \end{aligned}$$

Substitute for I_{BQ} gives:

$$V_{BB} - V_{BE} = \left(\frac{I_{CQ}}{\beta} - I_{CBO}\right)[R_B + R_E] + R_E I_{CQ}$$

or $$I_{CQ} = \frac{V_{BB} - V_{BE} + (R_B + R_E)I_{CBO}}{R_E + (R_B + R_E)/\beta}$$

then $$\frac{\partial I_{CQ}}{\partial I_{CBO}} = \frac{R_B + R_E}{R_E + (R_B + R_E)/\beta} = \frac{1}{\frac{1}{\beta} + \frac{R_E}{R_E + R_B}}$$

Similarly

$$\frac{\partial I_{CQ}}{\partial \beta} = \frac{[(V_{BB} - V_{BE}) + (R_B + R_E)I_{CBO}]}{R_B + R_E + \beta R_E} - \frac{\beta R_E[(V_{BB} - V_{BE}) + (R_B + R_E)I_{CBO}]}{((R_B + R_E) + \beta R_E)^2}$$

For $I_{CBO} \approx 0 \quad R_B \cong \beta R_E$

$$\frac{\partial I_{CQ}}{\partial \beta} = (V_{BB} - V_{BE})\left[\frac{1}{R_B + \beta R_E} - \frac{\beta R_E}{(R_B + \beta R_E)^2}\right]$$

$$= (V_{BB} - V_{BE})\left[\frac{R_B + \beta R_E - \beta R_E}{(R_B + \beta R_E)^2}\right]$$

$$= \frac{R_B(V_{BB} - V_{BE})}{\beta^2 R_E^2}$$

Also from the output circuit:

$$I_{CQ} = \frac{V_{CC} - V_{CEQ}}{R_E + R_C}$$

then $$\frac{\partial I_{CQ}}{\partial V_{CC}} = \frac{1}{R_E + R_C}$$

Substituting expressions for the partial derivatives gives:

$$\Delta I_{CA} = \frac{-\Delta V_{BE}}{R_E + \frac{R_B}{\beta}} + \frac{\beta \Delta I_{CBO}}{1 + \beta\frac{R_E}{R_B}} + \frac{R_B(V_{BB} - V_{BE})}{\beta^2 R_E^2} + \frac{\Delta V_{CC}}{R_E + R_C}$$

(Stability)

Grade Yourself

Circle the numbers of the questions you missed. Then fill in the total incorrect for each topic. If you answered more than three questions incorrectly, you need to focus on that topic. If a topic has less than three questions and you had at least one wrong, we suggest you study that topic also. Read your textbook, a review book, or ask your teacher for help.

Subject: Bipolar Junction Transfer Biasing Circuits

Topic	Question Numbers	Number Incorrect
BJT configurations	1	
Common-base characteristics	2, 3	
Common-emitter biased	4, 5, 6, 7, 8, 9, 10, 11, 16	
Common-emitter with feedback	12	
Emitter follower bias	13	
Common-emitter with temperature compensation	14	
Common-base bias	15	
Stability	17	

Field Effect Transistor Biasing Circuits

3

Brief Yourself

There are different types of Field Effect Transistors (FETs). Some examples are the Junction Field Effect Transistor (JFET), the Metal-Oxide Semiconductor FET (or MOSFET), the Complimentary MOS (CMOS) FET, the Vertical MOS (VMOS) FET, and the Metal-Semiconductor FET (MESFET). These transistors can operate in two modes, depletion and enhancement, except for the JFET, which operates only as a depletion mode device. The analysis of circuits incorporating FETs also can be broken down into dc and ac, similar to the BJT circuit analysis. Practical dc biasing circuits are classified into: a) fixed-biasing; b) voltage-divider biasing; c) voltage-feedback biasing; d) un-bypassed source-resistor biasing; e) bypassed source-resistor biasing; and f) beta-independent biasing. FET circuits can be configured as common-gate, common-source, or common-drain.

Analysis of FET dc biasing circuits entails writing equations for the input and output circuits and solving for the desired circuit parameters. The transfer relationship for the enhancement mode and depletion is used as appropriate in analyzing these circuits.

Test Yourself

1. Sketch the transfer characteristics of a P-channel E-MOSFET. What device paramaters can be determined from the intercepts with the axes?
2. Repeat problem 1 for a D-MOSFET.
3. The transconductance of a depletion-mode MOSFET is $g_m = 2.5mS$ at a Q-point given by $V_{GSQ} = -1.5V$, $I_{DSQ} = 8mA$. Calculate the pinch-off voltage, V_P, and the drain saturation current, I_{DSS}, of the transistor.

4.

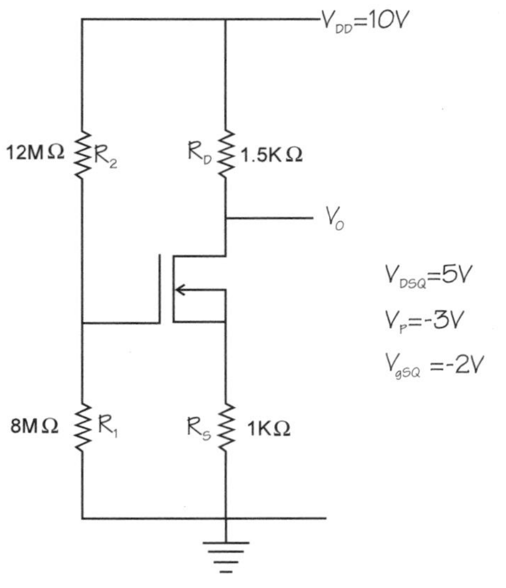

Fig. P3.4a

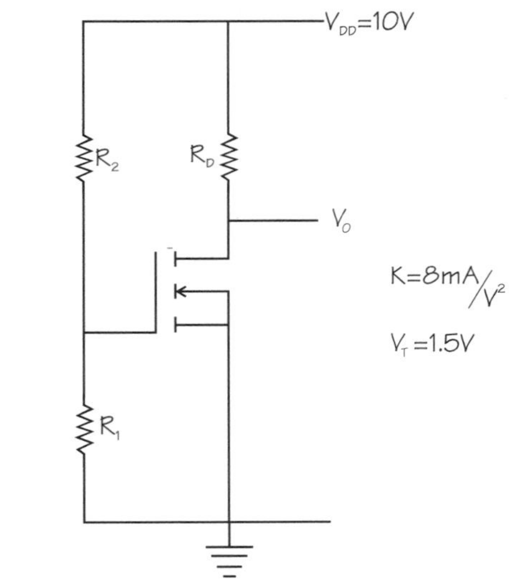

Fig. P3.4b

The depletion-mode MOSFET of Fig. P3.4a has a Q-point of $V_{DSQ} = 5V$, $V_{GSQ} = -2V$ and $V_P = -3V$. It is replaced by an enhancement-mode MOSFET with $k = 8mA/V^2$ and $V_T = 1.5V$, as shown in Fig. P3.4b. Determine the value of R_D such that the drain current remains unchanged.

5. Find:
   a) I_{DSQ}
   b) V_{GSQ}
   c) V_{DSQ}

   for the circuit shown in Fig. P3.5.

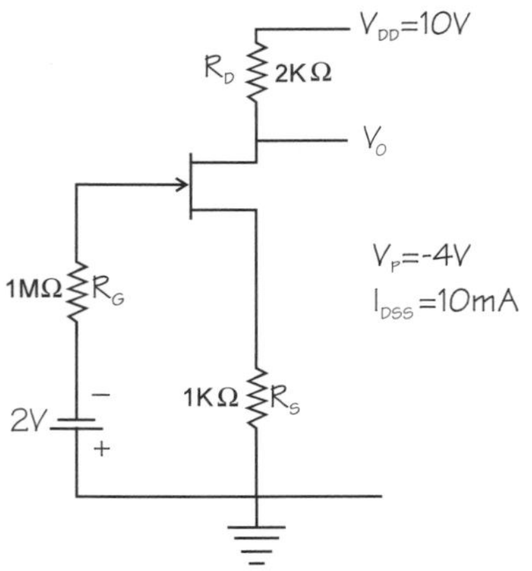

Fig. P3.5

6. Determine the coordinates of the Q-point and the d.c. power dissipation of the transistor in Fig. P3.6.

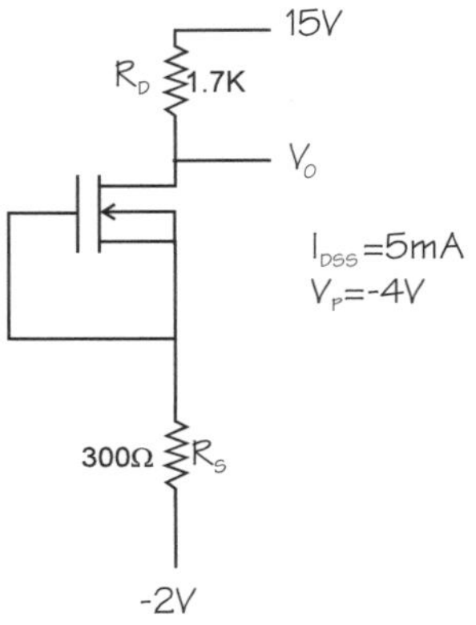

Fig. P3.6

7. Determine the coordinates of the Q-point and the d.c. power dissipation of the transistor in Fig. P3.7.

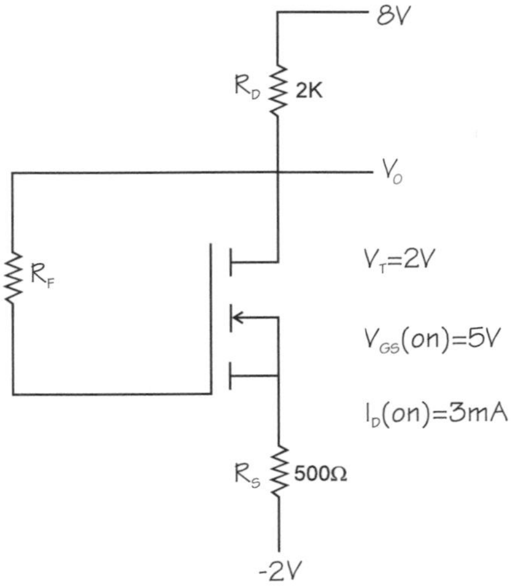

Fig. P3.7

8. Determine the coordinates of the Q-point and the d.c. power dissipation of the transistor in Fig. P3.8.

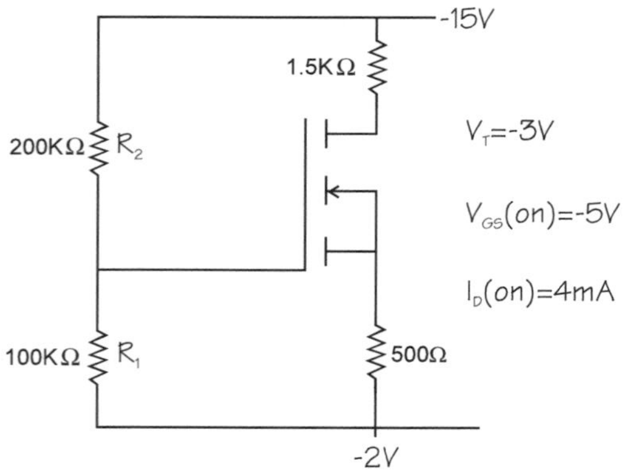

Fig. P3.8

9. Calculate I_D, V_{GS}, and V_{DS} for the circuit of Fig. P3.9.

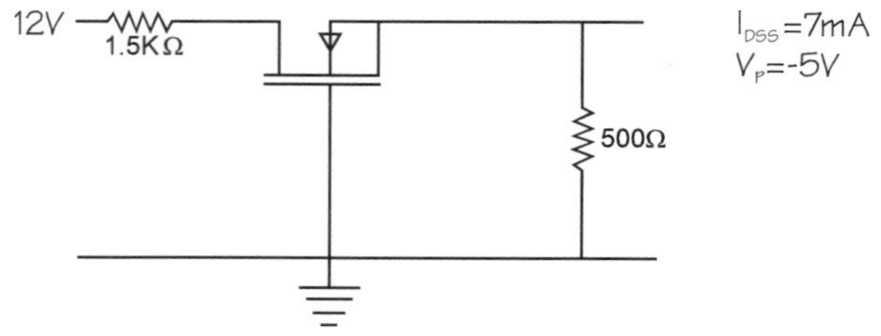

Fig. P3.9

10. Repeat problem 9 for the circuit of Fig. P3.10.

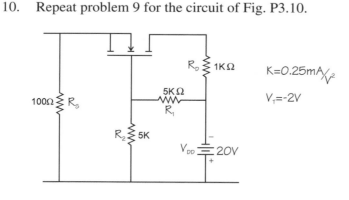

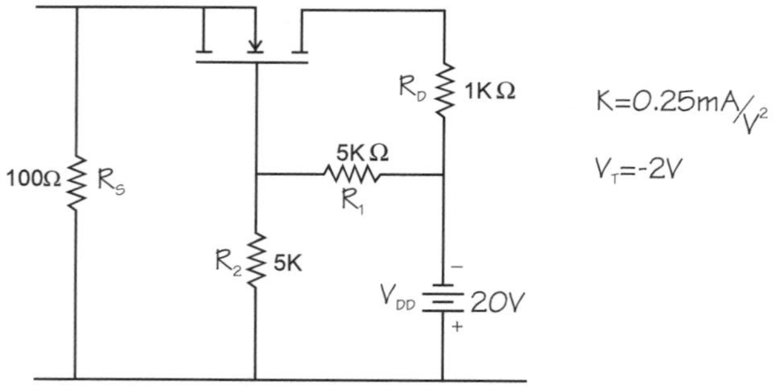

Fig. P3.10

11. An npn BJT is connected in series with an n-channel depletion-mode MOSFET as shown in Fig. P3.11. The current gain, β, of the BJT is 100. The drain saturation current, and pinch-off voltage, V_P, of the MOSFET are I_{DSS} = 8mA and V_P = –5V. Determine:

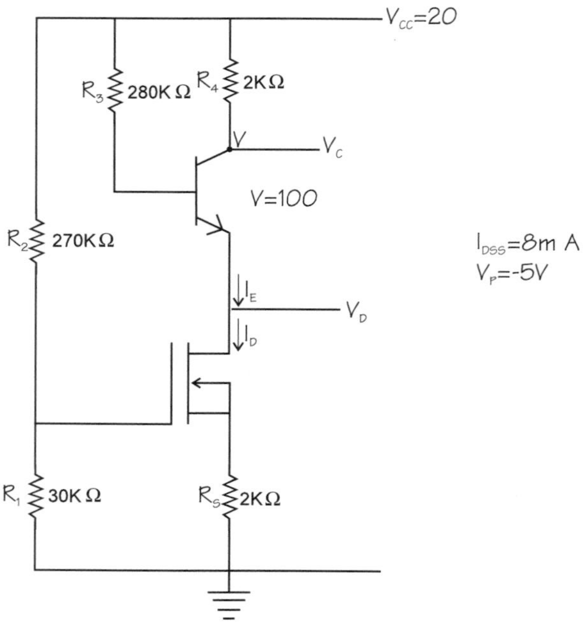

Fig. P3.11

a) V_{GSQ}, I_{DQ} and V_{DSQ} of the MOSFET.
b) I_B, I_E and V_{CE} of the BJT.
c) the d.c. power dissipated by each transistor.

12. Repeat problem 11 for the circuit of Fig.

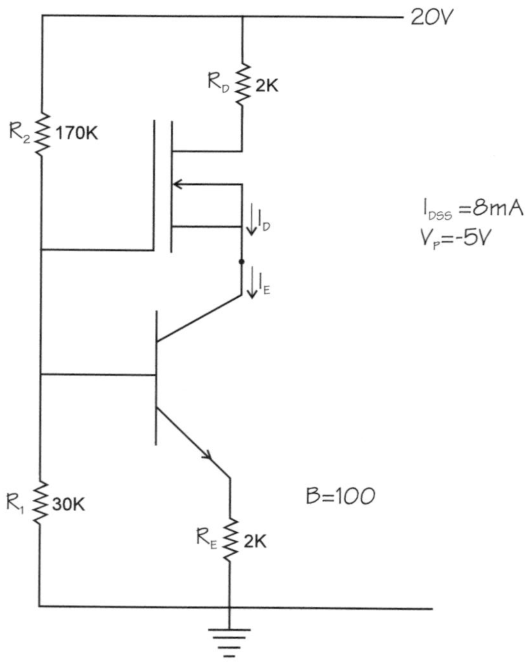

Fig. P3.12

P3.12.

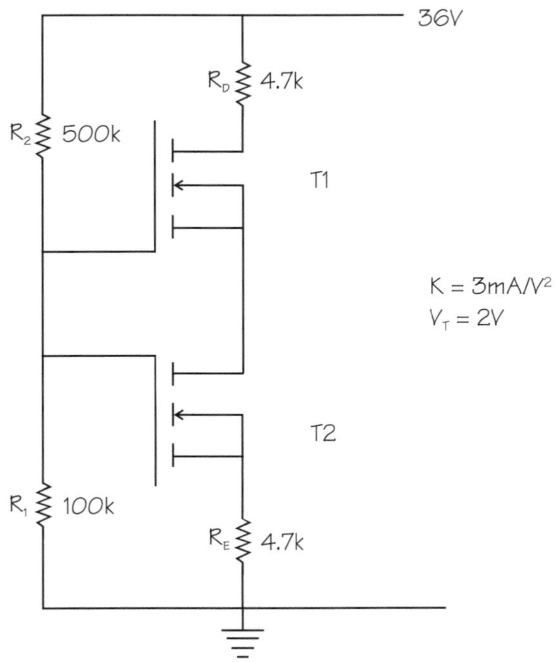

Fig. P3.13

13. Two identical n-channel enhancement-mode MOSFET, T1 and T2, are connected in series as shown in Fig. P3.13. Determine the coordinates of the Q-point for each transistor.

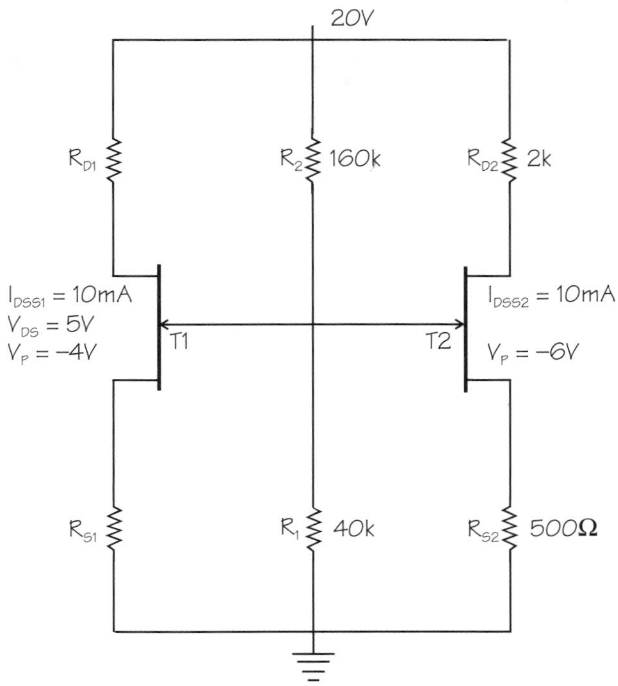

Fig. P3.14

14. Find the value of R_{S1} and R_{D1}, in the circuit of the Fig. P3.14, such that the drain currents of the transistors are equal.

Check Yourself

1. The following parameters can be determined from the transfer characteristics for a given Q-point:
   i) the threshold voltage, V_T
   ii) the drain current, I_{DQ}
   iii) the gate-to-source voltage, V_{GSQ}
   iv) the transconductance, $g_m = \dfrac{\Delta I_D}{\Delta V_{GS}}$

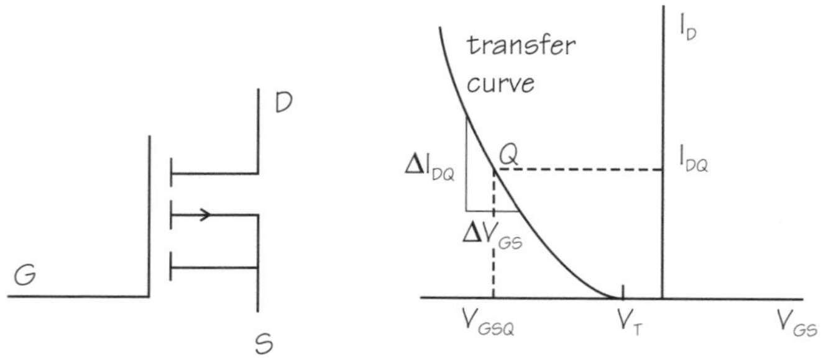

Fig. S3.1

(FET characteristics)

2. The following parameters can be determined from the transfer characteristics for a given Q-point:
   i) pinch-off voltage, V_P
   ii) drain saturation current, I_{DSS}
   iii) drain current, I_{DQ}
   iv) gate-to-source voltage, V_{GS}
   v) transconductance

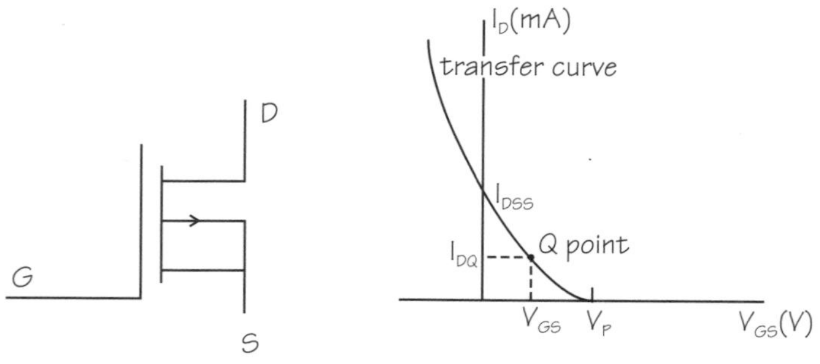

Fig. S3.3

(FET characteristics)

3. The expresssion for the drain current, I_D, and transconductance, g_m, are:

$$I_D = I_{DSS}\left(1 - \frac{V_{GS}}{V_P}\right)^2$$

$$g_m = g_{mo}\left(1 - \frac{V_{GS}}{V_P}\right); \qquad g_{mo} = \left|\frac{2I_{DSS}}{V_p}\right|$$

at the Q-point, $I_D = 7.5mA$, $V_{GS} = -1.5V$, $g_m = 2.5mS$

then $7.5 = I_{DSS}\left(1 - \frac{-15}{V_P}\right)^2$

$$2.5 = -\frac{2I_{DSS}}{V_P}\left(1 - \frac{-1.5}{V_P}\right)$$

Dividing the two equations gives:

$$\frac{7.5}{2.5} = -\frac{V_P}{2}\left(1 - \frac{-1.5}{V_P}\right)$$

or $6 = -V_p \frac{(V_P + 1.5)}{V_p}$

$$V_P = -7.5V$$

Thus $I_D = I_{DSS}\left(1 - \frac{-1.5}{-7.5}\right)^2$

i.e. $I_{DSS} = \dfrac{7.5mA}{\left(1 + \frac{1.5}{7.5}\right)^2} = 11.7mA$

(Transfer characteristics)

4. From the output circuit of Fig. 3.4a we write:

$$I_D = \frac{V_{DD} - V_{DS}}{R_D + R_S} = \frac{10V - 5V}{2.5V} = 2mA$$

But $I_D = K(V_{GS} - V_T)^2$

i.e. $2 = 8(V_{GS} - V_T)^2 = 8(V_{GS} - 1.0)^2$

implies $V_{GS} = 1.5V$

$$V_G = \frac{R_1}{R_1 + R_2} \times 10V = \frac{8}{20} = 4V$$

From the input circuit

$$V_G - V_{GS} - I_D R_S = 0$$

implies $R_S = \dfrac{V_B - V_{GS}}{I_D} = \dfrac{4V - 1.5V}{2mA} = 1.25k\Omega$

Using the expression for I_D, above, we get:

$$2mA = \frac{10V - 5V}{1.25k + R_D}$$

implies $R_D = 1.25k\Omega$

(CS biasing)

5. $$I_D = I_{DSS}\left(1 - \frac{V_{GS}}{V_P}\right)^2 = 10mA\left(1 - \frac{V_{GS}}{-4}\right)^2$$

KVL around input gives:

$$-1 - V_{GS} - 1000I_D = 0$$
$$V_{GS} = -1 - 1000I_D$$

Substitute the expression for VGS in previous equation for ID and solve for the quadratic equation in ID. That is

$$I_D = 10^{-2}\left(1 - \frac{(1 + 1000I_D)}{4}\right)^2$$

$$1600I_D = 9 - 6000I_D + 10^6 I_D^2$$

or $$10^6 I_D^2 - 6600I_D + 9 = 0$$

$$I_D = \frac{6600 \pm \sqrt{(6600)^2 - 4 \cdot 9 \cdot 10^6}}{2 \times 10^6}$$

$$I_D = 4.67mA, \text{ or } 1.93mA$$

neglect $I_D = 1.93mA$ since it does not satisfy the physical conditions.

$$V_{GS} = -1 - 4.67 = -5.67V$$

KVL around output gives:

$$V_{DD} - V_{DS} - I_D(R_D + R_S) = 0$$
$$V_{DS} = V_{DD} - I_D(R_D + R_S) = 10 - 3 = 7V$$

(Self-biasing)

6. $$I_D = I_{DSS}\left(1 - \frac{V_{GS}}{V_P}\right)^2$$

But $V_{GS} = V_G - V_S = 0$

Then $I_D = I_{DSS} = 5mA$

Also $V_{DS} = V_{DD} - V_{SS} - I_D(R_S + R_D)$

$= 15 - (-2) - 5mA(1.7k + .3k)$

$$V_{DS} = 17 - 10 = 7V$$

Power dissipation of transistor is:

$$P_{dc} = V_{DSQ}I_{DQ} = (5mA)7V = 35mW$$

(Fixed biasing)

7. $$K = \frac{I_D(ON)}{(V_{GS}(ON) - V_T)^2} = \frac{3mA}{(5-2)^2} = \frac{1mA}{3V^2}$$

$$I_D = K(V_{GSQ} - V_T)^2$$
$$= \frac{1mA}{3V^2}(V_{GSQ} - 2)^2$$

From the output circuit:

$$V_{DD} - I_D(2500) - V_{DS} + 2 = 0$$
$$10 - 2500I_D - V_{DS} = 0$$

But $V_{DS} = V_{GS}$ (Since $I_G = 0$)
Then $V_{GS} = 10 - 2500I_D$

$I_D = 10^{-3}(10 - 2500I_D - 2)^2$
$3I_D = 10^{-3}(8 - 2500I_D)^2$
$3I_D = 10^{-3}(64 - 40 \times 10^3 I_D + 625 \times 10^4 I_D^2)$
$3I_D = .064 - 40I_D + 6250I_D$

or $6250I_D^2 - 43I_D + 0.064 = 0$

$$I_D = \frac{43 \pm \sqrt{(43)^2 - 4(.064)(625)}}{2 \times 6250}$$

$$= \frac{43 \pm 41.1}{2 \times 6250} = .15\text{mA or } 2.69 \text{ mA}$$

$I_D = .15\text{mA}$

$V_{GS} = 2 - 2500(.15\text{mA}) = 1.63\text{V}$

$V_{DS} = V_{DD} + 2 - I_D(R_S + R_D)$
$= 8 + 2 - 1.63 = 8.38\text{V}$

(Feedback biasing)

8. $$K = \frac{I_D(ON)}{(V_{GS}(ON) - V_T)} = \frac{4\text{mA}}{(-5 - (-3))^2} = .25\frac{\text{mA}}{\text{V}}$$

$$V_{GG} = \frac{R_1}{R_1 + R_2} \times (-15) = \frac{200\text{k}}{300\text{k}}(-15\text{V}) = -10\text{V}$$

Also $V_{GG} - V_{GS} - I_D 500 = 0$

$V_{GS} - 10 + 500I_D$

But $I_D = K(V_{GS} - V_T)^2$
$= .25 \times 10^{-3}((-10 + 500I_D) - (-3))^2$
$4I_D = 10^{-3}(-7 + 500I_D)^2 = 0.049 - 70I_D + 250I_D^2$
$250I_D^2 - 73I_D^2 + 0.049 = 0$

$$I_D = \frac{73 \pm \sqrt{73^2 - 4(250)(.049)}}{2 \times 250} = .67\text{mA}$$

$V_{GS} = -10 + 500(.67 \times 10^{-3}) = -9.67\text{V}$
$V_{DS} = V_{DD} + I_D(2\text{k}) = -10 + 1.34 = -8.66\text{V}$
$P_{dc} = |V_{DS}I_D| = 8.66 \times .67 \times 10^{-3} = 5.8\text{mW}$

(CS biasing)

9. $$I_D = \frac{2400 \pm \sqrt{(2400)^2 - 4 \cdot (7 \times 10^4)(7)}}{2 \times 7 \times 10^4}$$

$I_D = 3.2\text{mA or } 31.1\text{mA}$

Neglect $I_D = 31.1\text{mA}$, as it does not satisfy the circuit conditions.
Therefore $I_D = 3.2\text{mA}$

$V_{GS} = -500I_D = -500 \times 3.2 \times 10^{-3} = -1.6V$
$V_{DS} = V_{DD} - I_D(R_S + R_D) = 12 - 3.2m(1.5k + .5k)$
$V_{DS} = 12 - 3.2(2) = 12 - 6.4 = 5.6V$

(CG biasing)

10. $$V_{GG} = \frac{R_2}{R_1 + R_2} \cdot V_{DD} = \frac{5k}{5k + 5k} \times (-20V) = -10V$$

$V_{GS} = V_{GG} + I_DR_S = -10 + 100I_D$
$I_D = K(V_{GS} - V_T)^2 = .25 \times 10^{-3}(-10 + 100I_D + 2)^2$
$4I_D = 10^{-3}[64 - 1600I_D + 10^4I_D^2]$
$0 = .064 - 5.6I_D + 10I_D^2$

$$I_D = \frac{5.6 \pm \sqrt{(5.6)^2 - 4(10)(.064)}}{2 \times 10} = 11.6mA$$

$V_{GS} = -10 + 100 \times 11.6 \times 10^{-3} = -8.8V$
$V_{DS} = V_{DD} - I_D(R_S + R_D) = -20 + 11.6mA(1.1k)$
$V_{DS} = -7.24V$

(CG biasing)

11. $$V_{GG} = \frac{R_1}{R_1 + R_2} \cdot V_{CC} = \frac{30k}{30k + 170k} \times 20V = 3V$$

$V_{GS} = V_{GG} - I_DR_5 = 3 - 2000I_D$

$$I_D = I_{DSS}\left(1 - \frac{V_{GS}}{V_P}\right)^2$$

$$= 8mA\left(1 - \frac{3 - 2000I_D}{-5}\right)^2$$

$$1000I_D = \frac{8}{25}[-8 + 2000I_D]^2$$

$25000I_D = 8[6.4 - 32000I_D + 4 \times 10^6I_D^2]$

or $0 = .512 - 281I_D + 32 \times 10^3I_D^2$

i.e. $$I_D = \frac{281 \pm \sqrt{(281)^2 - 4(.512)(32 \times 10^3)}}{2 \times 32 \times 10^3}$$

$= 2.58mA$ or $6.18mA$

neglecting $I_D = 6.18mA$, gives

$I_D = 2.58mA$
$V_{GS} = 3 - 2000I_D = 3 - (2000)2.58 \times 10^{-3}) = -2.16V$

From the circuit

$I_{DQ} = I_E \approx I_C$ implies $I_E = 2.58mA$

$$I_B = \frac{I_C}{\beta} = \frac{2.58mA}{100} = 25.8\mu A$$

$V_D = V_E = V_B - V_{BE}$
$= (V_{CC} - I_BR_3) - V_{BE}$
$= 20 - (-25.8A)(280k) - 0.7$
$V_D = 12V$

$V_{DS} = V_D - V_S = 12 - I_D R_2 = 12 - (2.58\text{mA})(2\text{k}) = 6.92\text{V}$
$V_{CE} = V_{CC} - I_C(2\text{k}) - V_D$
$= 20\text{V} - (2.58\text{mA})(2\text{k}) - 6.92$
$V_{CE} = 7.96\text{V}$

(Mixed configuration)

12. $$V_{BB} = \frac{R_1}{R_1 + R_2} \times V_{DD} = \frac{30\text{k}}{170\text{k} + 30\text{k}} \times 20\text{V} = 3\text{V}$$

$R_B = R_1//R_2 = 30\text{k}//170\text{k} = 25.5\text{k}$
$V_{BB} - I_B R_B - V_{BE} - (\beta + 1)I_B R_E = 0$
$$I_B = \frac{V_{BB} - V_{BE}}{R_B + (\beta + 1)R_E} = \frac{3 - 0.7}{25.5\text{k} + 202\text{k}} = 10\mu\text{A}$$
$I_C = \beta I_B = 100 \times 10\mu\text{A} = 1.0\text{mA}$
$$I_D = I_{DSS}\left(1 - \frac{V_{GS}}{V_P}\right)^2 = 8\text{mA}\left(1 - \frac{V_{GS}}{-5}\right)^2$$
i.e. $$V_{GS} = -5\left(1 - \sqrt{\frac{1}{8}}\right) = -32\text{V}$$
$V_S = V_G - V_{GS} = 3\text{V} - (-3.2\text{V}) = 6.2\text{V}$
$V_{DS} = V_{CC} - I_D R_D - V_S = 20 - 2 - 6.2 = 11.8\text{V}$
$V_{CE} = V_C - V_E = V_S - I_D R_E = 6.2 - 2 = 4.2\text{V}$

(Mixed configuration)

13. $$V_{GG} = \frac{100\text{k}}{100\text{k} + 500\text{k}} \times 36\text{V} = 6\text{V}$$

$V_{GS2} = V_{GG} - I_D R_S = 6 - 4700 I_D$
$I_{DS2} = K(V_{GS} - V_T)^2 = 3 \times 10^{-3}(4 - 470 I_D)^2$

or $6.87 \times 10^4 I_D{}^2 - 113.8 I_D + 0.048 = 0$
$$I_{DS2} = \frac{113.8 \pm \sqrt{(113.8)^2 - 4(6.87 \times 10^4)(.048)}}{2 \times 6.87 \times 10^4}$$
$I_{DS2} = 0.55\text{mA}$ or 1.1mA

implies $V_{GS2} = 3.42\text{V}$ or 0.83V
Neglect $V_{GS} = 0.83 < V_T$

$I_{DS2} = 0.55\text{mA}$ $\quad$ $V_{GS1} = 3.42\text{V}$

But $I_{DS2} = I_{DS1} = 3 \times 10^{-3}(V_{GS1} - V_T)^2$
i.e. $$V_{GS1} = 2 \pm \sqrt{\frac{0.55}{3}} = 2 \pm .43 = 2.4\text{V}$$
$V_{GS1} = 2.4\text{V}$

Also $V_{GG} - V_{GS1} - V_{DS2} - I_D R_S = 0$
implies $V_{DS2} = 6 - 2.4 - 0.55\text{mA}(2\text{k})$
$V_{DS2} = 2.5\text{V}$
$V_{DS1} = V_{DD} - I_D(R_D + R_S) - V_{DS2}$
$= 36\text{V} - 0.55\text{A}(4.7\text{k} + 4.7\text{k}) - 2.5\text{V}$
$= 36 - 5.16 - 2.5\text{V}$
$V_{DS1} = 28.4\text{V}$

(Compound configuration)

14. $$V_{GG} = \frac{R_1}{R_1 + R_2} \times 20 = \frac{40k}{40k + 160k} \times 20 = 4V$$

$$V_{GS2} = V_{GG} - I_{D2}R_{S2} = 4 - 500I_{D2}$$

But $$I_{D2} = I_{DSS2}\left(1 - \frac{V_{GS2}}{V_{P2}}\right)^2$$

$$= 10mA\left(1 - \frac{4 - 500I_{D2}}{-6}\right)^2$$

i.e. $$36I_{D2} = 10mA(100 - 10^4I_{D2} + 25 \times 10^4 I_{D2}^2)$$

or $$0 = 1 - 136I_{D2} + 2500I_{D2}^2$$

$$I_{D2} = \frac{136 \pm \sqrt{(136)^2 - 4(1)(2500)}}{2 \times 2500}$$

$$I_{D2} = 8.76mA$$

(Compound configuration)

Grade Yourself

Circle the numbers of the questions you missed. Then fill in the total incorrect for each topic. If you answered more than three questions incorrectly, you need to focus on that topic. If a topic has less than three questions and you had at least one wrong, we suggest you study that topic also. Read your textbook, a review book, or ask your teacher for help.

Subject: Field Effect Transistor Biasing Circuits

Topic	Question Numbers	Number Incorrect
FET characteristics	1, 2	
Transfer characteristics	3	
CS biasing	4, 8	
Self-biasing	5	
Fixed biasing	6	
Feedback biasing	7	
CG biasing	9, 10	
Mixed configuration	11, 12	
Compound configuration	13, 14	

BJT Single-Stage Amplifiers

4

Brief Yourself

The transistor can be used to amplify signals when the Q-point lies in the linear region of the current-voltage characteristics. The nomenclature of single-stage BJT amplifiers is based upon the transistor configuration (CB, CE, CC) and the dc bias network (fixed-bias, voltage divider, etc.), as described in chapter 2. Coupling capacitors are used to isolate the input signal and the output load so that the dc bias point of the transitor is not adversely affected during its operation. Also, bypass capacitors such as emitter bypass capacitors are added to improve the performance (i.e., stability) of the circuit. However, these capacitors determine the low-frequency response of the amplifier circuit. On the other hand, the transistor parasitic capacitances, resistances as well as parasistics due to the interconnection, determine the high frequency response of the circuit. The amplifier has its maximum gain in the so-called mid-frequencies. It is important to remember that for the mid-frequency ac analysis all capacitors are replaced by short circuits.

For the ac analysis the transistor must be replaced by its ac equivalent circuit. In this chapter we limit our analysis to the hybrid (or h-parameter) model for the ac equivalent circuit. Each transistor configuration (CB, CE, CC) has an associated h-parameter. However, the h-parameter of one configuration can be directly converted into the h-parameter of another configuration. The quantities to be determined are the current, voltage, and power gains, low- and high-frequency response.

Test Yourself

1. The characteristics of an npn transistor used to design the CE amplifier circuit of Fig. P4.1a are shown in Figs. P4.1b and P4.1c. The Q-point is at V_{CEQ} = 6V, I_{CQ} = 2.9mA, I_{BQ} = 20A.

   Determine :

   a) h_{fe}
   b) h_{oe}
   c) h_{ie}
   d) h_{re}

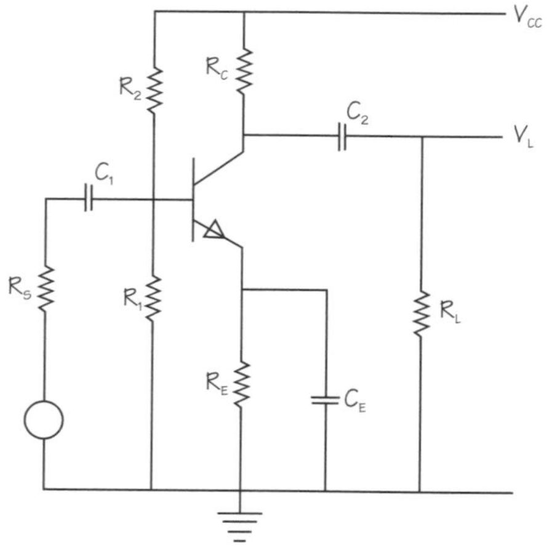

Fig. P4.1a

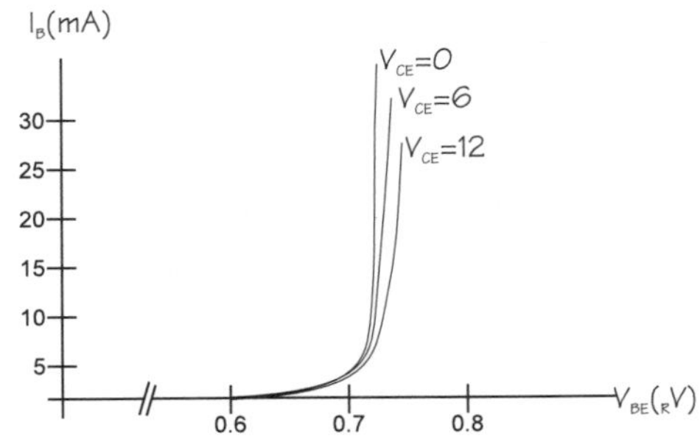

Fig. P4.1b

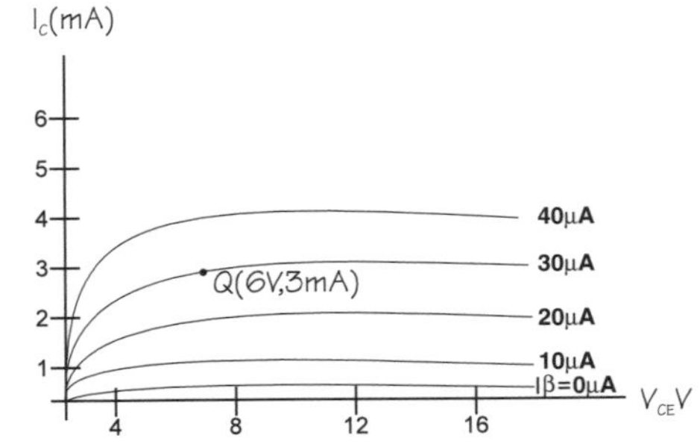

Fig. P4.1c

2. The h-parameter small-signal a.c. equivalent 42 circuit for CE, CB, and CC configuration are shown in Figs. P4.2a, P4.2b, and P4.2c.

   Deduce that:

   a) $h_{ie} = \dfrac{h_{ib}}{(1 + h_{fb})(1 - h_{rb}) + h_{ob}h_{ib}} = h_{ic}$

   b) $h_{re} = \dfrac{h_{ib}h_{ob} - h_{rb}(1 + h_{fb})}{(1 + h_{fb})(1 - h_{rb}) + h_{ob}h_{ib}} = 1 - h_{rc}$

   c) $h_{fe} = \dfrac{-h_{ib}(1 - h_{rb}) - h_{ob}h_{ib}}{(1 + h_{fb})(1 - h_{rb}) + h_{ob}h_{ib}}$
   $= -(1 + h_{fc})$

   d) $h_{oe} = \dfrac{h_{ob}}{(1 + h_{fb})(1 - h_{rb}) + h_{ob}h_{ib}} = h_{oc}$

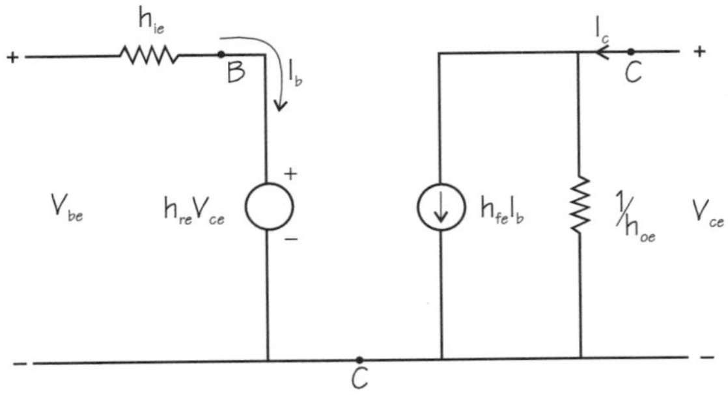

Fig. P4.2a

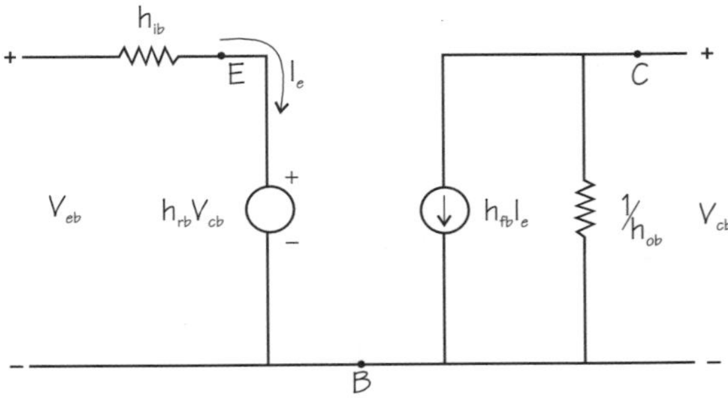

Fig. P4.2b

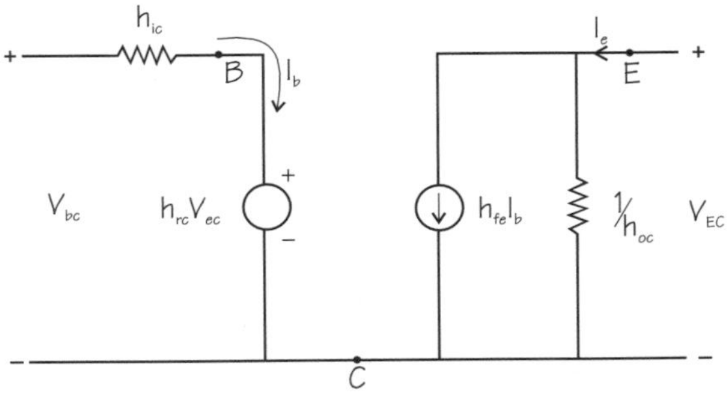

Fig. P4.2c

3. Draw the h-parameter small-signal ac equivalent circuit of Fig. P4.3 and determine expressions for:

   a) input impedence, Z_i
   b) output impedence, Z_o
   c) voltage gain, A_v
   d) current gain, A_i
   e) power gain, A_p

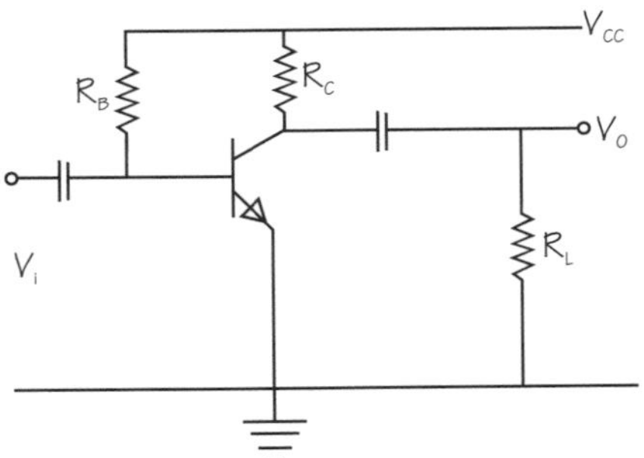

Fig. P4.3

4. For the circuit of Fig. P4.3, if $h_{fe} = 120$, $h_{re} = 5 \times 10^{-4}$, $h_{ie} = 2k$, $\dfrac{1}{h_{oe}} = 50k$, $R_B = 560k$, $R_C = 1k$, $R_L = 1k$, find:

   a) Z_i
   b) Z_o
   c) A_v
   d) A_i

5. For the network of Fig. P4.5 calculate:

   a) A_i
   b) A_v

   for $h_{oe} \to \infty$, $h_{re} = 0$, $h_{fe} = 100$, $h_{ie} = 1.4k$

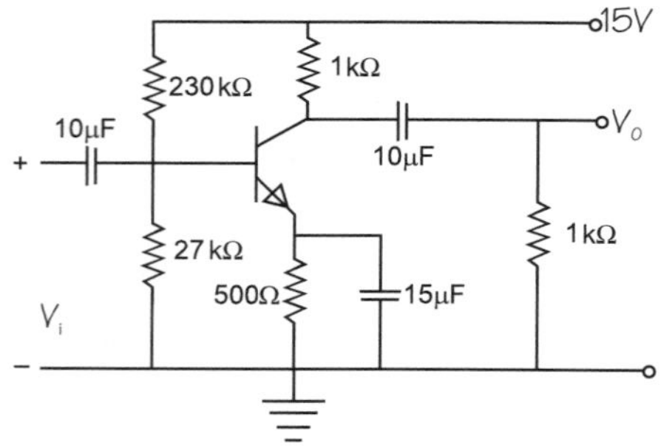

Fig. P4.5

6. Calculate:

   a) h_{ie}
   b) h_{fe}

   for the circuit of Fig. P4.6, given that $A_v = -25$, $A_i = 20$ and $R_{E1} = 0$

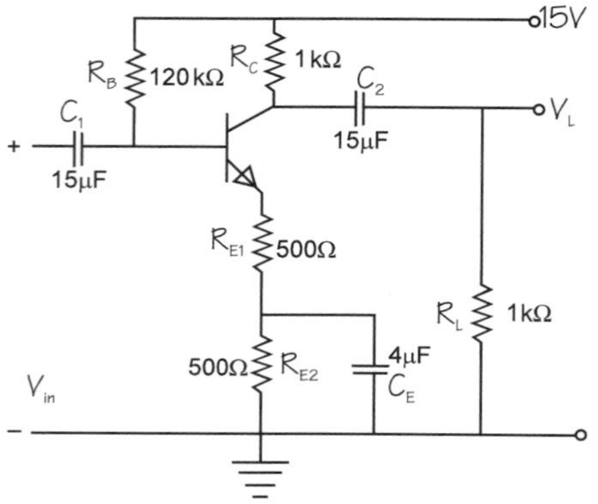

Fig. P4.6

7. Determine:

   a) Z_i b) Z_o
   c) A_i d) A_V

   for the emitter-follower amplifier circuit of Fig. P4.7 if $h_{fe} = 120$, $h_{ie} = 3k$, $h_{re} = 0$, $h_{oe} = 0$

8. Determine:

   a) Z_i b) Z_o
   c) A_i d) A_V

   for the circuit of Fig. P4.8 if $h_{fe} = 100$, $h_{ie} = 3k$, $h_{re} = 0$, $h_{oe} = 0$

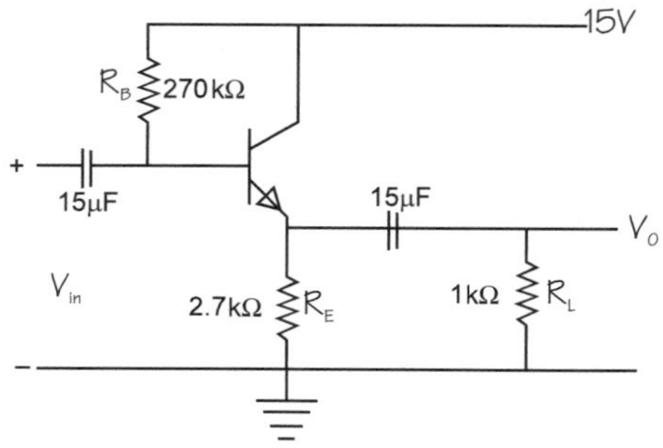

Fig. P4.7

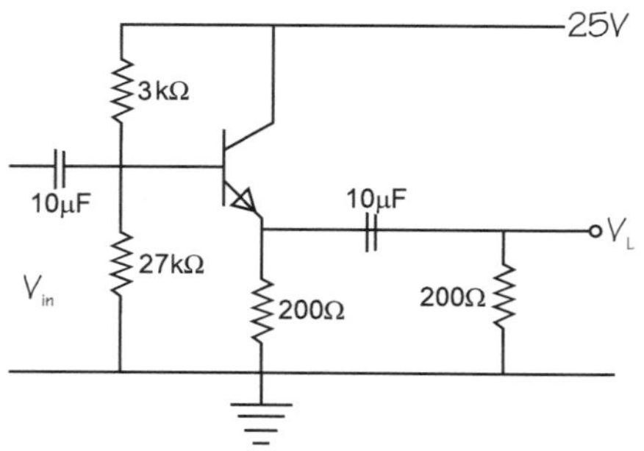

Fig. P4.8

9. a) Draw the h-parameter ac small-signal equivalent circuit for the network of Fig. P4.9.

   b) Show that the input impedence is

$$Z_I = R_E \| \left(h_{ib} + \frac{R_B}{\beta} \right)$$

   where β is the CE current gain.

   c) Show that the current gain is

$$A_i = \left(\frac{R_E}{R_E + h_{ib} + \dfrac{R_B}{\beta}} \right) \left(\frac{R_C}{R_C + R_L} \right)$$

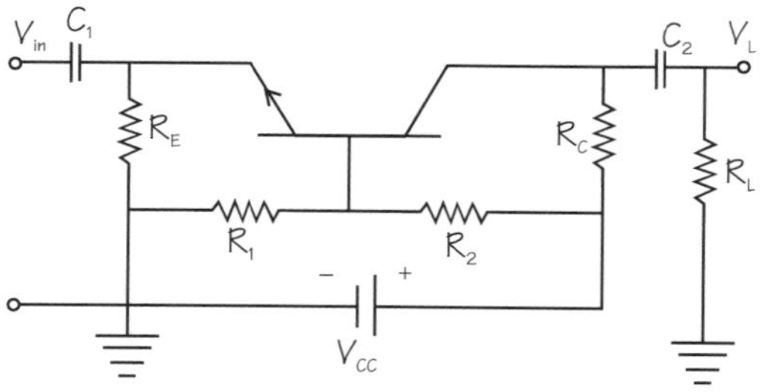

Fig. P4.9

10. For the circuit of Fig. P4.9 determine:

    a) A_v
    b) A_i

    if $R_c = R_L = 2k$, $R_E = 400\Omega$, $\beta = 100$, $R_1 = 5k$, $R_2 = 25k$, $V_{CC} = 18V$

11. Determine the power gain, A_p, for the network of Fig. P4.11.

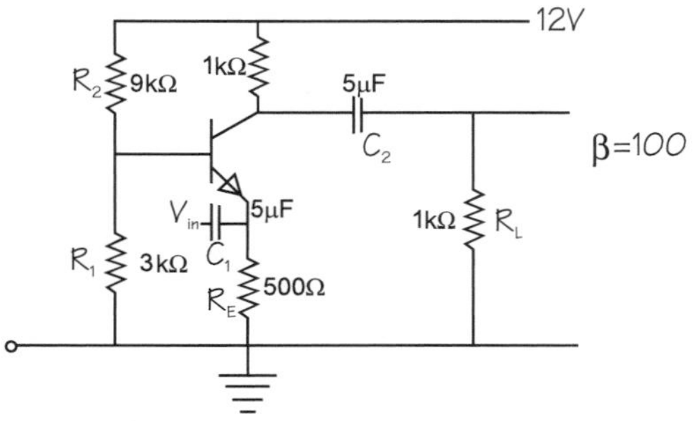

Fig. P4.11

12. The h-parameters for the transistor in Fig. P4.12 are h_{ie} = 1.4k, β = 100, h_{re} = 0, h_{oe} = 0.

    A load device with impedance 1k is connected at the output. Calculate the resistance of R_C than can result in the maximum transfer of power to the load. What is the power gain?

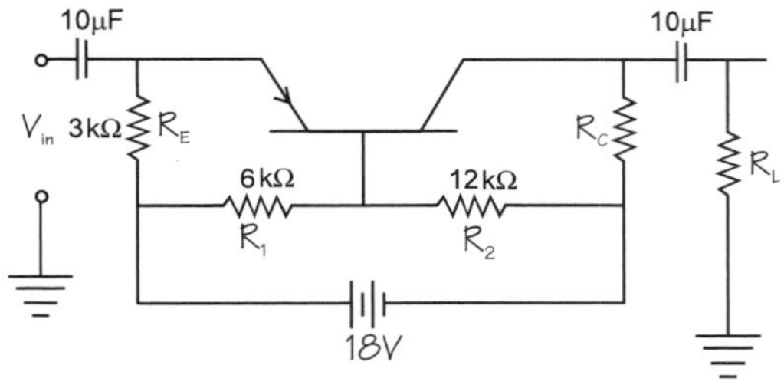

Fig. P4.12

13. Calculate the input impedance, Z_i, and the voltage gain, A_V, of the network in Fig. P4.13. Take β = 100, h_{ie} = 0, h_{re} = 0, h_{oe} = 0.

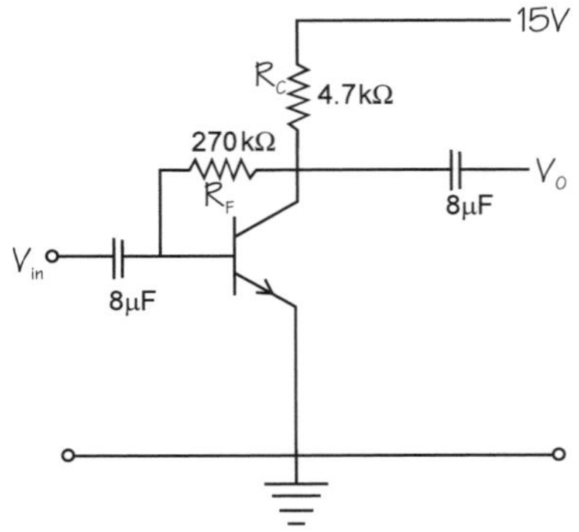

Fig. P4.13

14. Calculate the input impedance, Z_i, the output impedance, Z_o, the current gain, A_i, and the voltage gain, A_V, of the network in Fig. P4.14.

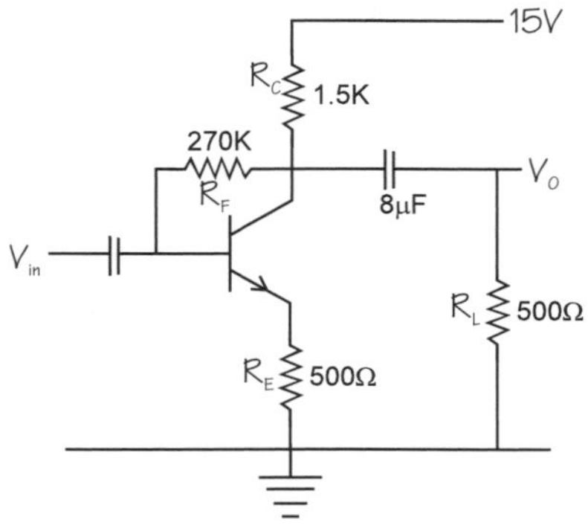

Fig. P4.14

15. A pnp transistor with β = 100 is used to design a CE voltage-divider amplifier circuit with a voltage-gain, AV = –10, as shown in Fig. P4.15. The circuit is to drive a load of 1k. Calculate the resistances R_1, R_2, and R_E.

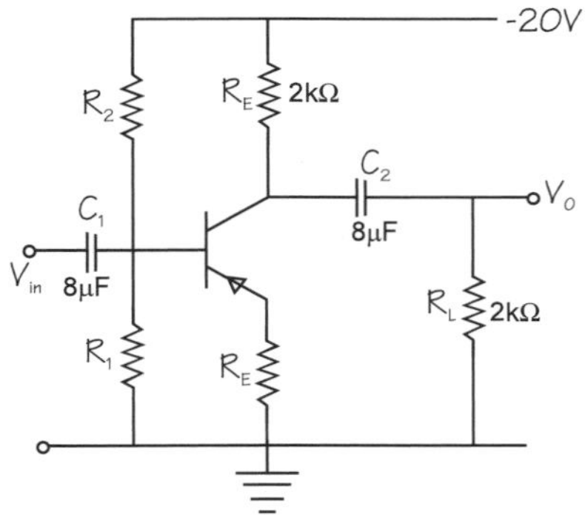

Fig. P4.15

Check Yourself

1. a) By definition, $h_{fe} = \left.\dfrac{\Delta I_C}{\Delta I_B}\right|_{V_{CE} = \text{constant}}$

Thus, draw a line $V_{CE} = 6V$, through the Q-point and determine the ratio of the change in I_C, ΔI_C, to the change in I_B, ΔI_B.

b) $$h_{oe} = \left.\frac{\Delta I_C}{\Delta V_{CE}}\right|_{I_B = \text{constant}} = \left.\frac{\Delta I_C}{\Delta V_{CE}}\right|_{I_B = 20\mu A} = \frac{3.0mA - 2.8mA}{4V} = 500\mu S$$

c) $$h_{ie} = \left.\frac{\Delta V_{BE}}{\Delta I_B}\right|_{V_{CE} = \text{constant}} = \frac{0.75V - 0.72V}{30\mu A - 20\mu A} = 3k$$

d) $$h_{re} = \left.\frac{\Delta V_{BE}}{\Delta V_{CE}}\right|_{V_{CE} = \text{constant}} = \frac{0.74V - 0.72V}{12V} = 1.67 \times 10^{-4}$$

(h-parameter)

2. a) By definition, $h_{fe} = \left.\dfrac{\Delta V_{be}}{\Delta I_b}\right|_{V_{ce} = 0}$

With reference to Fig. P4.2b, letting $V_{ce} = 0$ leads to:

$$V_{be} = V_{cb}$$

Also from the input circuit we get (KVL):

$$V_{be} = h_{ib}I_e - h_{rb}V_{cb} = h_{ib}I_e + h_{rb}V_{be}$$

or $$I_e = \frac{h_{rb} - 1}{h_{ib}}V_{be}$$

Also from Fig. P4.2b we get:

$$I_b = -I_e - h_{fb}I_e - h_{ob}V_{cb}$$

or $$Ib = -(1 + h_{fb})I_e - h_{ob}V_{cb}$$

i.e. $$I_b = -\left[(1 + h_{fb})\left(\frac{h_{rb}^{-1}}{h_{ib}}\right)V_{be}\right] + h_{ob}V_{be}$$

$$= \left[\frac{(1 + h_{fb})(1 - h_{rb})}{h_{ib}} + h_{ob}\right]V_{be}$$

Similarly by definition

$$h_{re} = \left.\frac{V_{be}}{I_{ce}}\right|_{I_b = 0}$$

with reference to Fig. P4.2c

$$V_{EC} = 0 \Rightarrow V_{bc} = V_{be}$$

i.e. $$h_{ic} = \frac{V_{bc}}{I_b} = \frac{V_{be}}{I_b} = h_{ie}$$

b) By definition, $h_{re} = \left.\dfrac{V_{be}}{V_{ce}}\right|_{I_b = 0}$

In Fig. P4.2b let $I_b = 0$

Then $I_c = -I_e$

Also from the output node

$$I_c = h_{fb}I_e + h_{ob}V_{cb}$$

Then $-I_e = h_{fb}I_e + h_{ob}V_{cb}$

or $$I_e = -\frac{h_{ob}V_{cb}}{1 + h_{fb}}$$

$$\begin{aligned} V_{ce} &= V_{cb} - V_{be} \\ &= V_{cb} - h_{rb}V_{cb} - h_{ib}I_e \\ &= (1 - h_{rb})V_{cb} - h_{ib}I_e \\ &= (1 - h_{rb})V_{cb} + h_{ib}\left(\frac{h_{ob}}{1 + h_{fb}}\right)V_{cb} \end{aligned}$$

or

$$V_{ce} = \left[(1 - h_{rb}) + \frac{h_{ib}h_{ob}}{1 + h_{fb}}\right]V_{cb}$$

$$V_{ce} = \left[(1 - h_{rb}) + \frac{h_{ib}h_{ob}}{1 + h_{fb}}\right][V_{ce} - V_{be}]$$

$$1 = \left[(1 - h_{rb}) + \frac{h_{ib}h_{ob}}{1 + h_{fb}}\right]\left[1 - \frac{V_{be}}{V_{ce}}\right]$$

$$\frac{V_{be}}{V_{ce}} = \left[(1 - h_{rb}) + \frac{h_{ib}h_{ob}}{1 + h_{fb}}\right] = \left[1 - \left\{(1 - h_{rb}) + \frac{h_{ib}h_{ob}}{1 + h_{fb}}\right\}\right]$$

$$\frac{V_{be}}{V_{ce}} = \frac{h_{rb} - h_{ib}h_{ob}}{1 + h_{fb}} \Big/ \frac{(1 - h_{rb})(1 + h_{fb}) + h_{ib}h_{ob}}{1 + h_{fb}}$$

$$\frac{V_{be}}{V_{ce}} = \frac{h_{rb}(1 + h_{fb}) - h_{ib}h_{ob}}{(1 - h_{rb})(1 + h_{fb}) + h_{ib}h_{ob}}$$

$$\therefore h_{re} = \frac{h_{rb}(1 + h_{fb}) - h_{ib}h_{ob}}{(1 - h_{rb})(1 + h_{fb}) + h_{ib}h_{ob}}$$

$$h_{rc} = \frac{V_{bc}}{V_{ce}} = \frac{V_{ce} - V_{be}}{V_{ce}} = 1 - \frac{V_{be}}{V_{ce}}$$

$$h_{rc} = 1 - h_{re}$$

or $$h_{re} = 1 - h_{rc}$$

c) By definition, $h_{fe} = \left.\frac{I_c}{I_b}\right|_{V_{ce} = 0}$

Using the circuit of Fig. P4.2b, we have for $V_{ce} = 0$, $V_{cb} = V_{be}$

$$I_b = (1 + h_{fb})I_e - h_{ob}V_{cb}$$
$$I_b = -(1 + h_{fb})I_e + h_{ob}V_{be}$$

but $\quad I_e = I_b - I_c = \dfrac{h_{rb} - 1}{h_{ib}} V_{be}$

Then $\quad I_b = (1 + h_{fb})(I_b + I_c) + \dfrac{h_{ib}h_{ob}}{1 - h_{rb}}(I_b + I_c)$

$$I_c\left[(1 + h_{fb}) + \frac{h_{ib}h_{ob}}{1 - h_{rb}}\right] = I_b\left[1 - (1 + h_{fb}) - \frac{h_{ib}h_{ob}}{1 - h_{rb}}\right]$$

$$\therefore\ h_{fe} = \frac{I_c}{I_b} = \frac{-h_{fb}(1 - h_{rb}) - h_{ib}h_{ob}}{(1 + h_{fb})(1 - h_{rb}) + h_{ib}h_{ob}}$$

Similarly by definition

$$h_{fc} = \frac{I_E}{I_b} = \frac{-(I_c + I_b)}{I_b} = -\left(1 + \frac{I_c}{I_b}\right)$$

or $\quad hfc = -(1 + h_{fe})$

or $\quad hfe = (1 + h_{fc})$

$$\therefore\ h_{fe} = \frac{I_c}{I_b} = \frac{-h_{fb}(1 - h_{rb}) - h_{ib}h_{ob}}{(1 + h_{fb})(1 - h_{rb}) + h_{ib}h_{ob}} = -(1 + h_{fc})$$

d) By definition $h_{re} = \left.\dfrac{I_c}{V_{ce}}\right|_{I_b = 0}$

Let $I_b = 0$ in Fig. P4.2b.

Then $\quad I_c = I_e$

$$V_{ce} = V_{cb}(1 - h_{rb}) - h_{ib}I_e$$

$$V_{ce} = V_{cb}(1 - h_{rb}) + h_{ib}I_c$$

$$V_{cb} = \left[(I_c - h_{fb}I_e)\frac{1}{h_{ob}}\right] = \frac{(1 + h_{fb})I_c}{h_{ob}}$$

Then $\quad V_{ce} = \left[\dfrac{(1 - h_{rb})(1 + h_{fb})}{h_{ob}} + h_{ib}\right]I_c$

$$\therefore\ \frac{I_c}{V_{ce}} = \frac{h_{ob}}{(1 - h_{rb})(1 + h_{fb}) + h_{ib}h_{ob}} = h_{oe}$$

Similarly by definition

$$h_{oc} = \left.\frac{I_e}{V_{eb}}\right|_{I_b = 0} = \frac{-I_c}{-V_{ce}} = h_{oe}$$

$$\therefore\ h_{oe} = \frac{h_{ob}}{(1 - h_{rb})(1 + h_{fb}) + h_{ib}h_{ob}} = h_{oe}$$

(h-parameter)

3. a) $Z_i = h_{ie}//R_B$

b) $Z_o = R_c//\dfrac{1}{h_o}{}_e$

c) $A_V = \dfrac{V_L}{V_i} = \dfrac{I_L R_L}{h_{ie} I_B}$, at node c

$$V_L = I_L R_L = (I_L + R_c)R_c$$

$$\Rightarrow I_c = -\left(\frac{R_L + R_c}{R_L}\right)I_L$$

Also $\quad I_c = h_{fe}I_B + h_{oe}I_L R_L$

equating the two expressions for I_c gives:

$$I_L = \frac{-R_c h_{fe} I_B}{R_c + R_L + R_c R_L R_{oe}}$$

Thus $A_V = \dfrac{I_L R_L}{h_{ie} I_B} = \dfrac{-R_c R_L h_{fe} I_B}{h_{ie}(R_c + R_L + R_c R_L h_{oe}) I_B}$

$\therefore \quad A_V = \dfrac{-R_c R_L h_{fe}}{h_{ie}(R_c + R_L + R_c R_L h_{oe})}$

d) $\quad A_i = \dfrac{I_L}{I_i} = \dfrac{I_L}{I_B} \cdot \dfrac{I_B}{I_i} = \dfrac{h_{ie}}{R_L}\left(\dfrac{I_L R_L}{I_B h_{ie}}\right) \cdot \dfrac{I_B}{I_i}$

$$= \frac{h_{ie} I_B}{R_L I_i} A_v$$

Current division at the input gives:

$$I_B = \frac{R_B}{R_B + h_{ie}} I_i \Rightarrow \frac{I_B}{I_i} = \frac{R_B}{R_B + h_{ie}}$$

$\therefore \quad A_i = \dfrac{-R_B h_{ie}}{R_L(R_B + h_{ie})}\left[\dfrac{h_{fe} R_L R_c}{h_{ie}(R_c + R_L + R_c R_L h_{oe})}\right]$

$$A_i = \frac{-h_{fe} R_c R_B}{(R_B + h_{ie})(R_C + R_L + R_c R_L h_{oe})}$$

e) $\quad A_p = A_i A_V$

$$= \frac{h_{fe}{}^2 R_c{}^2 R_B R_L}{h_{ie}(R_B + h_{ie})(R_c + R_L + R_c R_L h_{oe})^2}$$

(h-parameter)

4. a) $\quad Z_i = h_{ie} // R_B = 2k//560k = 1.99k$

b) $\quad R_c // \dfrac{1}{h_{oe}} = 1k//50k = 980\Omega$

c) $\quad A_V = \dfrac{-R_c R_L h_{fe}}{h_{ie}(R_c + R_L + R_c R_L h_{oe})} = \dfrac{1k \cdot 1k \cdot 100}{2k\left(1k + 1k + \dfrac{1k \cdot 1k}{50k}\right)} = -25$

d) $\quad A_i = \dfrac{R_B h_{ie} A_V}{R_L(R_B + h_{ie})} = \dfrac{560k \times 2k \times 25}{1k \times 562k} = -49.8$

(h-parameter)

5. a) $\quad A_V = \dfrac{-R_c R_L h_{fe}}{h_{ie}(R_c + R_L)} = \dfrac{-2k \times 1k \times 100}{1.4k(2k + 2k)} = -47.6$

b) $\quad A_i = \dfrac{R_B h_{ie} A_V}{R_L(R_B + h_{ie})} = \dfrac{20.7k \times 1.4k}{1k(22.1k)}(-47.6) = -62.4$

(CE amplifier)

6. $\quad A_V = \dfrac{-R_c R_L h_{fe}}{h_{ie}(R_c + R_L)} = \dfrac{-h_{fe}}{h_{ie}}\left(\dfrac{1k \times 1k}{2k}\right) = \dfrac{-h_{fe}}{2h_{ie}} = -25$

$$A_i = \frac{R_B h_{ie} A_V}{R_L(R_B + h_{ie})} = \frac{-120k \times 25 h_{ie}}{1k(120k + h_{ie})} = -20$$

$$\frac{h_{ie}}{(120k + h_{ie})1k} = \frac{20}{120k \times 25} \Rightarrow \frac{1k \cdot 120k}{h_{ie}} + 1k = \frac{120k \times 25}{20}$$

$$\frac{1k \cdot 120k}{h_{ie}} = \frac{120k \times 25}{20} - 1k = 149k$$

$$\Rightarrow h_{ie} = \frac{149k}{120k} \times 1k = 1.3k$$

$$h_{fe} = \frac{h_{ie}(R_c + R_L)}{R_c R_L} A_V = \frac{1.3k \times 2k \times 25}{1k \cdot 1k} = 65$$

(CE amplifier)

7. a) $Z_b = \frac{V_i}{I_b} = h_{ie} + (h_{fe} + 1)(R_E // R_L)$

$= h_{ie} + h_{fe}(R_E//R_L) \quad \text{for} \quad h_{fe} >> 1$

$Z_i = R_B//Z_b = 270k//(3k + 100(2.7k//1k))$

$Z_i = 270k//(3k + 72.97k) = 270k//75.97k = 59k$

b) $Z_o = R_E//R_L = 2.7k//1k = 730\Omega$

c) $A_i = \frac{I_L}{I_i}$, but $I_L R_L = R_E(I_E - I_L)$

At the input:

$R_B(I_i - I_b) = I_b h_{ie} + h_{fe}(R_E//R_L)I_b$

$\Rightarrow I_i = \frac{I_b}{R_B}(h_{ie} + R_B + h_{fe}(R_E//R_L))$

$\therefore \quad A_i = \frac{h_{fe} R_E R_B}{(R_E + R_L)(h_{ie} + R_B + h_{fe}(R_E//R_L))}$

d) $A_V = \frac{-A_i Z_L}{Z_i} = \frac{-77.1 \times 10^3 \times 730}{59 \times 10^3} = 880$

(Emitter-follower amplifier)

8. a) $R_B = 27k//3k = 2.7k$

$Z_i = R_B(h_{ie} + h_{fe}(R_E//R_L))$

$= 2.7k//(3k + 100(100)) = 2.2k$

b) $Z_o = R_E//R_L = 200\Omega//200\Omega = 100\Omega$

c) $A_i = \frac{h_{fe} R_B R_E}{(h_{ie} + R_B + h_{fe}(R_E // R_L))(R_E + R_L)}$

$= \frac{100 \times 2.7k \times .200k}{(3k + 2.7k + 10k)(.4k)} = 8.6$

d) $A_i = -\frac{Z_L}{Z_i} A_i = \frac{100\Omega}{2.2 \times 10^3} 8.6 = .39$

(Emitter-follower amplifier)

9. a)

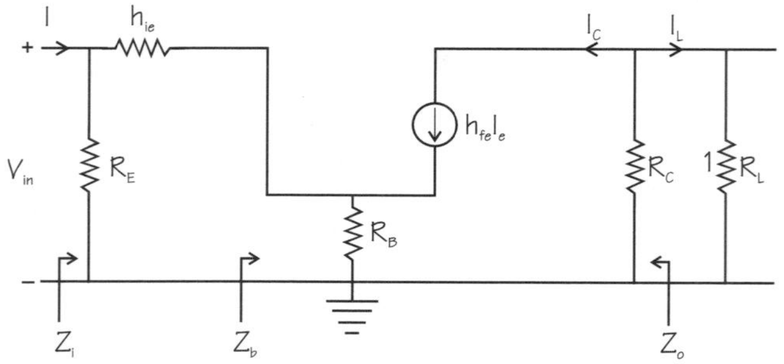

Fig. S4.9

b) $$Z_b = \frac{V_{in}}{I_b} = \frac{I_e h_{ib} + R_B[I_e + h_{fb}I_e]}{I_e}$$

$$Z_b = h_{ib} + R_B(1 + h_{fb})$$

$$= h_{ib} + R_B\left(1 - \frac{h_{fe}}{h_{fe}+1}\right); \; h_{fb} = \frac{-h_{fe}}{h_{fe}+1}$$

$$Z_b = h_{ib} + R_B\left(\frac{1}{h_{fe}+1}\right) = h_{ib} + \frac{R_B}{h_{fe}}$$

$$Z_i = R_E // Z_b = R_E // \left(h_{ib} + \frac{R_B}{h_{fe}}\right)$$

c) $$A_i = \frac{I_L}{I_i} = \frac{I_L}{I_c} \cdot \frac{I_c}{I_E} \cdot \frac{I_E}{I_i}$$

At the output

$$-I_L R_L = R_C(I_L + I_c) \Rightarrow \frac{I_L}{I_c} = \frac{-R_c}{R_c + R_L}$$

At the input

$$R_E I_i - R_E I_E = I_E\left(h_{ib} + \frac{R_B}{h_{fe}}\right)$$

i.e. $$\frac{I_E}{I_i} = \frac{R_E}{R_E + h_{ib} + \frac{R_B}{h_{fe}}}$$

Also $h_{fb} = \frac{I_C}{I_E}$, then

$$A_i = h_{fb}\left(\frac{R_E}{R_E + h_{ib} + \frac{R_B}{h_{fe}}}\right)\left(-\frac{R_c}{R_c + R_L}\right) = -\left(\frac{h_{fe}}{h_{fe}+1}\right)\left(\frac{R_E}{R_E + h_{ib} + \frac{R_B}{h_{fe}}}\right)\left(-\frac{R_c}{R_c + R_L}\right)$$

$\therefore$ $$A_i = \left(\frac{R_E}{R_E + h_{ib} + \frac{R_B}{h_{fe}}}\right)\left(\frac{R_c}{R_c + R_L}\right)$$

(h-parameter)

10. $$V_{BB} = \frac{R_1}{R_1 + R_2} \times V_{CC} = \frac{5k}{25k + 5k} \times 18V = 3V$$

$$R_{BB} = R_1 // R_2 = 5k // 25k = 4.2k$$

$$I_{CQ} = \frac{V_{BB} - V_{BE}}{R_E + \frac{R_B}{\beta}} = \frac{3 - 0.7}{.4k + \frac{4.2k}{100}} = 6.1mA$$

$$h_{ib} = \frac{26mV}{I_E(mA)} = \frac{26mV}{I_C(mA)} = \frac{26mV}{6.1} = 4.1\Omega$$

a) $$A_i = \left(\frac{R_E}{R_E + h_{ib} + \frac{R_B}{h_{fe}}}\right)\left(-\frac{R_c}{R_c + R_L}\right) = \left(\frac{.4k}{.4k + .0042 + \frac{.42k}{100}}\right)\left(\frac{2k}{2k + 2k}\right) = .089$$

b) $$Z_i = R_E // \left(h_{ib} + \frac{R_B}{h_{fe}}\right) = 400(4.2 + 42) = 41$$

$$A_V = \frac{A_i}{Z_i Z_L} = \frac{.089 \times 2 \times 10^3}{41} = 4.3$$

(CB-amplifier)

11. The circuit can be redrawn to show that it has a common-base configuration, as shown in Fig. S4.11.

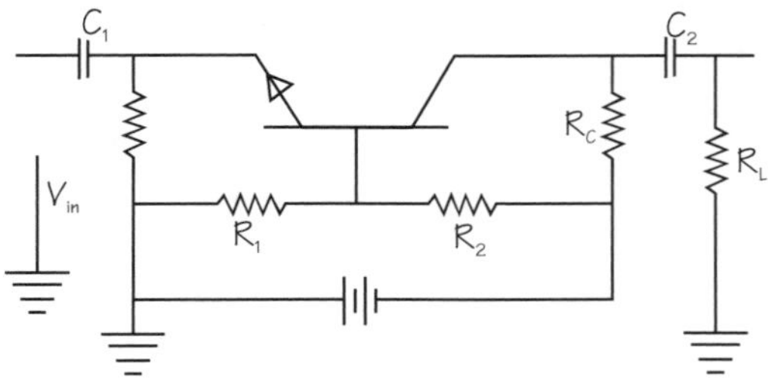

Fig. S4.11

$$V_{BB} = \frac{3k}{3k + 9k} \times 12V = 3V$$

$$R_B = 3k//9k = 2.3k$$

$$I_{CQ} = \frac{V_{BB} - V_{BE}}{R_E + \frac{R_B}{h_{fe}}} = \frac{3 - 0.7}{500 + \frac{2.3 \times 10^3}{100}} = 4.4mA$$

$$h_{ib} = \frac{26mV}{I_c(mA)} = \frac{26mV}{4.4mA} = 5.9A$$

$$Z_i = R_E//\left(h_{ib} + \frac{R_B}{h_{fe}}\right) = 500//(23 + 5.9) = 26.9\Omega$$

$$Z_o = R_c = 1k$$

$$A_i = \left(\frac{R_E}{R_E + h_{ib} + \frac{R_B}{h_{fe}}}\right)\left(\frac{R_c}{R_c + R_L}\right) = \left(\frac{500}{500 + 5.9 + 23}\right)\left(\frac{1000}{2000}\right) = 0.47$$

$$A_V = \frac{A_i Z_L}{Z_L} = \frac{.47 \times 10^3}{26.9} = 17.5$$

$$A_P = A_i A_V = 17.5 \times 0.47 = 8.3$$

(Emitter-follower amplifier)

12. $$\frac{h_{ib}}{h_{fe}} + 1 = \frac{1.4k}{100} + 1 = 13.9\Omega$$

$$R_B = R_1//R_2 = 6k//12k = 4k$$

a) $$R_c = R_L = 1k$$

$$A_i = \left(\frac{R_E}{R_E + h_{ib} + \frac{R_B}{h_{fe}}}\right)\left(\frac{R_c}{R_c + R_L}\right) = \left(\frac{3k}{3k + .0139k + .004}\right)\left(\frac{1}{2}\right) = .49$$

b) $$A_P = \frac{Z_L A_i^2}{Z_i} = \frac{(.49)^2 10^3}{Z_i}$$

$$Z_i = R_E//\left(h_{ib} + \frac{R_B}{h_{fe}}\right) = 3k//(.0139 + 0.04)$$

$$Z_i = 52.9$$

(CB amplifier)

13. $$I_B = \frac{V_{CC} - V_{BE}}{R_F + \beta R_c} = \frac{15 - 0.7}{270k + 100 \times 4.7k} = 19.3\mu A$$

$$I_E = (\beta + 1)I_B = 101 \times 19.3\mu A = 1.95mA$$

$$r_e = \frac{26mV}{I_E} = \frac{26mV}{1.9mA} = 133\Omega$$

$$A_V = \frac{-R_c}{r_e} = \frac{-4.7k}{13.3} = -352.8$$

$$Z_i = \beta R_e//\frac{R_F}{|A_V|} = (100 \times 13.3)//\frac{270 \times 10^3}{352.8}$$

$$= 13300//765.3$$

$$= 723.6\Omega$$

(CE with feedback amplifier)

14. a) $$Z_i = \frac{\beta R_F R_E}{R_F + \beta R_E\left(1 + \frac{R_c}{R_E}\right)} = \frac{100 \times 200 \times 10^3 \times 500}{200 \times 10^3 + 100 \times 500\left(1 + \frac{1500}{500}\right)}$$

$Z_i = 25k$

b) $Z_o = R_c // R_F = 200k//1.5k = 1.49k$

c) $$A_i = \frac{R_F}{R_E + R_c + \frac{R_F}{\beta}} = \frac{200k}{.5k + 1.5k + \frac{200k}{100}} = 50$$

d) $$A_v = -\frac{A_i}{Z_i} Z_o = \frac{50 \times 1.49k}{25k} = 2.98$$

(CE with feedback)

15. $$A_V = -10 = \frac{R_c R_L}{R_c + R_L}\left(\frac{1}{R_E + \frac{h_{ie}}{\beta}}\right)$$

$$10 = \frac{2k \times 2k}{4k}\left(\frac{1}{\frac{h_{ie}}{\beta} + R_E}\right)$$

i.e. $\frac{h_{ie}}{\beta} + R_E = R'_E = 100$

$R_{dc} = R_c + R'_E = 2k + .1k = 2.1k$

$R_{ac} = R'_E + R_c // R_L = .1k + 1k = 1.1k$

$$I_{CQ} = \frac{V_{CC}}{R_{dc} + R_{ac}} = \frac{-20}{3.2k} = -6.25mA$$

$$\frac{h_{ie}}{\beta} = \frac{26mV}{I_{CQ}} = 4.16\Omega$$

$R_E = 100 \quad 4.16 = 95.8$

Using the design rule $R_B = 0.1\beta R_E$

$R_B = 0.1 \times 100 \times 95.8 = 958$

$$I_C = \frac{V_{BB} + V_{BE}}{\frac{R_B}{\beta} + R_E}$$

$$-6.25mA = \frac{V_{BB} + V_{BE}}{\frac{958}{100} + 95.8};$$

$V_{BB} = -0.7 - 6.25(.0958 + .00958) = -1.36V$

But $$V_{BB} = \frac{R_1}{R_1 + R_2}(-20) = -1.36V$$

$$R_B = \frac{R_1 R_2}{R_1 + R_2} = 958\Omega$$

From the last two equations we get:

$R_1 = 1k, \qquad R_2 = 14.2k$

(CE amplifier)

Grade Yourself

Circle the numbers of the questions you missed. Then fill in the total incorrect for each topic. If you answered more than three questions incorrectly, you need to focus on that topic. If a topic has less than three questions and you had at least one wrong, we suggest you study that topic also. Read your textbook, a review book, or ask your teacher for help.

Subject: BJT Single-Stage Amplifiers

Topic	Question Numbers	Number Incorrect
h-parameter	1, 2, 3, 4	
CE amplifier	5, 6, 15	
Emitter-follower amplifier	7, 8, 11	
h-parameter	9	
CB amplifier	10, 12	
CE with feedback amplifier	13	
CE with feedback	14	

FET Single-Stage Amplifiers

5

Brief Yourself

The transistor can be used to amplify signals when the Q-point lies in the linear region of the current-voltage characteristics. The nomenclature of single-stage FET amplifiers is based upon the transistor configuration (CG, CD, CS) and the dc bias network (fixed-bias, voltage divider, etc.), as described in chapter 2. Coupling capacitors are used to isolate the input signal and the output load so that the dc bias point of the transistor is not adversely affected during its operation. Also, bypass capacitors such as emitter bypass capacitors are added to improve the performance (i.e., stability) of the circuit. However, these capacitors determine the low-frequency response of the amplifier circuit. On the other hand, the transistor parasitic capacitances, resistances as well as parasistics due to the interconnection, determine the high-frequency response of the circuit. The amplifier has its maximum gain in the so-called mid-frequencies. It is important to remember that for the mid-frequency ac analysis all capacitors are replaced by short circuits.

For the ac analysis the transistor must be replaced by its ac equivalent circuit. In this chapter we limit our analysis to the hybrid (or h-parameter) model for the ac equivalent circuit. Each transistor configuration has an associated h-parameter. However, the h-parameter of one configuration can be directly converted into the h-parameter of another configuration. The quantities to be determined are the current, voltage, power gains, and low- and high-frequency response.

Test Yourself

FET Single-Stage Amplifiers

1. The JFET transistor of Fig. P5.1 has an output admittance Y_{OS} of 20 μS and transconductance g_m = 2mS. When the switch S is in position 1, the capacitor C_S bypasses the resistor R_S. The capacitor C_S is shorted out when S is in position 2. Compare:

   a) the ac equivalent circuits
   b) the input impedance
   c) the output impedance
   d) amplifier gain

   for the switch S in position 1 and position 2.

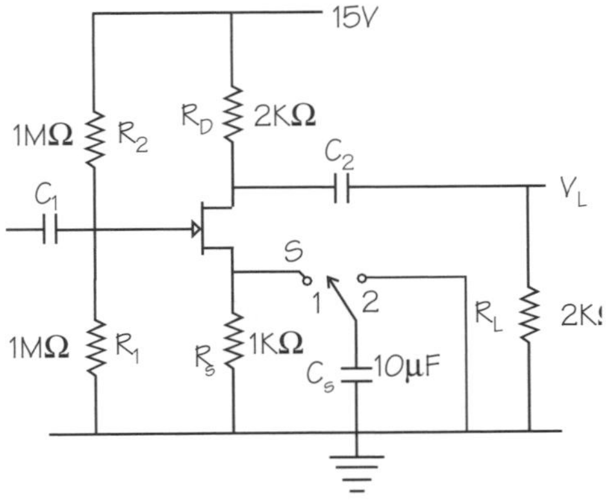

Fig. P5.1

2. The n-channel MOSFET of Fig. P5.2 has a drain-to-source saturation current $I_{DSS} = 10mA$ and a pinch-off voltage $V_P = -2V$. Calculate the voltage gain A_V if the output admittance $Y_{OS} = 0$.

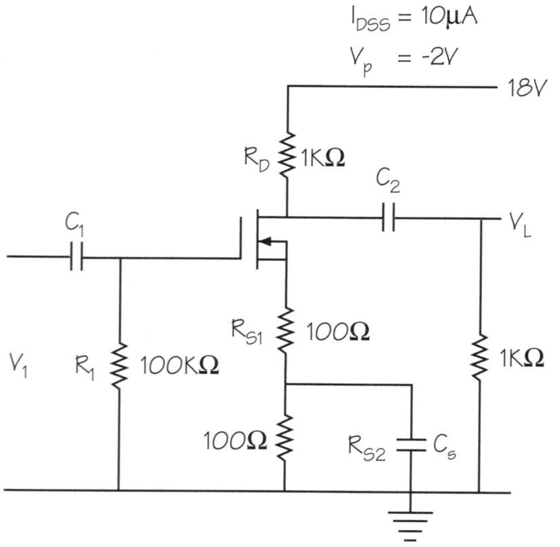

Fig. P5.2

3. The JFET shown in Fig. P5.3 has a drain-to-source saturation current $I_{DSS} = 10mA$, pinch-off voltage $V_P = -5V$, and output admittance 100k.

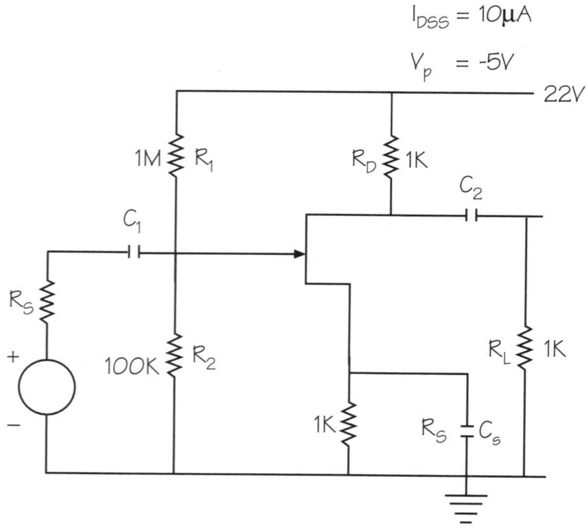

Fig. P5.3

a) Find the Q-point of the amplifier.
b) Calculate the voltage gain, A_V.
c) Calculate the current gain, A_i.
d) Calculate the power gain, A_P.
e) Calculate the input impedance, Z_i.
f) Calculate the output impedance, Z_o.

4. The circuit shown in Fig. P5.4 has a voltage gain of –2, and an output impedance of 2kΩ. Calculate the value of R_D.

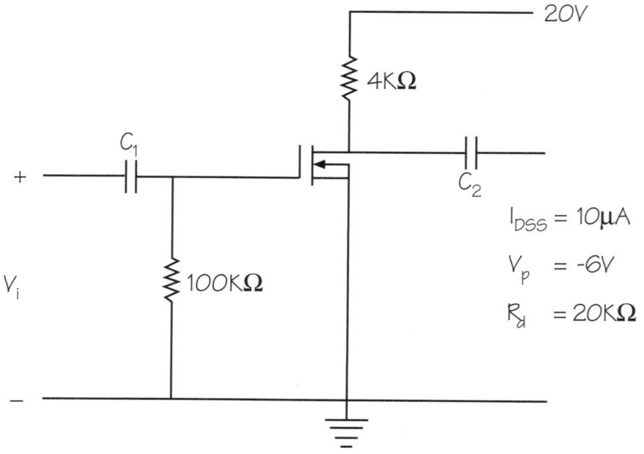

Fig. F5.4

5. The voltage-divider circuit in Fig. P5.5 has a gain of –2 and an output impedance of 1kΩ. The transistor has a pinch-off voltage of –6V, a drain-saturation current of 8mA, and a negligible output admittance. Calculate the value of R_D and R_S and the dc Q-point.

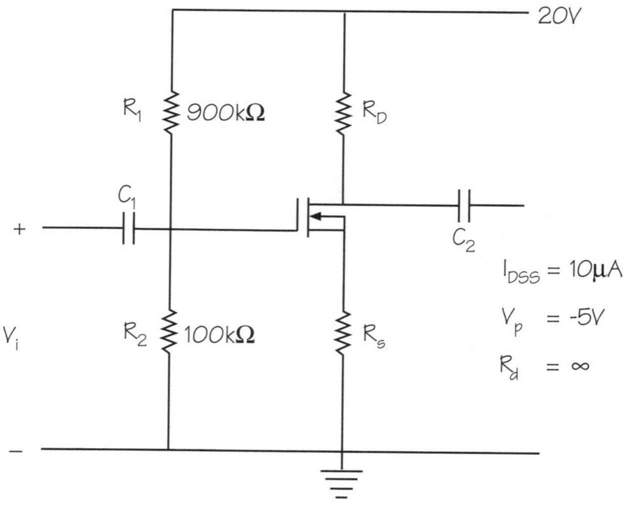

Fig. P5.5

6. Compute the small-signal parameters C_{gd} and C_{gs} for the 2N3495 JFET transistor shown in the CS amplifier circuit of Fig. P5.6.

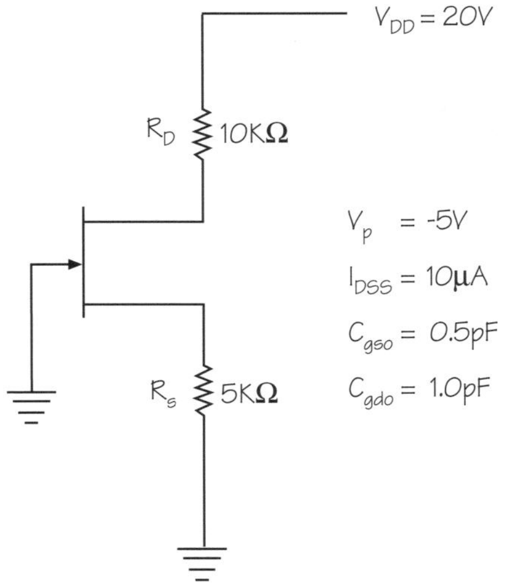

Fig. P5.6

7. The MOSFET transistor of the common-gate amplifier circuit of Fig. P5.7 has a drain-to-source saturation current of 16mA and a pinch-off voltage of –4V and an input impedance r_d = 50kΩ. Calculate the power gain of the circuit.

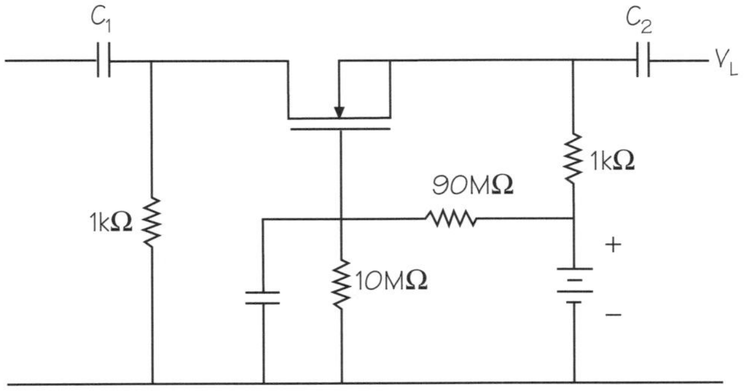

Fig. P5.7

8. The enhancement-mode MOSFET shown in Fig. P5.8 has $I_{DS}(on)$ = 6mA, $V_{GS}(on)$ = 8V, $V_{GS}(th)$ = 3V, r_d = 50kΩ. Calculate:

   a) the output impedance, Z_o
   b) the input impedance, Z_i
   c) the voltage gain A_V

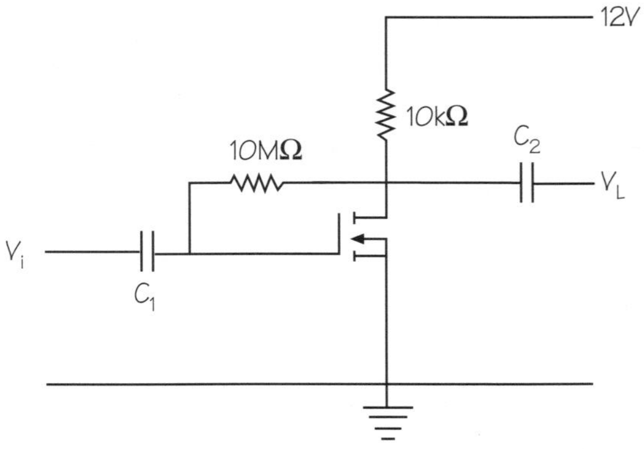

Fig. P5.8

9. Show that the low-frequency response of the amplifier circuit of Fig. P5.2 can be expressed in terms of the mid-frequency gain A_{Vmid} and the parameters

$$\gamma_1 = C_2(+ R_D)$$

$$\gamma_2 = C_S R_{S2}$$

$$\gamma_3 = \frac{\gamma_2}{1 + g_M R_{S2}/(1 + g_M R_{S1})}$$

as

$$A_V = A_{Vmid}\left(\frac{\gamma_1\gamma_3}{\gamma_2}\right)\left(\frac{S}{1 + S\gamma_1}\right)\left(\frac{S + S\gamma_2}{1 + S\gamma_3}\right)$$

10. The FET in the amplifier circuit of Fig. P5.10 has C_{dg} = 2pF, C_{gs} = 10pF, C_{ds} = 2pF. I_{DSS} = 16mA, V_P = –4V, r_{ds} = 100k.

    Determine:

    a) the mid-frequency gain.
    b) the low-frequency cutoff.
    c) the high-frequency cutoff.

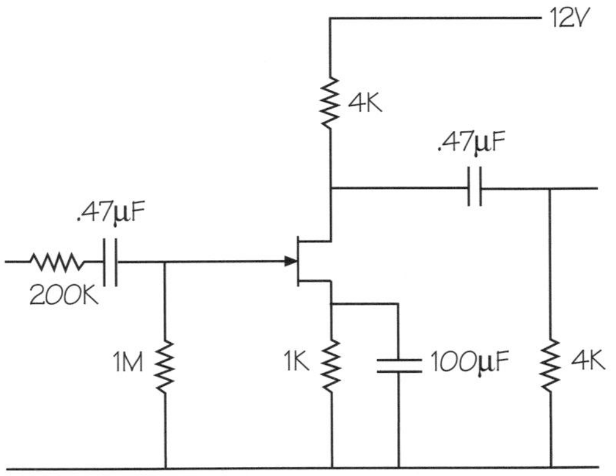

Fig. P5.10

Check Yourself

1. a)

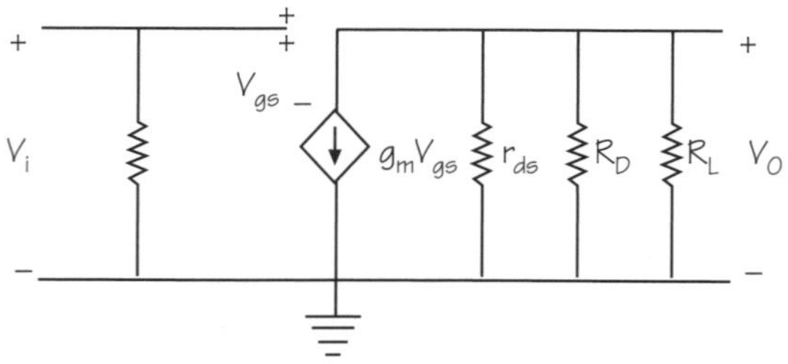

Fig. S5.1a

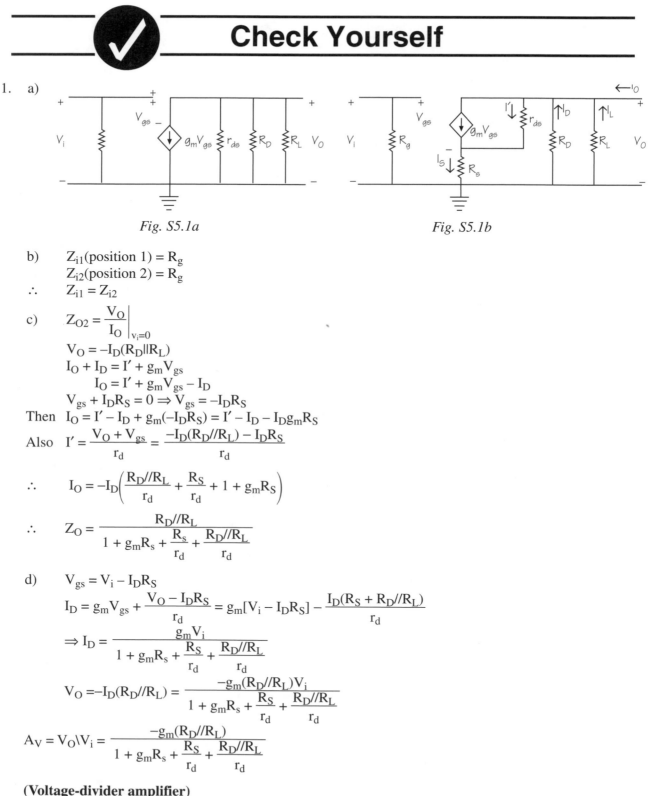

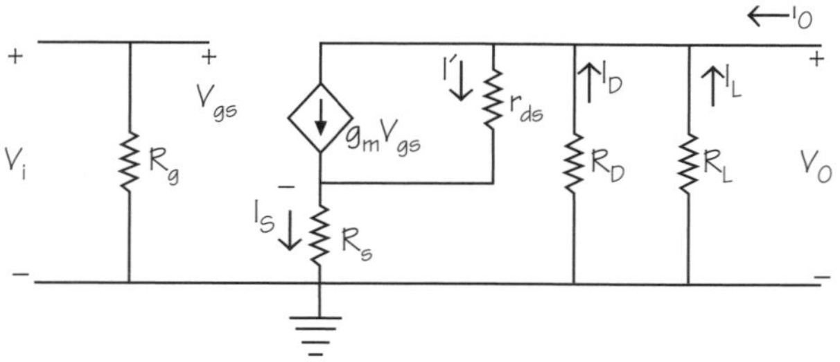

Fig. S5.1b

b) $Z_{i1}(\text{position 1}) = R_g$

$Z_{i2}(\text{position 2}) = R_g$

$\therefore \quad Z_{i1} = Z_{i2}$

c) $$Z_{O2} = \left.\frac{V_O}{I_O}\right|_{v_i=0}$$

$V_O = -I_D(R_D||R_L)$

$I_O + I_D = I' + g_mV_{gs}$

$I_O = I' + g_mV_{gs} - I_D$

$V_{gs} + I_DR_S = 0 \Rightarrow V_{gs} = -I_DR_S$

Then $I_O = I' - I_D + g_m(-I_DR_S) = I' - I_D - I_Dg_mR_S$

Also $$I' = \frac{V_O + V_{gs}}{r_d} = \frac{-I_D(R_D//R_L) - I_DR_S}{r_d}$$

$$\therefore \quad I_O = -I_D\left(\frac{R_D//R_L}{r_d} + \frac{R_S}{r_d} + 1 + g_mR_S\right)$$

$$\therefore \quad Z_O = \frac{R_D//R_L}{1 + g_mR_s + \dfrac{R_s}{r_d} + \dfrac{R_D//R_L}{r_d}}$$

d) $V_{gs} = V_i - I_DR_S$

$$I_D = g_mV_{gs} + \frac{V_O - I_DR_S}{r_d} = g_m[V_i - I_DR_S] - \frac{I_D(R_S + R_D//R_L)}{r_d}$$

$$\Rightarrow I_D = \frac{g_mV_i}{1 + g_mR_s + \dfrac{R_S}{r_d} + \dfrac{R_D//R_L}{r_d}}$$

$$V_O = -I_D(R_D//R_L) = \frac{-g_m(R_D//R_L)V_i}{1 + g_mR_s + \dfrac{R_S}{r_d} + \dfrac{R_D//R_L}{r_d}}$$

$$A_V = V_O \backslash V_i = \frac{-g_m(R_D//R_L)}{1 + g_mR_s + \dfrac{R_S}{r_d} + \dfrac{R_D//R_L}{r_d}}$$

(Voltage-divider amplifier)

	Switch in Position 1	Switch in Position 2
Z_i	R_g	R_g
Z_O	990Ω	331Ω
A_V	3.96	1.32

2. The voltage gain, A_V, is:

$$A_V = \frac{-g_m R_D // R_L}{1 + g_m R_{S1}}$$

But g_m is:

$$g_m = \frac{2I_{DSS}}{V_p}\left(1 - \frac{V_{gs}}{V_p}\right)$$

$$V_{gs} = -0.2I_D$$

$$I_{DQ} = I_{DSS}\left(1 - \frac{-0.2I_{DQ}}{-2}\right)^2$$

$$= 10\text{mA}(1 - 0.01\,I_{DQ})^2$$

$$= 10\text{ mA}(1 - 0.2I_{DQ} + 0.01\,I_{DQ}^2)$$

$$0.1\,I_{DQ}^2 - 3I_{DQ} + 10 = 0$$

$$I_{DQ} = \frac{3 \pm \sqrt{9 - 4(.1)(10)}}{2 \times 1}$$

$$I_{DQ} = 3.82\text{mA or } 26.15\text{mA}$$

Thus $V_{gs} = -0.2I_{DQ} = -0.2(3.82) = 0.76\text{V}$

$$g_m = \frac{2I_{DSS}}{V_p}\left(1 + \frac{0.76}{2}\right) = \frac{2 \times 10}{2}(1 + 0.38)$$

$$g_m = 6.18\text{mS}$$

$$A_v = \frac{-(6.18 \times 10^{-3})(0.5 \times 10^3)}{1 + (6.18 \times 10^{-3})(.1)}$$

$$A_V = -1.91$$

(Voltage-divider amplifier)

3.

$$R_g = R_1 // R_2 = 1\text{M} // 100\text{k} = 90.9\text{k}$$

$$V_g = \frac{R_2}{R_1 + R_2}15\text{V} = \frac{100\text{k}}{100\text{k} + 1\text{M}}15\text{V} = 2\text{V}$$

$$V_{gs} = 2 - I_D R_S$$

$$I_D = I_{DSS}\left(1 - \frac{V_{gs}}{V_p}\right)^2 = I_{DSS}\left(1 - \frac{2 - I_D R_S}{-5}\right)^2$$

$$I_D^2 - 19I_D + 49 = 0 \Rightarrow I_D = 3.07\text{mA or } 15.92\text{mA}$$

$$V_{gs} = 2 - I_D R_S = 2 - 3.07 = -1.07\text{V}$$

$$V_{DS} = 22 - (3.07)(2) = 15.86\text{V}$$

$$g_m = \frac{2I_{DSS}}{|V_p|}\left(1 - \frac{V_{gs}}{V_p}\right) = \frac{2 \times 5}{5}\left(1 - \frac{-1.07}{-5}\right) = 1.57\text{mS}$$

a) $Z_i = R_g = 90.9\text{k}$

b) $A_V = -g_m(R_D // R_L // r_d)$

$= -1.57\text{mS }(500//100\text{k}) = -0.78$

c) $Z_o = R_D // R_L // r_d = 497\Omega$

d) $A_i = \dfrac{-A_V}{Z_o} Z_i = \dfrac{781}{497} \times 90.0\text{k} = 142$

e) $A_P = |A_i||A_V| = 142 \times .78 = 112$

(Voltage-divider amplifier)

4.

$$A_V = -2 = \frac{-g_m R_D}{1 + g_m R_S + \dfrac{R_D + R_S}{2}}$$

$$Z_o = 2\text{k} = \frac{R_D}{1 + g_M R_S + \dfrac{R_D + R_S}{2}}$$

$$\Rightarrow g_m = 1\text{mS}$$

$$2\text{k} = \frac{R_D}{1 + \dfrac{R_D}{r_d}} \quad \text{for } R_S = 0$$

$$2\text{k} = \frac{R_D}{1 + \dfrac{R_D}{20\text{k}}}$$

$$R_D = 2.2\text{k}$$

(Fixed-bias amplifier)

5.

$$g_m = \frac{A_V}{20} = \frac{2}{1\text{k}} = 2\text{mS}$$

But $g_m = \dfrac{2I_{DSS}}{V_P}\left(1 - \dfrac{V_{gs}}{V_P}\right)$

$$2\text{mS} = \frac{2 \times 10\text{mA}}{5}\left(1 - \frac{V_{gs}}{-5}\right) \Rightarrow V_{gs} = -2.5\text{V}$$

$$V_g = \frac{100\text{k}}{100\text{k} + 900\text{k}} \times 20\text{V} = 2\text{V}$$

$$V_{gs} = V_g - V_S \Rightarrow V_S = V_g - V_{gs} = 2 - (-2.5) = 4.5\text{V}$$

$$I_D = 10\text{mA}\left(1 - \frac{-2.5}{-5}\right)^2 = 2.5\text{mA}$$

$$R_S = \frac{V_S}{I_S} = \frac{V_S}{I_D} = \frac{4.5\text{V}}{2.5\text{mA}} = 1.8\text{k}$$

$$Z_o = \frac{R_D}{1 - g_m R_S} \Rightarrow 1\text{k} = \frac{R_D}{1 + (2\text{mS})(1.8\text{k})} \Rightarrow R_D = 4.6\text{k}$$

(Voltage-divider amplifier)

6.

$$V_{gs} = -5I_D$$

$$I_D^2 = 10\left(1 - \frac{-5I_D}{-5}\right)^2 = 10(1 - 2I_D + I_D^2)$$

$$I_D^2 - 2.1I_D + 1 = 0 \Rightarrow I_D = .73\text{V or } 1.69\text{V}$$

$$V_{gs} = -5 \times 0.73\text{V} = -3.65\text{V}$$

$$g_m = \frac{2 \times 10}{5}\left(1 - \frac{-3.65}{-5}\right) = 1.08\text{mS}$$

$$V_{DD} = I_D R_D - V_{DG} = 0$$

$$V_{DG} = 20 - 10\text{k}(0.73) = 12.7\text{V}$$

a) $$C_{gd} = \frac{C_{gdo}}{\left(1 + \frac{V_{DG}}{V_P}\right)^{1/3}} = \frac{1pF}{\left(1 + \frac{12.7}{.7}\right)^{1/3}} = 0.37pF$$

b) $$C_{gs} = \frac{C_{gso}}{\left(1 + \frac{V_{gs}}{V_P}\right)^{1/3}} = \frac{0.5pF}{\left(1 + \frac{.73}{0.7}\right)^{1/3}} = 0.37pF$$

(CS amplifier)

7. $$V_g = \frac{10M}{10M + 90M} \times 20V = 2V$$

$$V_{gs} = V_g - 1kI_D = 2 - I_D$$

i.e. $$I_D = I_{DSS}\left(1 - \frac{V_{gs}}{V_P}\right)^2 = 16\left(1 - \frac{2 - I_D}{-4}\right)^2$$

$$I_D^2 - 13I_D + 36 = 0 \Rightarrow I_D = 4mA \text{ or } 9mA$$

$$V_{gs} = 2 - 4 = -2V$$

$$g_m = \frac{2I_{DSS}}{V_P}\left(1 - \frac{V_{gs}}{V_P}\right) = \frac{2 \times 16}{4}\left(1 - \frac{1}{2}\right) = 2mS$$

$$A_V = g_m R_D \text{ (for } r_d >> 10R_D)$$

$$= 2mS \times 1k = 2$$

$$Z_i = R_S // \frac{1}{g_m} = 1k // \frac{1}{2mS} = 333\Omega$$

$$Z_o = 1k$$

$$A_i = \frac{A_V}{Z_o} Z_i = \frac{2 \times 333}{1k} = .67$$

$$A_P = 2 \times 0.67 = 1.3$$

(CG amplifier)

8. $$K = \frac{I_D(on)}{(V_{gs}(on) - V_{TH})^2} = \frac{10mA}{(8-3)^2} = 0.4mS$$

$$V_{gs} = V_{DS} = V_{DD} - I_D R_D = 12 - I_D$$

$$I_D = K(V_{gs} - V_T)^2 = .4mS(12 - I_D - 3)^2$$

$$0.4I_D^2 - 8.2I_D + 32.4 = 0$$

$$\Rightarrow I_D = 1.04mA \text{ or } 19mA$$

$$V_{gs} = 12 - 1.04 = 10.96V$$

$$g_m = 2 \times .4(10.96 - 3) = 6.4mS$$

$$Z_i = \frac{R_F + r_d // R_D}{1 + g_m(r_d // R_D)} = \frac{10M + 50k//1k}{1 + 6.4(50k//1k)} = 1.38M$$

$$Z_o = R_F // r_d // R_D = 10M//50k//1k = 980\Omega$$

$$A_V = -g_m(R_F // r_d // R_D) = -6.4mS \times .98k = -6.24$$

(CS with feedback amplifier)

9. The voltage gain

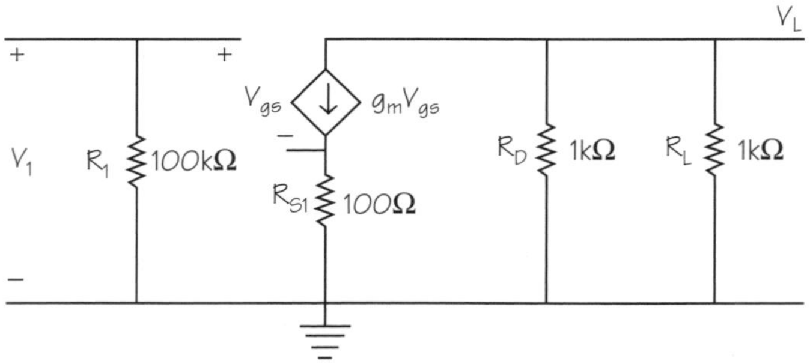

Figure S5.2

$$A_V = \frac{V_o}{V_i} = \frac{I_L R_L}{V_i}$$

Current division at the output

$$I_L = \left(\frac{R_D}{R_D + R_L + \frac{1}{SC_2}}\right)(-g_m V_{gs})$$

Then $A_V = \left(\frac{R_D \cdot R_L}{R_D + R_L + \frac{1}{SC_2}}\right)\left(\frac{-V_{gs}g_m}{V_i}\right)$

$$V_{gs} = V_i - g_m V_{gs}\left(R_{S1} + R_{S2} // \frac{1}{SC_2}\right)$$

$$A_V = \left[\frac{R_D R_L}{R_D + R_L + \frac{1}{SC_2}}\right]\left[\frac{-g_m}{1 + g_m\left(R_{S1} + R_{S2}//\frac{1}{SC_S}\right)}\right]$$

$$= \frac{-g_m R_L R_D}{\left[R_D + R_L + \frac{1}{SC_2}\right]\left[1 + g_m R_{S1} + \frac{g_m R_{S2}}{SC_2}\left(\frac{1}{R_{S2} + \frac{1}{SC_S}}\right)\right]}$$

$$= \left[\frac{-R_L R_D SC_2}{SC_2(R_L + R_D) + 1}\right]\left[\frac{g_m}{1 + g_m R_{S1} + \frac{g_m R_{S2}}{1 + SC_S R_{S2}}}\right]$$

$$= \left[\frac{-R_L R_D SC_2}{1 + SC_2(R_L + R_D)}\right]\left[\frac{g_m}{1 + g_m R_{S1}}\right]\left[\frac{1}{1 + \frac{g_m R_{S2}}{(1 + g_m R_{S1})(1 + SC_S R_{S2})}}\right]$$

$$= \left[\frac{-g_m R_L R_D SC_2}{1 + SC_2(R_L + R_D)}\right]\left[\frac{1}{1 + g_m R_{S1}}\right]\left[\frac{1 + SC_S R_{s2}}{SC_S R_{S2} + \left(1 + \frac{g_m R_{S2}}{1 + g_m R_{S1}}\right)}\right]$$

or $$V_{gs} = \frac{V_i}{1 + g_m\left(R_{S1} + R_{S2} // \frac{1}{SC_S}\right)}$$

(Frequency response)

10. $$V_{gs} = -I_D R_S = -1k(I_D mA) = I_D$$

$$I_D = I_{DSS}\left(1 - \frac{V_{gs}}{V_P}\right)^2 = 16\left(1 - \frac{I_D}{4}\right)^2$$

$$I_D = \frac{16}{16}(4 - I_D)^2 = 16 - 8I_D + I_D^2$$

$$I_D = I_D^2 - 9I_D + 16 = 0$$

$$I_D = \frac{9 \pm \sqrt{81 - 4.16}}{2}$$

$$I_D = 2.06mA$$

i.e. $$V_{gs} = (2.06mA)(1k) = 2.06V$$

$$g_m = \frac{2I_{DSS}}{V_P}\left(1 - \frac{V_{gs}}{V_P}\right) = \frac{2 \times 16}{4}\left(1 - \frac{2.06}{4}\right)mS$$

$$g_m = 3.88mS$$

a) The mid-frequency gain,

$$A_V = g_m(r_{ds}//R_D//R_L)$$

$$= -3.88 \times 10^{-3}(100k//4k//4k)$$

$$= -3.88 \times 10^{-3}(100k//11k)$$

$$= -3.88 \times 10^{-3}\left(\frac{100}{101}\right) \times 10^3$$

$$= -3.84$$

b) $$\gamma_1 = C_1(R_L + r_{ds}//R_D)$$

$$= .47\mu F\ (4k + 100k//4k)$$

$$= .47\mu F\ (4k + 3.84k) = 3.7ms$$

$$\gamma_2 = R_S C_S = 3k \times 100\mu F = 200ms$$

$$\gamma_3 = \left(R_S // \frac{1}{g_m}\right)C_S = \left(1k // \frac{1}{3.88 \times 10^{-3}}\right)(100\mu F)$$

$$= (1k//.257k)(100\mu F) = 20ms$$

$$f_1 = \frac{1}{2\pi\gamma_1} = \frac{1}{2\pi(3.7ms)} = 43Hz$$

$$f_2 = \frac{1}{2\pi\gamma_2} = \frac{1}{2\pi(200ms)} = .78Hz$$

$$f_3 = \frac{1}{2\pi\gamma_3} = \frac{1}{2\pi(20ms)} = 7.36Hz$$

$\therefore$ Low-frequency cutoff is 43Hz

c) $$C_{in} = 10pF + 2pF(1 - (A_V))$$

$$= 20pF + 2(4.84)pF = 19.7pF$$

$$\gamma_1 = C_{in}(R_i//R_G) = 19.7pF(200k) = 3.94\mu s$$

Grade Yourself

Circle the numbers of the questions you missed. Then fill in the total incorrect for each topic. If you answered more than three questions incorrectly, you need to focus on that topic. If a topic has less than three questions and you had at least one wrong, we suggest you study that topic also. Read your textbook, a review book, or ask your teacher for help.

Subject: FET Single-Stage Amplifiers

Topic	Question Numbers	Number Incorrect
Voltage-divider amplifier	1, 2, 3, 5	
Fixed-bias amplifier	4	
CS amplifier	6	
CG amplifier	7	
CS with feedback amplifier	8	
Frequency response	9, 10	

$C_{out} = 4pF$

$\gamma_2 = C_{out}(R_D//r_{ds}//R_L) = 4pF(4k//4k//100k) = 7 \times 10^{-9}S$

$\therefore$ High-frequency cutoff is 40kHz

(Frequency response)

Compound Configurations

6

Brief Yourself

When two or more transistors are coupled to each other, directly or by using coupling capacitors, the configuration is referred to as a compound configuration. Compound configurations are widely used in either discrete or integrated circuits. One type of compound configuration is the cascade connection, which provides stages in series. In such a connection the output of a given stage is coupled to the input of the next stage, as shown in problems 1 through 7. The current gain Ai and the voltage gain A_V of a multistage amplifier increase with the increase in the number of stages used and the amplification of each stage. The cascode connection is another example of the compound configuration. There is a variety of these configurations as shown in problems 10 and 14. Two common cascode configurations are the Darlington pair and Differential amplifiers. Problems 11 through 13 and 16 through 18 are examples of Darlington-pair differential amplifiers, respectively. Problem 19 is an example of compound configuration widely used in some integrated circuits as a constant current source.

Test Yourself

1. Fig. P6.1 shows a cascaded amplifier of two stages. Assume that the transistors are identical and that h_{fe} [β] for each one is 150. The biasing resistors are: $R_C = 2.5k\Omega$, $R_B = 400k\Omega$, $R_E = 1.5k\Omega$. Assume that $C_1 = C_2 = C_3 = 1\mu f$, and $C_E = 10\mu f$. If a load resistance of $10k\Omega$ is connected to the output:

   a) Draw the small-signal model for the circuit. (Consider that $h_{oe} = \frac{1}{r_o} = 0$, and that the coupling and bypass capacitors can be replaced by short circuits at the signal frequency.)

   b) Find the total voltage gain (in dB).

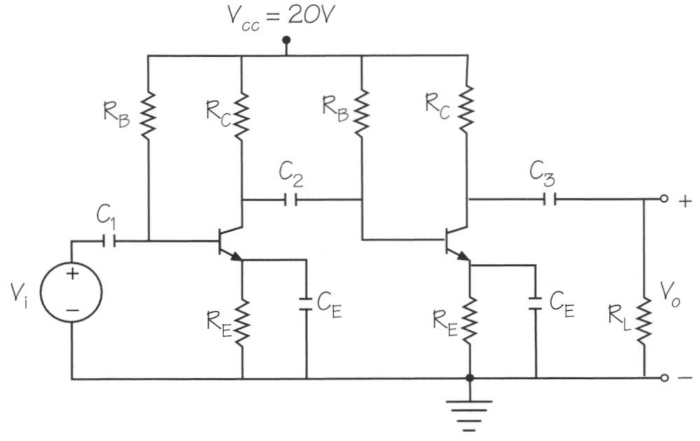

Fig. P6.1

c) If the input voltage, V_i, is 20μV, find the output voltage, V_o.

d) If the combination of R_E and the bypass capacitor, C_E, for each stage are replaced by a short circuit, then the voltage gain will be the same as in part b. What is the disadvantage of this method?

2. In problem 1:

a) Find the input and the output impedances.

b) If the bypass capacitors are removed from the two stages, redraw the small-signal model and find the input and output impedances for the new circuit.

c) Find the voltage gain for the circuit in part b. Compare the voltage-gain value with that of problem 1, part b. What do you conclude from that comparison?

3. For the circuit shown in Fig. P6.3, both transistors have h_{fe} = 100, h_{ie} = 1.214kΩ, h_{oe} = 10μS.

a) Calculate the input and the output impedances.

b) Determine the total voltage gain with respect to the voltage source [V_o / V_s].

c) Determine the total current gain of the amplifier.

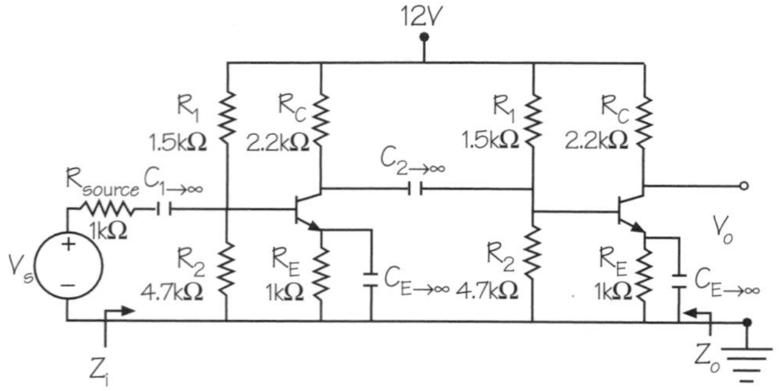

Fig. P6.3

4. The two-stage amplifier shown in Fig. P6.4 consists of CE and CC [Emitter Follower] amplifiers. The hybrid parameters for each stage are: h_{ie} = 2kΩ and h_{fe} =100.

a) Draw the small-signal model, assuming that all capacitors may be replaced by short circuits at the signal frequency.

b) Compute the input impedance and the output impedance for each stage.

c) The current gain and the voltage gain for each stage amplifier and the overall current and voltage gains.

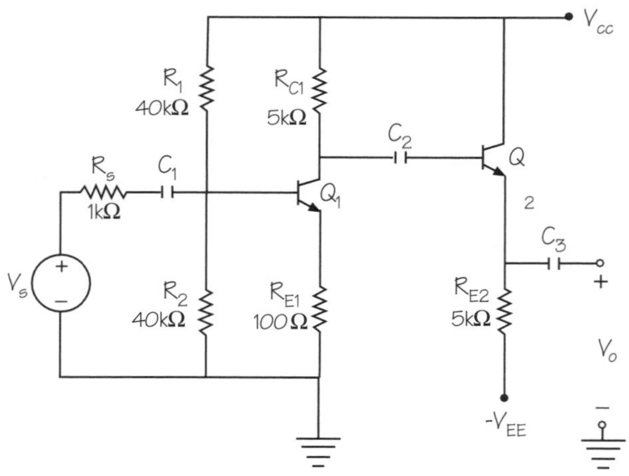

Fig. P6.4

5. Consider the cascade amplifier shown in Fig. P6.5 with h_{ie} = 3kΩ and h_{fe} = 100 for each transistor.

a) Draw the small-signal model, assuming all capacitors can be replaced by short circuit approximation.

b) Find the input and output impedances and the overall voltage and current gains of the amplifier.

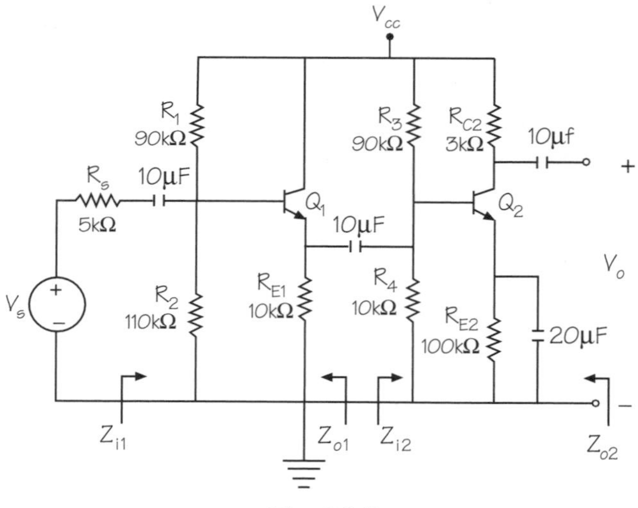

Fig. P6.5

6. For the JFET cascade amplifier shown in Fig. P6.6, assume that both transistors are identical with I_{Dss} = 8mA, V_p = –4V. Consider that r_d is very large.

a) Calculate the dc bias conditions.

b) Draw the small-signal model for the amplifier (replace all capacitors by short circuits at the signal frequency); then compute the input and output impedances.

c) Calculate the voltage gain for each stage and the overall voltage gain.

d) Compute the output voltage if a 10mV signal is applied to the input.

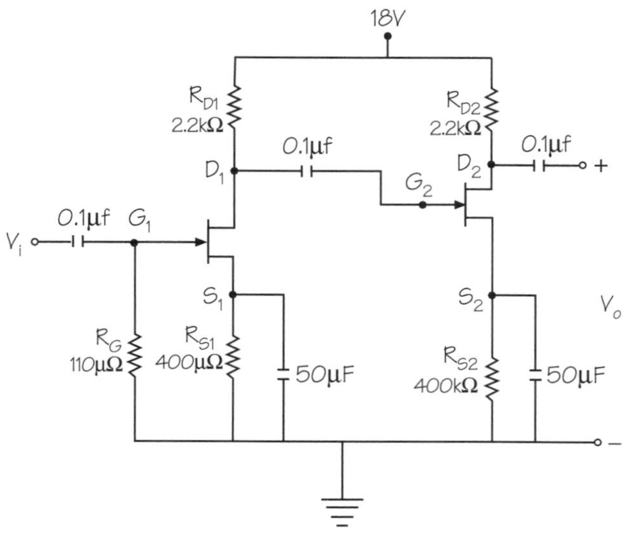

Fig. P6.6

7. The cascade amplifier shown in Fig. P6.7 has the following parameters:

For the JFETs, $g_m = 2.6\text{mS}$, $r_d = 25\text{k}\Omega$.

For the BJTs, $h_{ie} = 1.2\text{k}\Omega$, $h_{fe} = 200$,

$$h_{oe} = \frac{1}{r_o} = 5\mu\text{S}.$$

a) Find the input and output impedance of each stage.

b) The voltage gain of every stage and the overall voltage gain.

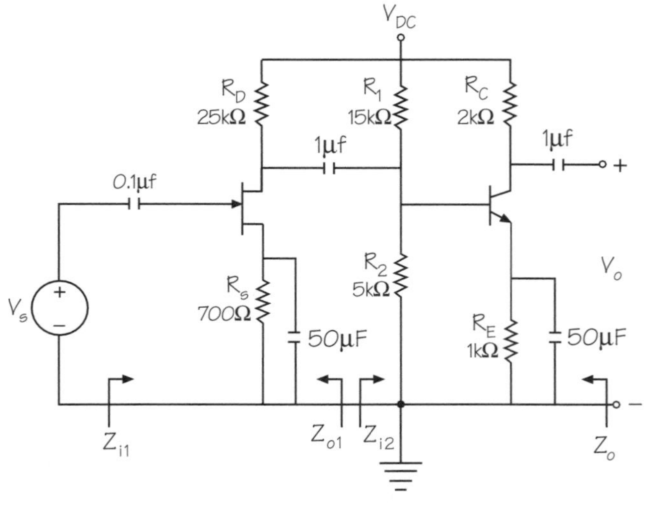

Fig. P6.7

8. The CE and CB cascade amplifier shown in Fig. P6.8 has the following parameters: $h_{ie} = 2\text{k}\Omega$, $h_{fe} = 100$, $h_{ib} = 10$, $h_{fb}[\alpha] = 0.98$.

a) Draw the ac small-signal model.

b) Find Z'_{i1}, Z_{i1}, Z_{o1}, Z'_{i2} and Z_{o2}.

c) The overall voltage gain V_o / V_s and the overall current gain.

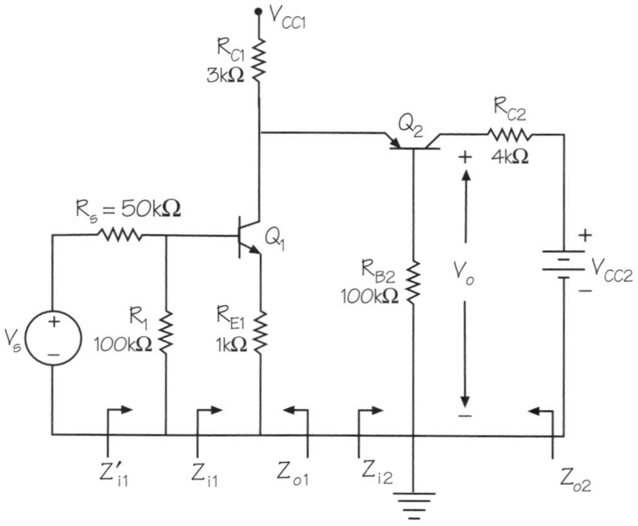

Fig. P6.8

9. Consider the circuit in Fig. P6.9 with $h_{fe} = 100$ and $h_{ie} = 4\text{k}\Omega$ for each transistor.

a) Draw the ac small-signal model.

b) Compute A_i, A_v, A_{vs}, Z_i and Z_o

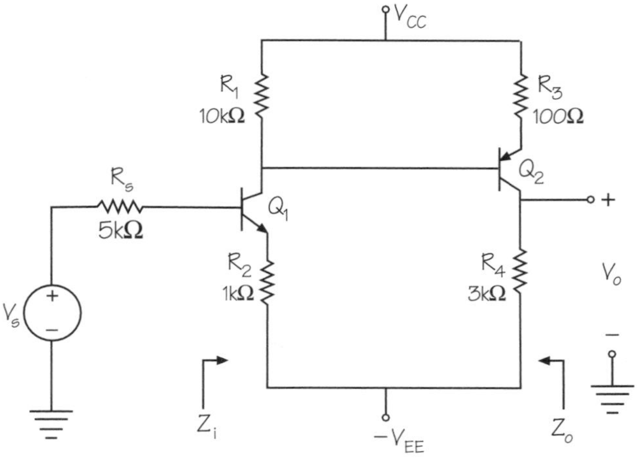

Fig. P6.9

10. Given: $h_{fe} = 100$ for both transistors in Fig. P6.10, $h_{oe} = 2.9\mu S$ for the CE amplifier and $h_{oe} = 33\mu S$ for the CC amplifier. Determine the lower cutoff frequency and sketch the Bode plot.

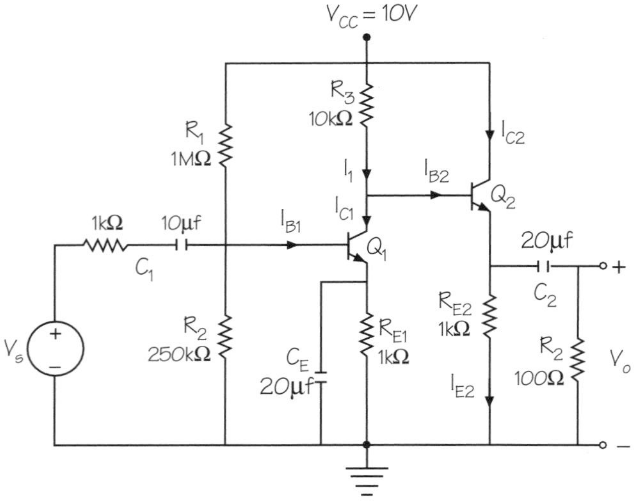

Fig. P6.10

11. Show that the transistor Q_2 of a Silicon Darlington pair shown in Fig. P6.11 can never be saturated.

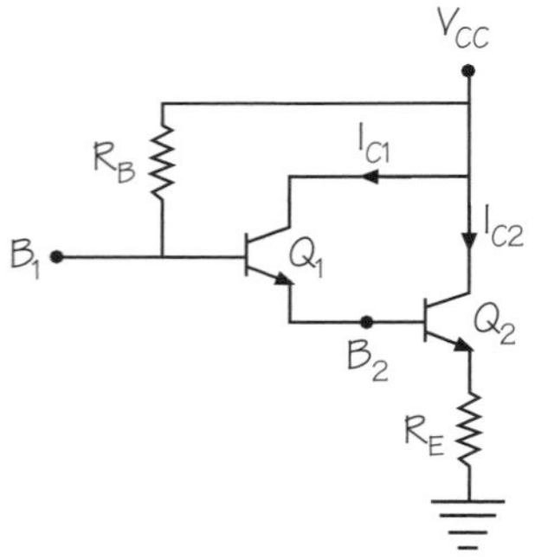

Fig. P6.11

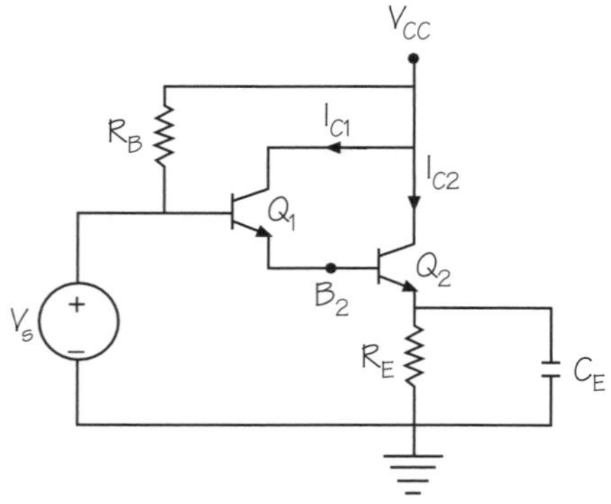

Fig. P6.12

12. Prove that the current gain of Darlington pair shown in Fig. P6.12 is given by: $\beta_D \approx \beta_1\beta_2$.

13. The Darlington emitter follower circuit is shown in Fig. P6.13. Assume that the two transistors are identical such that $\beta_1 = \beta_2$ and $h_{ie1} = h_{ie2}$. Derive relations for:

a) the input impedance of the pair.
b) the voltage gain.
c) the current gain.

In all of the above cases, assume that the capacitors can be replaced by short circuits at the signal frequency.

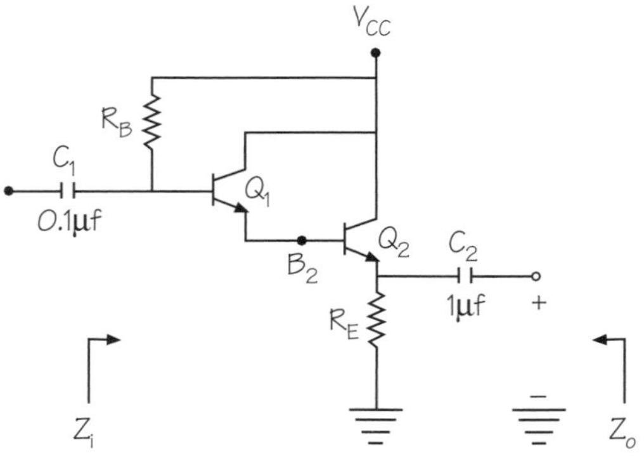

Fig. P6.13

14. For the cascade circuit shown in Fig. P6.14:

a) Draw the ac small-signal model. Consider all bypass and coupling capacitors are large enough so that they can be replaced by short circuits in the small-signal model.
b) Find the input impedance, the output impedance, the overall voltage and current gains. Take β for both transistors as 200.

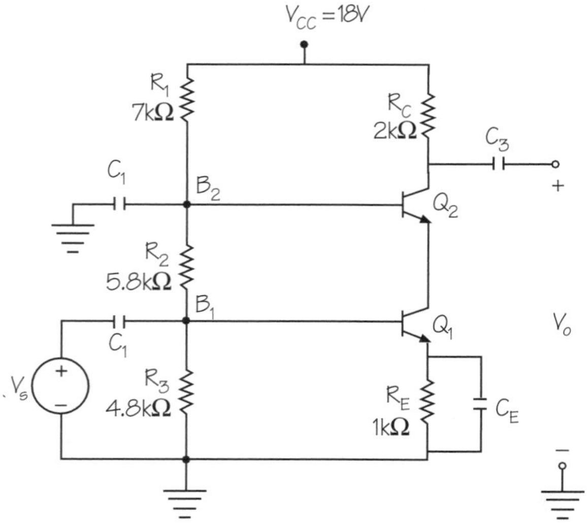

Fig. P6.14

15. The circuit shown in Fig. P6.15 is called the "Difference Amplifier." It is the basic building block of the emitter-coupled Logic [ECL] family of the integrated circuit. V_R is a reference voltage and the input is applied to the terminal, V_i. The output is taken out of the collectors C_1 and/or C_2. Assume that the transistors are identical; find a relation between V_{C1} and V_{C2} for the following cases:

    a) $V_i = V_R$

    b) $V_i = V_R \mp \Delta V$, where ΔV is the difference between the input voltage and reference voltage. Typically, $\Delta V \approx 120\text{mV}$

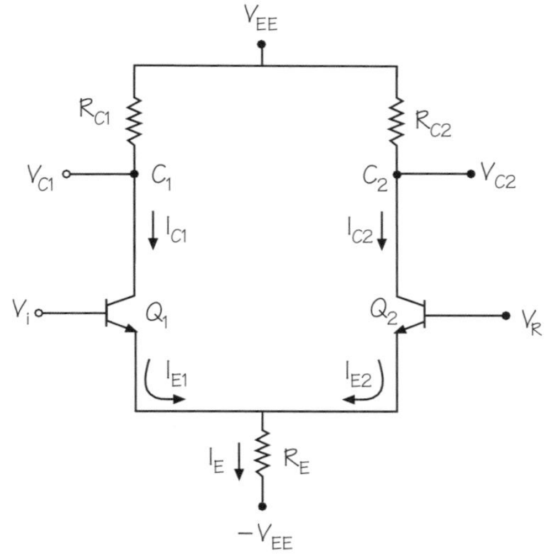

Fig. P6.15

16. In the circuit of problem P6.15, let $R_{C1} = R_{C2} = 1\text{k}\Omega$, $R_E = 2\text{k}\Omega$, $V_R = 1\text{V}$, $\Delta V = \mp 120\text{mV}$, $V_{CC} = |V_{EE}| = 5\text{V}$ and $\beta = 50$. Determine I_{C1}, I_{C2}, V_{C1}, V_{C2}, and I_E for:

    a) $V_i = V_R$

    b) $V_i = V_C \mp \Delta V$. (Take $V_{BE} = 0.7\text{V}$).

    c) If β changes by 10%, how much I_E will vary?

17. a) Draw the ac small-signal model for the differential amplifier shown in Fig. P6.17. Assume that the transistors are identical and that $h_{oe} = \infty$.

    b) Derive an expression for the differential voltage gain, A_d.

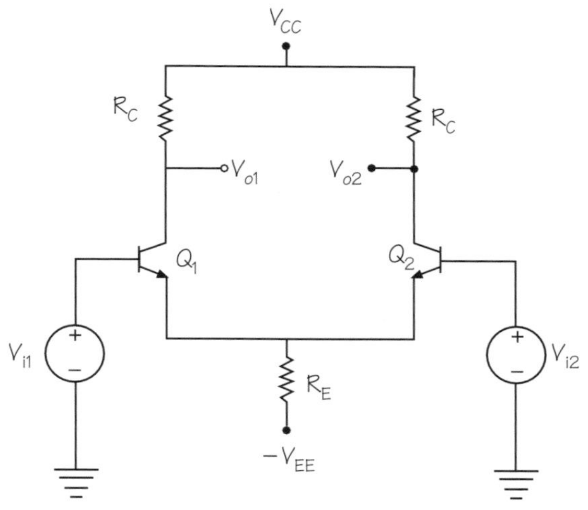

Fig. P6.17

18. Draw the ac small signal for the common-mode differential amplifier shown in Fig. P6.18; then derive a relation for the common-mode voltage gain, A_C.

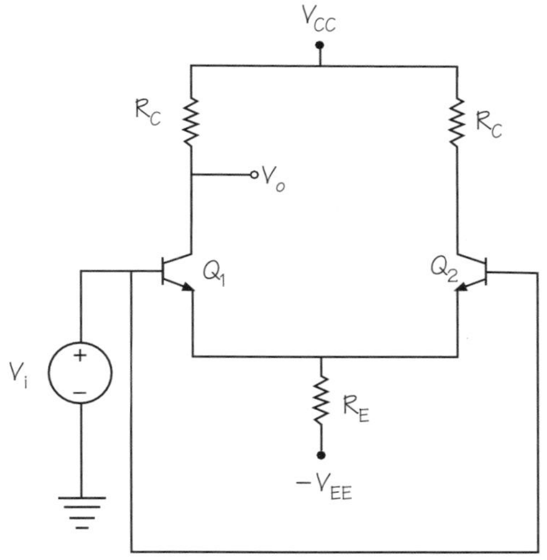

Fig. P6.18

19. The circuit shown in Fig. P6.19 is known as the "Widlar Current Source." It replaces the common-emitter resistance, R_E, in the differential pair in advanced ECL family and provides, almost, a constant current source regardless of temperature variation.

a) Prove that $I_o = \left(\frac{\beta}{\beta + 2}\right)\left(\frac{V_{ac} - V_{BE}}{R}\right)$.

b) If $V_{ac} = 5V$, $R = 2.5k\Omega$, $V_{BE} = 0.7V$, $\beta = 100$, calculate I_o.

c) If β varies by 10% due to temperature variations, how much will I_o vary? Compare your result with that of part c in problem 16.

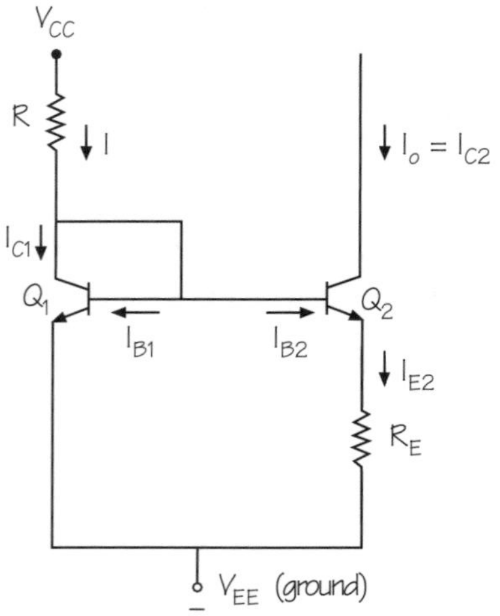

Fig. P6.19

Check Yourself

1. a)

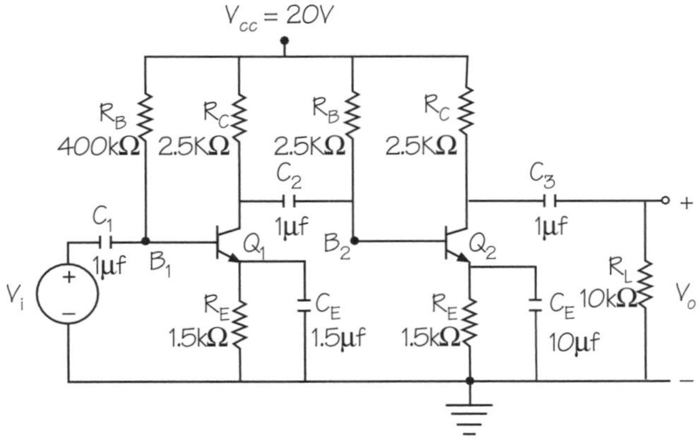

Fig. S6.1

Replace all the capacitors by short circuits, and dc supplies by a zero potential equivalent (short circuit). Therefore, the ac equivalent small-signal model is shown in Fig.S6.1a.

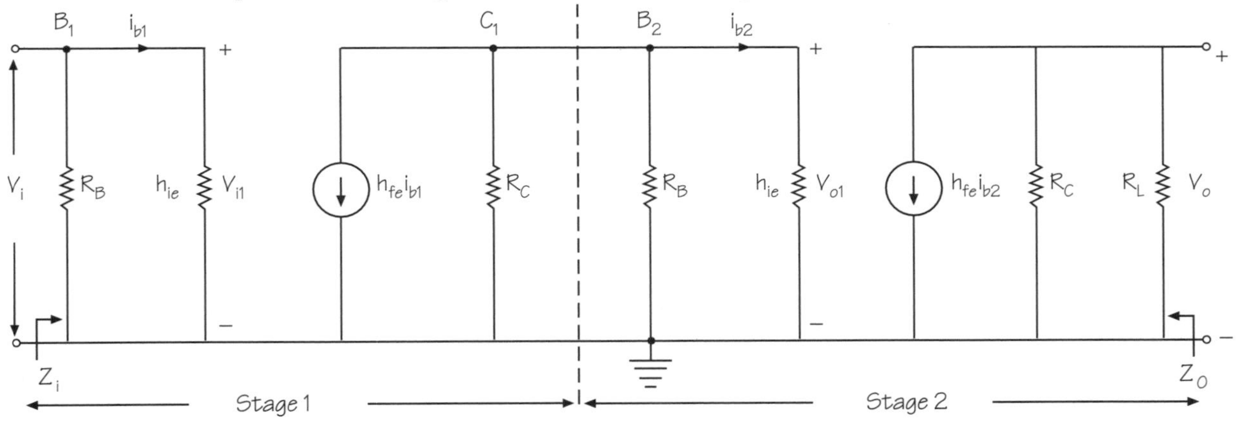

Fig. S6.1A

b) First we have to find h_{ie}. From the dc analysis:

$$I_b = \frac{V_{CC} - V_{BE}}{R_B + (\beta + 1)R_E}$$

$$I_b = \frac{20 - 0.7}{400 + 151 \times 1.5} = 0.031\text{mA}$$

$$h_{ie} = \frac{26\text{mV}}{I_b} = \frac{26\text{mV}}{0.031\text{mA}} = 0.844\text{k}\Omega$$

$$A_{V1} = \frac{V_{o1}}{V_{i1}} = \frac{-h_{fe}i_{b1}[R_C // R_B // h_{ie}]}{i_{b1}h_{ie}}$$

$$A_{V1} = \frac{-h_{fe}[R_C // R_B // h_{ie}]}{h_{ie}} = \frac{-150[2.5 // 400 // 0.844]}{0.844}$$

$$A_{V1} = -112$$

By similar method:

$$A_{V2} = \frac{h_{fe}[R_C \,//\, R_L]}{h_{ie}} = \frac{-150[2.5 \,//\, 10]}{0.844}$$

$A_{V2} = -355.45$

$A_V = A_{V1}A_{V2} = (-112)(-355.45) = 39810.4$

$A_V[db] = 20 \log_{10}A_V = 20 \log_{10}39810.4 = 92dB$

c) $V_o = A_V V_i$

$V_o = 39810.4 \times 20 \times 10\text{-}6 = 0.8V$

d) (1) The circuit without R_E has less stability level toward the dc biasing than the circuit with R_E.

(2) The circuit without R_E draws more power from the power supply than the circuit with R_E.

(Cascade amplifier)

2. a) From Fig.S6.1b:

$Z_i = R_B \,//\, h_{ie}$

$Z_i = 400 \,//\, 0.844 = 0.842k\Omega$

$Z_o = R_C \,//\, R_L$

$Z_o = 2.5 \,//\, 10 = 2k\Omega$

b) The output impedance is the same as in part a. For the input impedance, we have to redraw the ac small-signal model with the bypass capacitors being removed.

$Z_i = R_B \,//\, [h_{ie} + (h_{fe} + 1)\, R_E]$

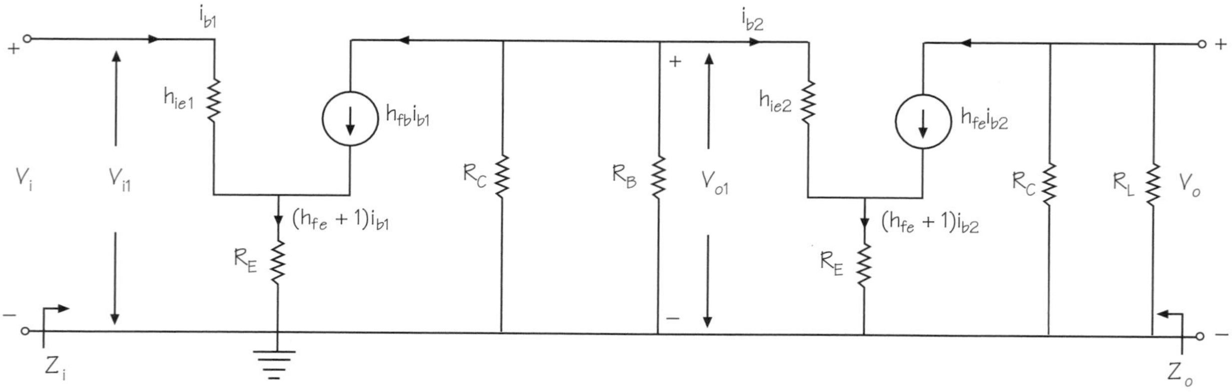

Fig. S6.2a

But $(h_{fe} + 1)\, R_E >> h_{ie}$

Therefore, $Z_i \approx R_B \,//\, R_E\,(h_{fe}+1)$

Since $h_{fe} + 1 \approx h_{fe}$, then

$Z_i = R_B \,//\, R_E\, h_{fe}$

$Z_i = 400 \,//\, (2.5)(150) = 193.55$

[exact value 194.44]

$Z_o = 2.0k\Omega$ as before.

c) $$A_{V1} = \frac{h_{fe}[R_C \,//\, R_B \,//\, (h_{ie2} + (h_{fe} + 1)R_E)]}{h_{ie1} + (h_{fe} + 1)R_E}$$

The load on the first stage consists of the parallel combination of R_C, R_B, and the input impedance of the second stage, which is $[h_{ie2} + (h_{fe} + 1)R_E]$.

Using the approximation of part b results in:

$$A_{V1} = \frac{-R_C\, //\, R_B\, //\, R_E h_{fe}}{R_E}$$

$$A_{V1} = \frac{-2.5\, //\, 400\, //\, (1.5)(150)}{1.5} = -1.638 \quad \text{(exact value} = -1.622\text{)}$$

$$A_{V2} = \frac{-(R_C\, //\, R_L)h_{fe}}{R_E} = \frac{-R_C\, //\, R_L}{R_E}$$

$$A_{V2} = \frac{-2.5\, //\, 10}{1.5} = -1.333 \quad \text{(exact value} = -1.32\text{)}$$

$$A_V = A_{V1}A_{V2} = (-1.638)(-1.333) = 2.18$$

Comparing this value of the voltage gain with that of problem P6.1, we notice that the voltage gain, with the bypass capacitors being removed from both stages, has been reduced by a ratio of

$$\frac{2.18}{39810.4} = 5.476 \times 10^{-5}. \text{ What a difference!}$$

In conclusion, the presence of the bypass capacitors in the emitter circuits increases the voltage gain to a very high value. **(Cascade amplifier)**

3. a) Fig. S6.3a shows the ac small-signal model of the circuit in Fig. S6.3

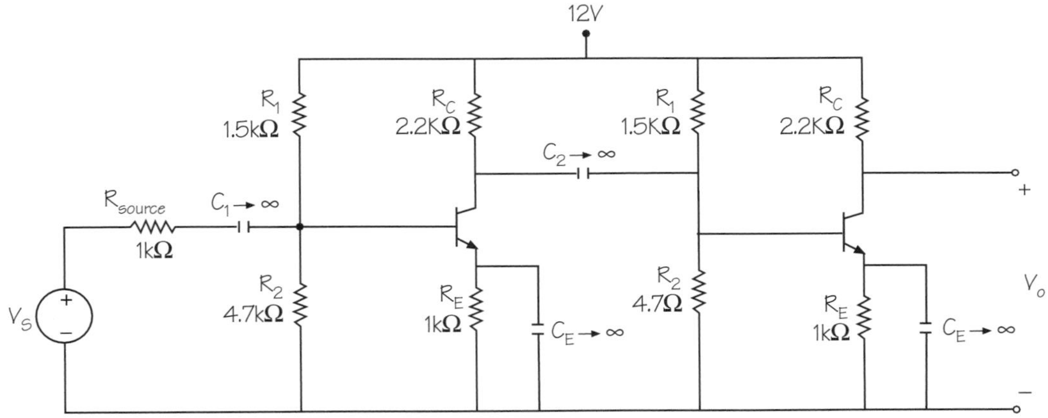

Fig.S6.3

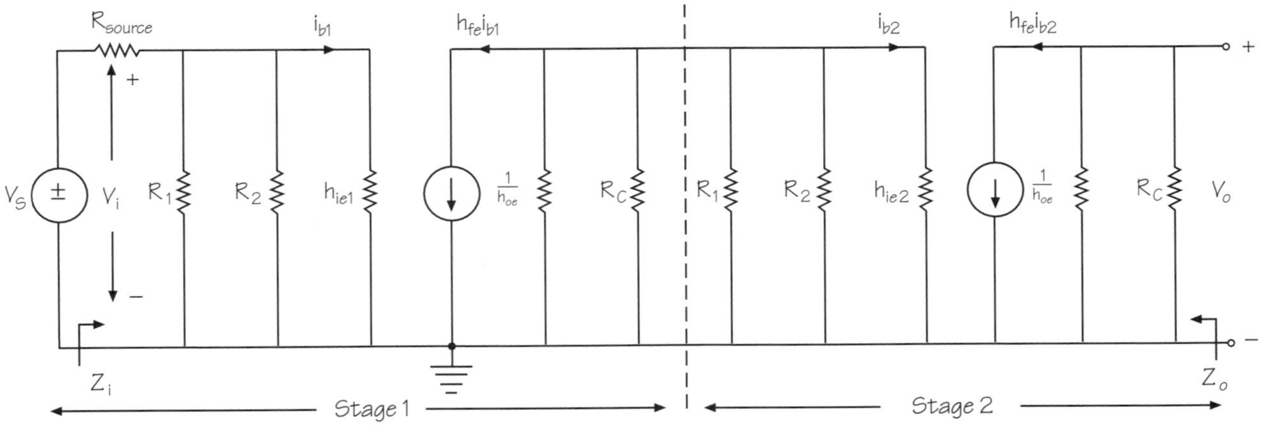

Fig. S6.3a

From Fig. S6.3a:

$$Z_i = R_1 // R_2 // h_{ie1}$$

$$Z_i = 1.5 // 4.7 // 1.214 = 0.59k\Omega$$

$$Z_o = R_C // \frac{1}{h_{oe}}$$

$$Z_o = 2.2k\Omega // \frac{1}{10 \times 10^{-6}S} = 2.2k\Omega \ \ 100k\Omega = 2.15k\Omega$$

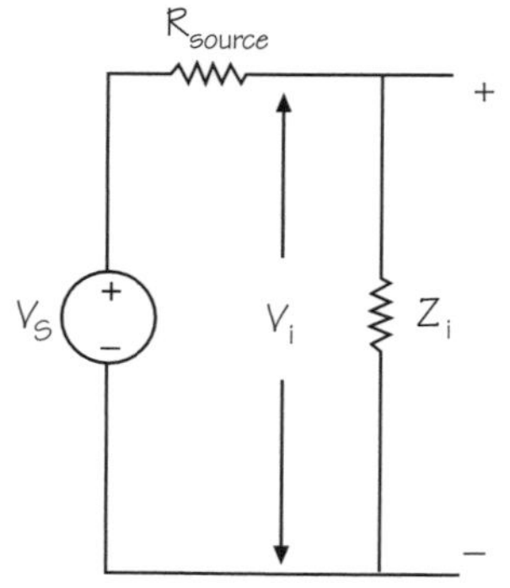

Fig. S6.3b

b) $$\frac{V_o}{V_S} = \frac{V_o}{V_i} \cdot \frac{V_i}{V_S} = A_V \frac{V_i}{V_S}$$

$$\frac{V_i}{V_S} = \frac{Z_i}{Z_i + R_{source}} \quad \text{[see Fig.S6.3b]}$$

Therefore,

$$\frac{V_o}{V_S} = \frac{Z_i A_V}{Z_i + R_{source}}$$

But A_V is given by [see S6.1]

$$A_V = A_{V1}A_{V2} = \left[\frac{-h_{fe}(R_C // R_B // h_{ie2})}{h_{ie1}}\right]\left[\frac{-h_{fe}\left(R_C // \frac{1}{h_{oe}}\right)}{h_{ie2}}\right]$$

where $R_B = R_1 // R_2$

$$A_V = \left[\frac{-100(2.2 // (1.5 // 4.7) // 1.214}{1.214}\right]\left[\frac{-100(2.2 // 100)}{1.214}\right]$$

$$A_V = 67969.3$$

Therefore, the voltage gain with respect to the voltage source V_o / V_S is:

$$A_{VS} = V_o/V_S = 67969.3 \times \frac{0.59}{0.59 + 1} = 2511.9$$

c) To find the total current gain of the amplifier, let us simplify Fig. S6.3a. The simplified figure is shown in Fig. S6.3c.

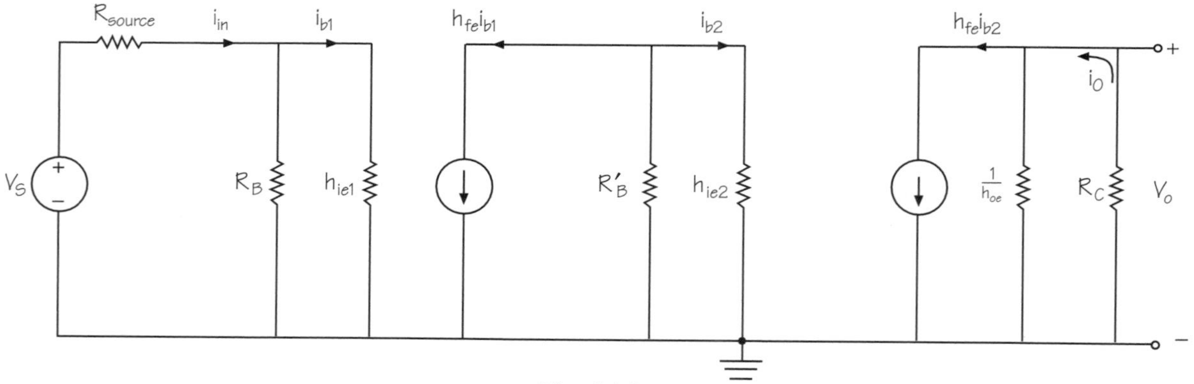

Fig. S6.3c

In Fig. S6.3c:

$R_B = R_1 // R_2 = 1.137k\Omega$, $R'_B = R_1 // R_2 // \frac{1}{h_{oe}} = 1.124k\Omega$

$\frac{1}{h_{oe}} = 100k\Omega$, $h_{ie1} = h_{ie2} = 1.214k\Omega$, and $R_C = 2.2k\Omega$.

By using a chain of current divider rules:

$$i_{b1} = \frac{i_{in}R_B}{R_B + h_{ie1}} = 0.484 i_{in}$$

$$i_{b2} = \frac{-h_{fe} i_{b1} R'_B}{R'_B + h_{ie2}} = 23.27 i_{in}$$

$$i_o = \frac{h_{fe} i_{b2}\left(\dfrac{1}{h_{oe}}\right)}{\dfrac{1}{h_{oe}} + R_C} = -2276.75 i_{in}$$

Therefore, the current gain $A_i = \dfrac{i_o}{i_{in}} = -2276.75$ **(Cascade amplifier)**

4. a)

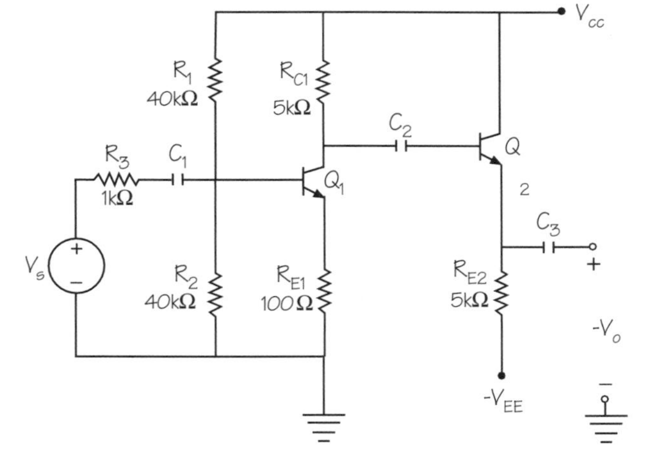

Fig. S6.4

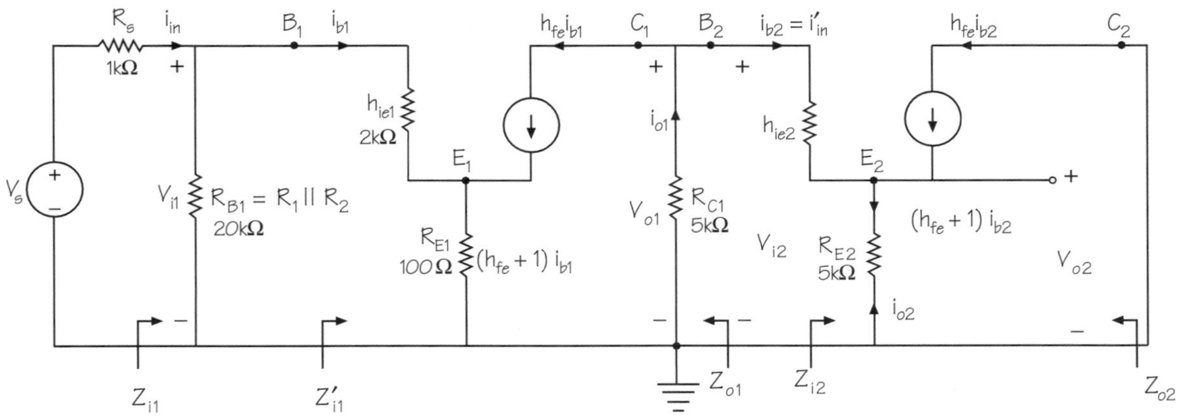

Fig. S6.4a

b) $Z_{i1} = R_{B1} \,//\, Z_{i1} = R_1 \,//\, R_2 \,//\, [h_{ie1} + (h_{fe} + 1) R_{E1}]$

$Z_{i1} = 40 \,//\, 40 \,//\, [2 + (101) \times 0.1] = 7.54\text{k}\Omega$

$Z_{o1} = R_{C1} = 5\text{k}\Omega$

$Z_{i2} = h_{ie}2 + (h_{fe} + 1) R_{E2}$

$Z_{i2} = 2 + (101)(5) = 507\text{k}\Omega$

To find Z_{o2} for the CC amplifier, Z_{o1} is considered as a source resistance for the second stage. The ac equivalent circuit for the CC stage is shown in Fig. S6.4b and the equivalent impedance with respect the load resistance, R_{E2}, is shown in Fig. S6.4c.

From Fig. S6.4c, the output impedance Z_{o2} is given by:

$$Z_{o2} = R_{E2} \,//\, \left[\frac{h_{ie2}}{h_{fe} + 1} + \frac{Z_{ol}}{h_{fe} + 1}\right]$$

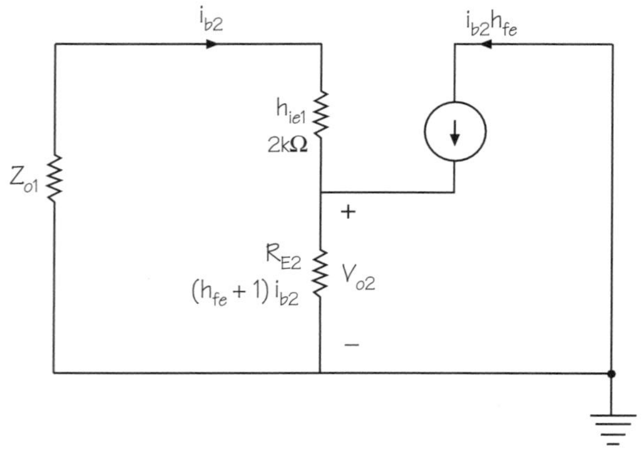

Fig. S6.4b

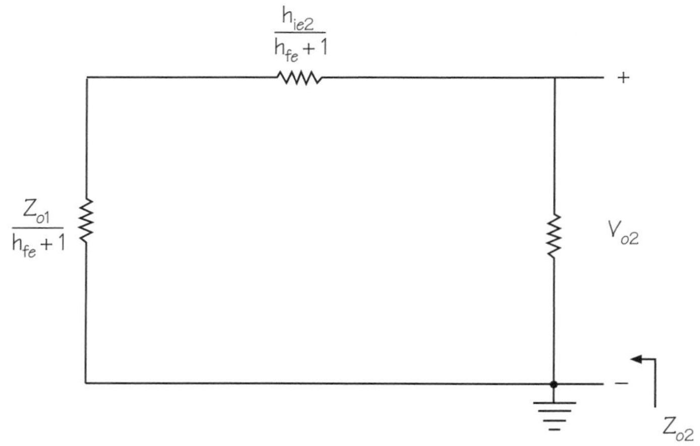

Fig. S6.4c

$$= 5 \,//\, \left[\frac{2}{101} + \frac{5}{101}\right]$$

$$Z_{o2} = 68.36\Omega$$

c) Referring to Fig. S6.4a and using current divider rule, we have:

$$i_{in} = \frac{i_{b1}[R_{B1} + h_{ie1} + (h_{fe} + 1)R_{E1}]}{R_{B1}} \qquad \text{1C}$$

$$i_{o1} = h_{fe}i_{b1} + i_{b2} \approx h_{fe}i_{b1} \qquad \text{2C}$$

$$A_{i1} = \frac{i_{o1}}{i_{in}} = \frac{h_{fe}R_{B1}}{R_{B1} + h_{ie1} + (h_{fe} + 1)R_{E1}} \qquad \text{3C}$$

$$A_{i1} = \frac{(100)(20)}{20 + 2 + (101)(0.1)} = 62.3$$

The current gain of the CC amplifier is given by:

$$A_{i2} = \frac{i_{o2}}{i'_{in}} = \frac{-(h_{fe} + 1)i_{b2}}{i_{b2}} = -(h_{fe} + 1) \qquad \text{4C}$$

$\therefore \quad A_{i2} = -101$

The overall current gain, A_i, is calculated as follows:

$$A_i = \frac{i_{o2}}{i_{in}} = \frac{-i_{b2}(h_{fe} + 1)}{i_{b1}[R_{B1} + h_{ie1} + (h_{fe} + 1)R_{E1}]/R_{B1}} \qquad \text{5C}$$

i_{B2} can be determined by using current divider as:

$$i_{b2} = \frac{-h_{fe}i_{b2}R_{C1}}{R_{C1} + [h_{ie2} + (h_{fe} + 1)R_{E2}]} \qquad \text{6C}$$

Equations 5C and 6C give:

$$A_i = \frac{h_{fe}(h_{fe} + 1)R_{C1}R_{B1}}{[R_{C1} + h_{ie2} + (h_{fe} + 1)R_{E2}][R_{B1} + h_{ie1} + (h_{fe} + 1)R_{E1}]} \qquad \text{7C}$$

$$A_i = \frac{(100)(101)(5)(20)}{[5 + 2 + (101)(5)][20 + 2 + (101)(0.1)]} = 61.45$$

To find the voltage gain, A_V, we find the voltage gain for each amplifier as follows:

$$A_{V1} = \frac{V_{o1}}{V_{i1}} \quad 8C$$

$$V_{i1} = i_{b1}[h_{ie1} + (h_{fe} + 1)R_{E1}]$$

The effective load on the first-stage amplifier is given as:

$$Z_{L1} = Z_{o1} \,//\, Z_{i2} \quad 9C$$

Thus,

$$V_{o1} = -h_{fe} i_{b1} Z_{L1} \quad 10C$$

Equations 8C and 10C give:

$$A_{V1} = \frac{-h_{fe}Z_{L1}}{h_{ie1} + (h_{fe} + 1)R_{E1}} = \frac{-h_{fe}Z_{o1} \,//\, Z_{i2}}{h_{ie1} + (h_{fe} + 1)R_{E1}} \quad 11C$$

$$= \frac{(-100)(5 \,//507)}{2 + (101)(0.1)} = -40.9$$

$$A_{V2} = \frac{V_{o2}}{V_{i2}} = \frac{-(h_{fe} + 1)R_{E2}}{h_{ie1} + (h_{fe} + 1)R_{E1}} \quad 12C$$

$$A_{V2} = \frac{-(101)(5)}{2 + (101)(5)} = -41.74$$

The overall voltage gain A_v is $A_v = A_{v1}A_{v2}$

$$A_v = (-40.9)(-41.74) = 1707$$

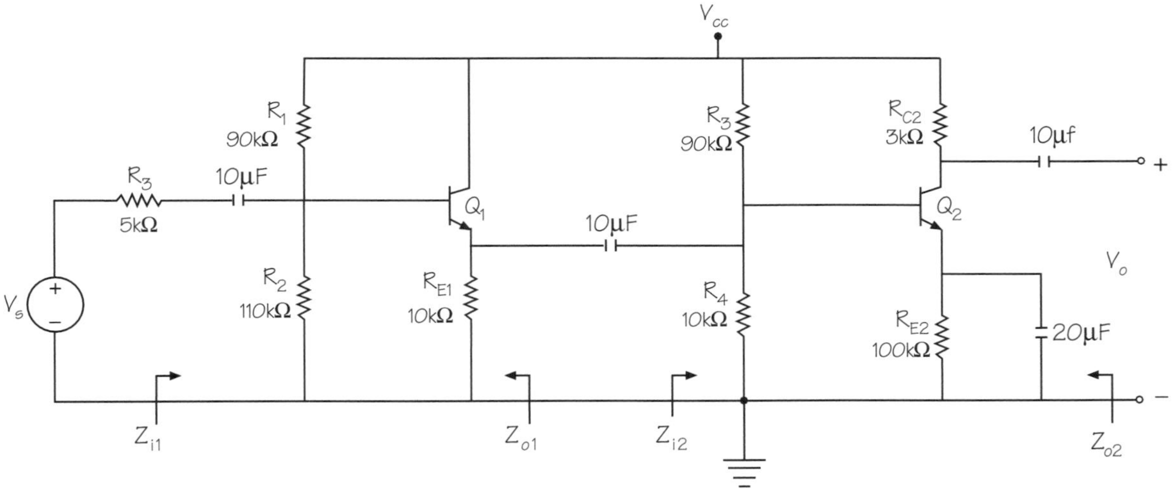

Fig. S6.5

(Cascade amplifier)

5. a) We notice from Fig. S6.5a that R_{E1}, R_{B2}, and h_{ie2} can be replaced by a single equivalent resistance in the emitter circuit, E_1, as shown in Fig. S6.5b.

$$R'_E = R_{E1} \,//\, R_{B2} \,//\, h_{ie2}$$
$$= 10 \,//\, 9 \,//\, 3 = 1.84 \text{ k}\Omega$$
$$Z_{i1} = R_{B1} \,//\, [h_{ie1} + R'_E\,(h_{fe} + 1)]$$
$$= 49.5 \,//\, [4 + (101)(1.84)] = 39.2 \text{ k}\Omega$$

To find Z_{o1}, refer to Fig. S6.5b and replace the voltage source by a short circuit (see Fig. S6.5c).

Notice that in Fig. S6.5c, h_{ie}, R_{B1}, and R_S are replaced by the effective values of each resistance.

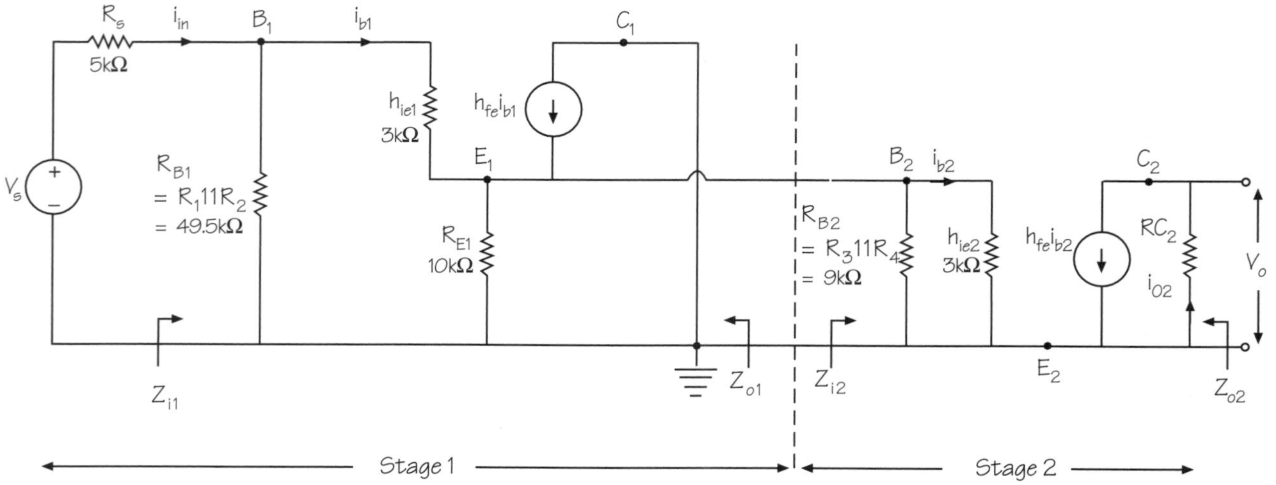

Fig. S6.5a

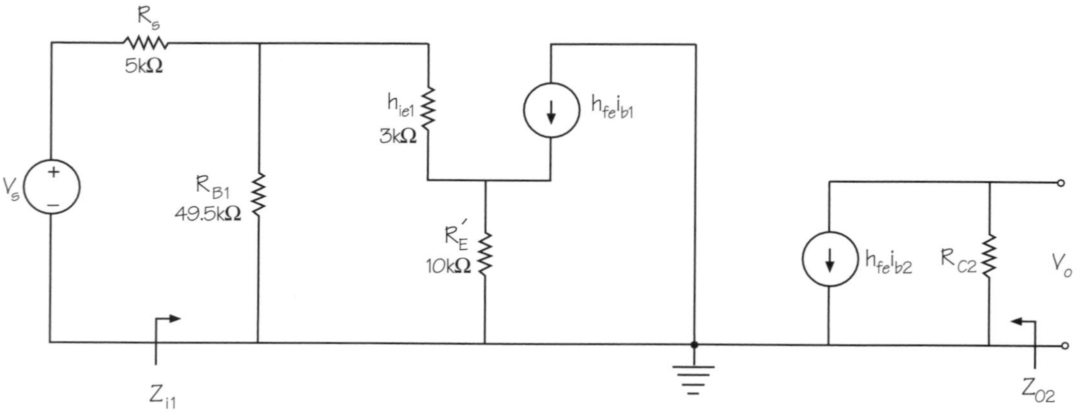

Fig. S6.5b

Then $Z_{o1} = R_E // \left[\dfrac{h_{ie1}}{h_{fe}+1} + \dfrac{R_{B1} // R_S}{h_{fe}+1}\right]$

$$Z_{o1} = 10 // \left[\frac{3}{101} + \frac{49.5 \times 5}{50(101)}\right] = 74.1\Omega$$

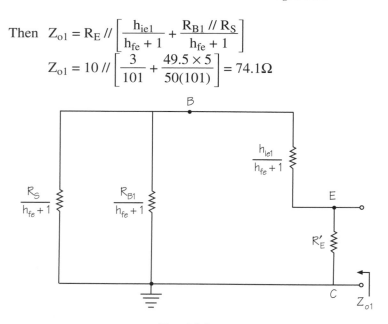

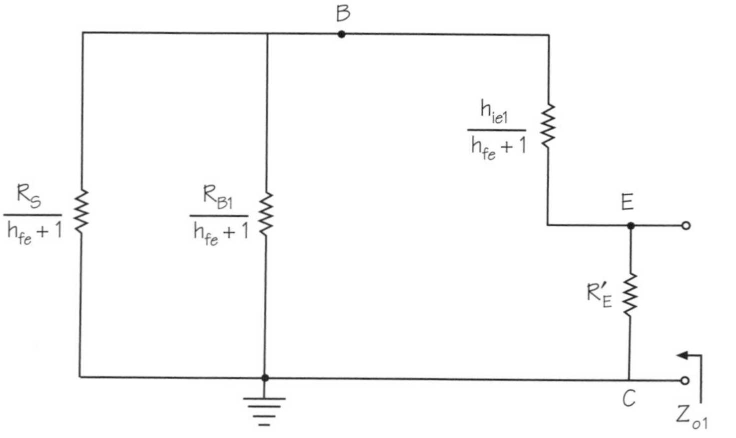

Fig. S6.5c

From Fig. S6.5b:

$$Z_{i2} = R_3 \,//\, R_4 \,//\, h_{ie2}$$
$$Z_{i2} = 90 \,//\, 10 \,//\, 3 = 2.25 \text{ k}\Omega$$
$$Z_{o2} = R_{C2} = 3 \text{ k}\Omega$$

b) The voltage gain of the first stage as calculated before is given by:

$$A_{v1} = \frac{\cancel{i_{b1}}(h_{fe} + 1)R'_E}{\cancel{i_{b1}}[h_{ie1} + R'_E(h_{fe} + 1)]} = \frac{(h_{fe} + 1)R'_E}{h_{ie1} + R'_E(h_{fe} + 1)}$$

$$A_{v1} = \frac{(101)(1.84)}{3 + (101)(1.84)} = 0.984$$

As expected, the voltage gain of CC amplifier is very close to unity.
The voltage gain of the second stage is given by:

$$A_{v2} = -\frac{R_{C2}h_{fe}}{h_{ie}} = -\frac{3 \times 100}{3} = -100$$

The overall voltage gain A_v is then:

$$A_v = A_{v1}A_{v2}$$
$$A_v = (0.984)(-100) = -98.4$$

The voltage gain with respect to the voltage source, as has been shown before,

$$A_{vs} = \frac{A_V Z_{il}}{Z_{il} + R_S} = -\frac{98.4 \times 39.2}{39.2 + 5} = -87.28$$

The overall current gain $A_i = \dfrac{i_o}{i_{in}} = \dfrac{V_o/Z_{o2}}{V_i/Z_{il}} = A_v\dfrac{Z_{il}}{Z_{o2}}$

$$A_i = -\frac{98.4 \times 39.2}{3} = -1285.76$$

The current gain with respect to the source can be found by:

$$A_{is} = \frac{i_o}{i_s} = \frac{i_o}{i_{in}} \cdot \frac{i_{in}}{i_s} = A_i\frac{i_{in}}{i_s}$$

where i_s is the current source due to the transformation of the voltage source, V_s, as shown in Fig. S6.5d.

From Fig. S6.5d:

$$\frac{i_{in}}{i_s} = \frac{R_S}{R_S + Z_{il}}$$

$$\therefore \quad A_{is} = A_i\frac{R_S}{R_S + Z_i}$$

$$A_{is} = -1286.76 \times \frac{5}{5 + 39.2} = 145.45$$ **(Cascade amplifier)**

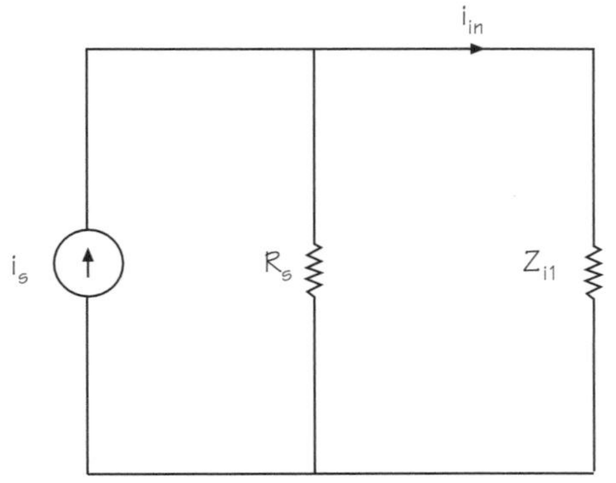

Fig. S6.5d

6. a) For any one of the two stages, KVL around the loop containing R_G, GS, and R_S:

$$V_{GS} = -I_D R_S$$
$$= -400 I_D$$

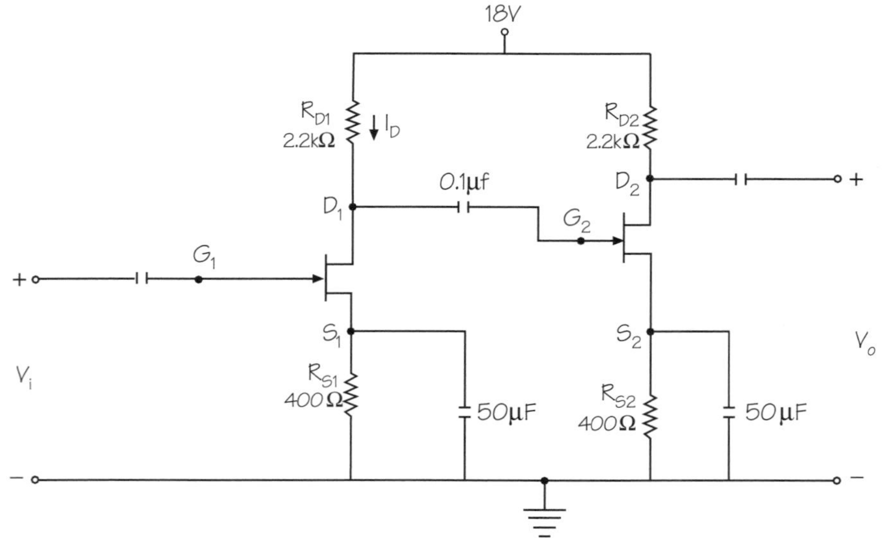

Fig. S6.6

From the current-voltage relationship of the JFET:

$$I_D = I_{DSS}\left[1 - \frac{V_{GS}}{V_P}\right]^2$$

Then $I_D = 8 \times 10^{-3}\left[1 - \dfrac{-400 I_D}{-4}\right]^2$

which results in the following quadratic equation:

$$80 I_D^2 - 2.601 I_D + 0.008 = 0$$

The solution of the quadratic equation results in two values for I_D, one of which is $I_D = 29$mA. This value is higher than I_{DSS} and therefore does not satisfy the circuit conditions. The other value is: $I_D = 3.44$mA.

Since $V_{GS} = -400 I_D$, $V_{GS} = -1.376$V.
Therefore, the operating points of each amplifier, *i.e.*,

I_{DSQ} and V_{GSQ} are [3.44mA, –1.376V] respectively.

b)

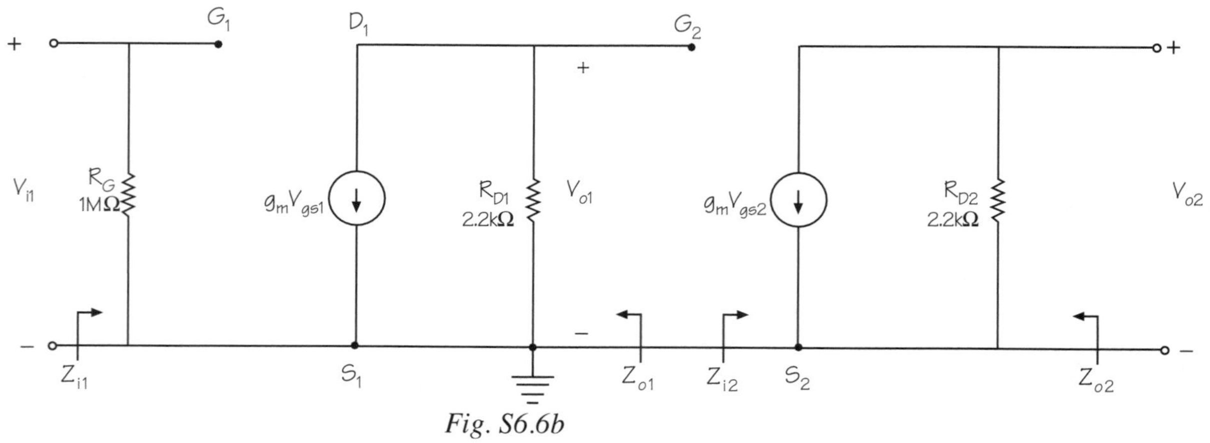

Fig. S6.6b

$Z_{i1} = R_G = 1M\Omega$
$Z_{o1} = R_{D1} = 2.2k\Omega$
$Z_{i2} = \infty$
$Z_{o2} = R_{D2} = 2.2k\Omega$

c) $V_{i1} = V_{gs1} = V_g - V_s = V_g$
$V_{o1} = g_m V_{gs} \cdot R_{D1}$

$$A_{v1} = \frac{V_{o1}}{V_{i1}} = \frac{-g_m V_{gs1} R_{D1}}{V_{gs1}} = -g_m R_{D1}$$

g_m [the transconductance] is given by:

$$g_m = g_m\left[1 - \frac{V_{GS}}{V_P}\right] = \frac{2I_{DSS}}{|V_P|}\left[1 - \frac{V_{GS}}{V_P}\right]$$

where g_{mo} is the value of g_m when $V_{GS} = 0$

$$\therefore \quad g_m = \frac{2 \times 8}{4}\left[1 - \frac{1.376}{4}\right]$$

$g_m = 2.264mS$

Therefore $A_{v1} = -2.264mS \times 2.2k\Omega = -5.77$
Similarly,

$$A_{v2} = -g_m R_{D2} = -5.77$$

and $A_v = A_{v1}A_{v2} = (-5.77)(-5.77) = 33.33$

d) Since $A_V = \frac{V_{o2}}{V_{il}}$,

$V_{o2} = A_v V_{i1} = 33.33 \times 10mV = 333.3mV$ **(JFETs cascade amplifier)**

7. a) To find the input and output impedances, we have to draw the small-signal model for the circuit in Fig. S6.7. Using the approximation that considers all coupling and bypass capacitors are replaced by short circuits, the small ac signal model is shown in Fig. S6.7a.

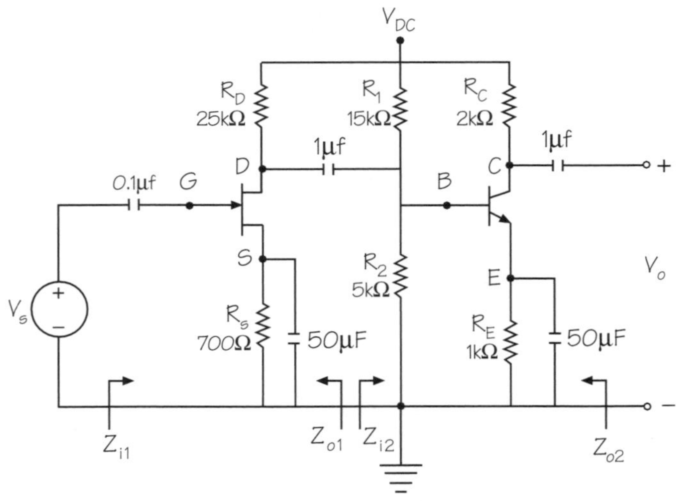

Fig. S6.7

b) $Z_{i1} = R_G = 3M\Omega$

$Z_{o1} = R_D // r_d$
$= 2.5 // 200 = 2.47k\Omega$

$Z_{i2} = R_B // h_{ie}$
$= 15 // 5 // 1.2 = 0.91k\Omega$

$Z_{o2} = 2k\Omega // 200 = 1.98k\Omega$

$A_{v1} = -g_m(Z_{o1} // Z_{i2})$
$= -2.6(2.47 // 0.91) = -1.73$

$$A_{v2} = \frac{-h_{fe}(r_o // R_C)}{h_{ie}} = \frac{-h_{fe}Z_{o2}}{h_{ie}} = \frac{-200 \times 1.98}{1.2}$$
$= -330$

$A_v = A_{v1}A_{v2} = (-1.73)(-330) = 570.9$

(JFET and BJT cascade amplifier)

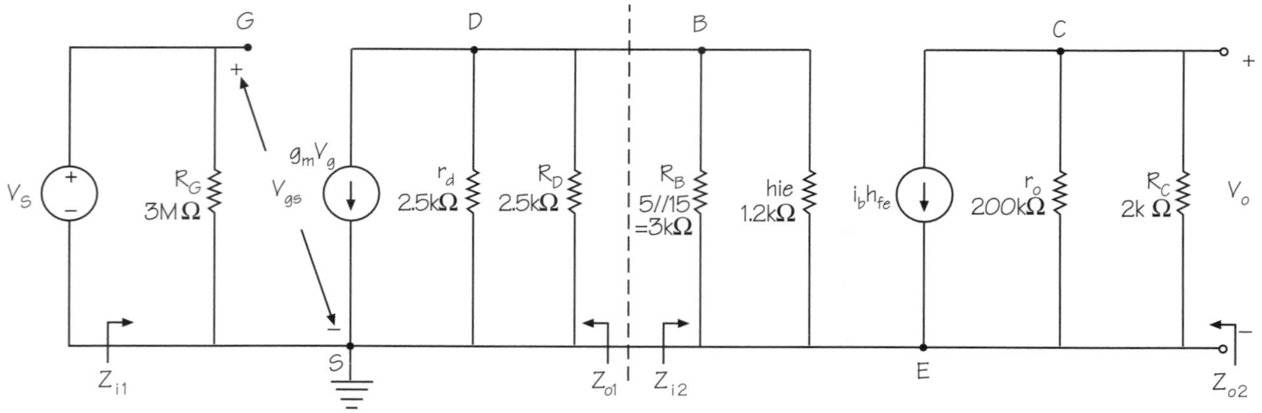

Fig. S6.7a

8.

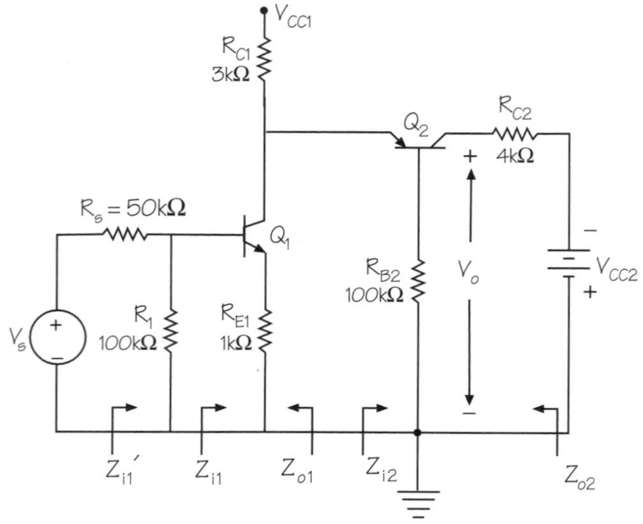

Fig. S6.8

a)

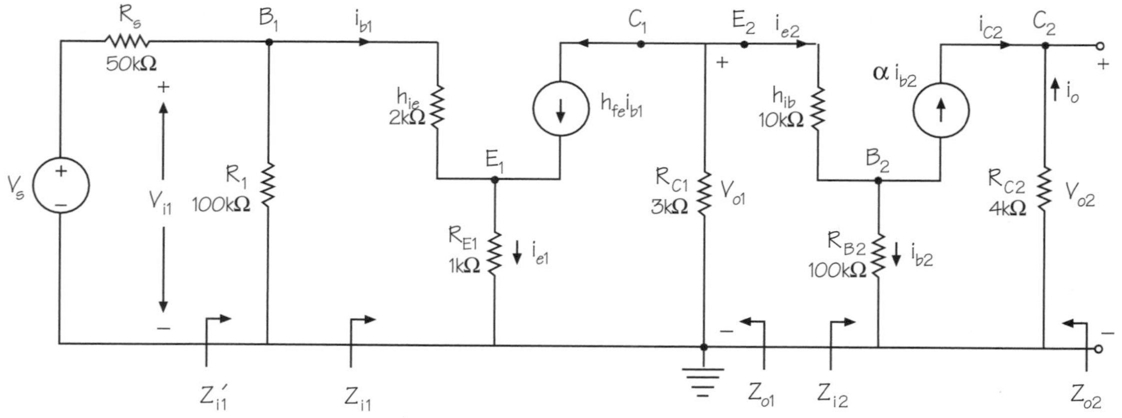

Fig. S6.8a

b) To find Z'_{i1}, let us first find Z_{i1}.

$$Z_{i1} = h_{ie} + (h_{fe1} + 1)R_{E1}$$
$$= 2 + 101 \times 1 = 103k\Omega$$

Then $Z'_{i1} = Z_{i1} // R_1$
$$= 103 // 100 = 50.25k\Omega$$
$$Z_{o1} = R_{C1} = 3k\Omega$$
$$Z_{i2} = h_{ib} + \frac{R_{B2}}{h_{fe2} + 1}$$

where $h_{fe2} = \frac{\alpha}{1 - \alpha} = \frac{0.98}{1 - 0.98} = 49$

Therefore $Z_{i2} = 10\Omega + \frac{100{,}000}{1 + 49} = 2k\Omega$
$$Z_{o2} = R_{C2} = 4k\Omega$$

c)
$$A_{V1} = \frac{V_{o1}}{V_{il}} = \frac{(R_{C1} // Z_{i2})h_{fe1}}{h_{ie1} + (h_{fel} + 1)R_{E1}}$$
$$A_{v1} = \frac{(3 // 2) \times 100}{2 + (101)(1)} = 1.165$$
$$A_{v2} = \frac{-R_{C2}h_{fe2}}{R_{B2} + (h_{fe2} + 1)h_{ib}}$$
$$= \frac{4 \times 49}{100 + 50 \times 0.01} = -1.95$$
$$A_v = A_{v1}A_{v2} = 1.165 \times (-1.95) = -2.72$$
$$A_{vs} = \frac{V_{o2}}{V_s} = \frac{V_{o2}}{V_{il}} \cdot \frac{V_{il}}{V_s} = A_v\frac{V_{il}}{A_s}$$
$$A_{vs} = A_v\frac{Z'_{il}}{Z'_{il} + R_S} = -2.27 \times \frac{50.25}{50.25 + 50} = -1.14$$

The overall current gain $A_i = A_v\frac{Z'_{il}}{Z_{o2}}$

$$A_i = -1.14 \times \frac{50.25}{4} = -14.32$$ **(CE-to-CB cascade amplifier)**

9. a)

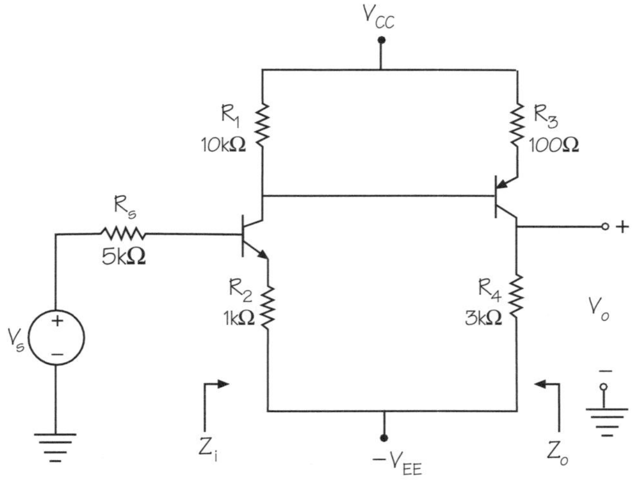

Fig. S6.9

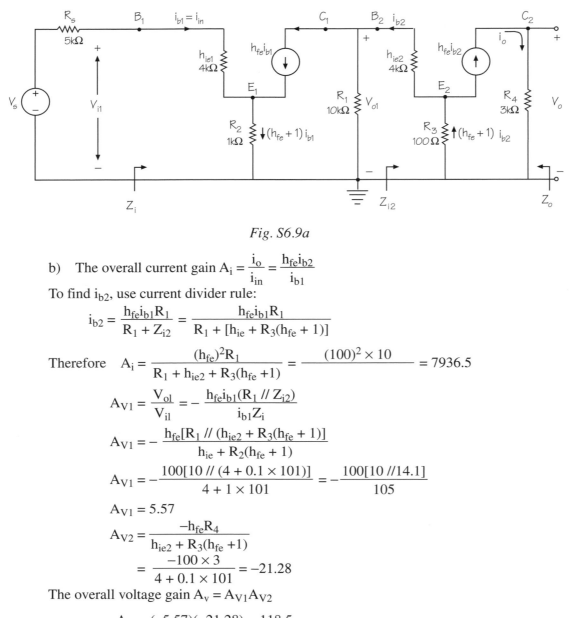

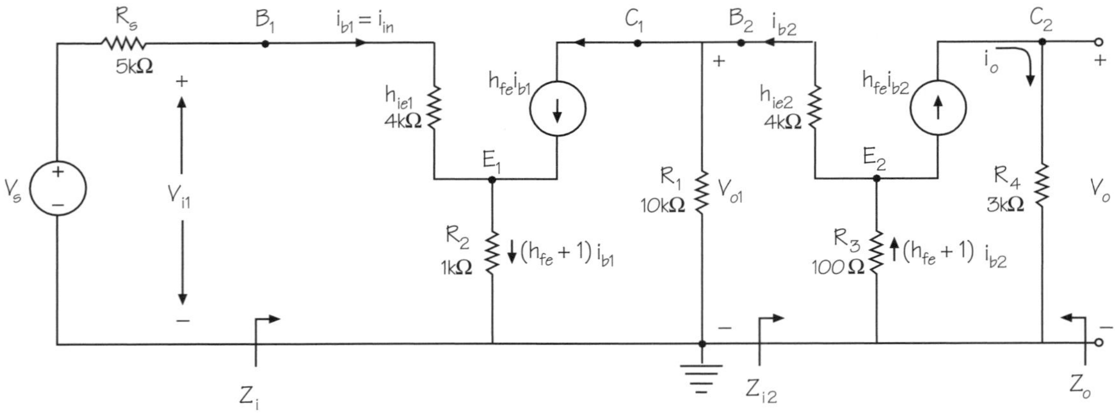

Fig. S6.9a

b) The overall current gain $A_i = \frac{i_o}{i_{in}} = \frac{h_{fe}i_{b2}}{i_{b1}}$

To find i_{b2}, use current divider rule:

$$i_{b2} = \frac{h_{fe}i_{b1}R_1}{R_1 + Z_{i2}} = \frac{h_{fe}i_{b1}R_1}{R_1 + [h_{ie} + R_3(h_{fe} + 1)]}$$

Therefore $$A_i = \frac{(h_{fe})^2 R_1}{R_1 + h_{ie2} + R_3(h_{fe} + 1)} = \frac{(100)^2 \times 10}{} = 7936.5$$

$$A_{V1} = \frac{V_{ol}}{V_{il}} = -\frac{h_{fe}i_{b1}(R_1 \,//\, Z_{i2})}{i_{b1}Z_i}$$

$$A_{V1} = -\frac{h_{fe}[R_1 \,//\, (h_{ie2} + R_3(h_{fe} + 1)]}{h_{ie} + R_2(h_{fe} + 1)}$$

$$A_{V1} = -\frac{100[10 \,//\, (4 + 0.1 \times 101)]}{4 + 1 \times 101} = -\frac{100[10 \,//14.1]}{105}$$

$$A_{V1} = 5.57$$

$$A_{V2} = \frac{-h_{fe}R_4}{h_{ie2} + R_3(h_{fe} + 1)}$$

$$= \frac{-100 \times 3}{4 + 0.1 \times 101} = -21.28$$

The overall voltage gain $A_v = A_{V1}A_{V2}$

$$A_V = (-5.57)(-21.28) = 118.5$$

$$A_{VS} = \frac{V_o}{V_S} = \frac{V_o}{V} \cdot \frac{V_{il}}{V_S} = A_v \frac{Z_i}{Z_i + R_S}$$

$$A_{VS} = A_V \frac{h_{ie1} + R_2(h_{fe} + 1)}{h_{ie1} + R_2(h_{fe} + 1) + R_S}$$

$$A_{VS} = 118.5 \times \frac{4 + 1 \times 101}{4 + 1 \times 101 + 5} = 113.11$$

Clearly $Z_i = h_{ie1} + R_2(h_{fe} + 1) = 105\text{k}\Omega$

and $Z_o = R_4 = 3\text{k}\Omega$

(Differential amplifier)

10. To determine the lower and higher cutoff frequencies, we have to find first h_{ie} for both transistors. Those can be found by solving for the dc bias conditions.

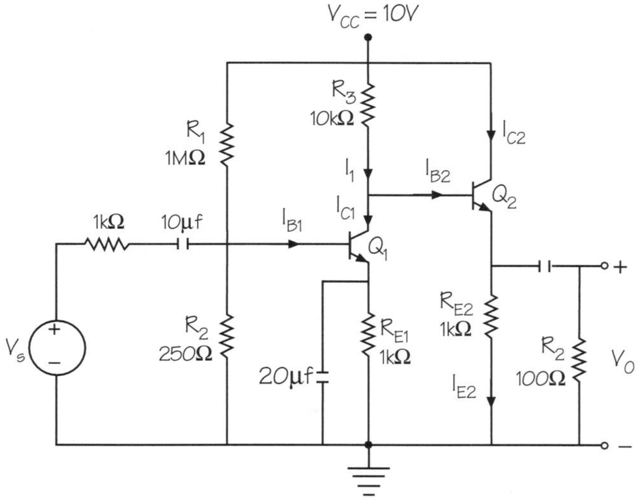

Fig. S6.10

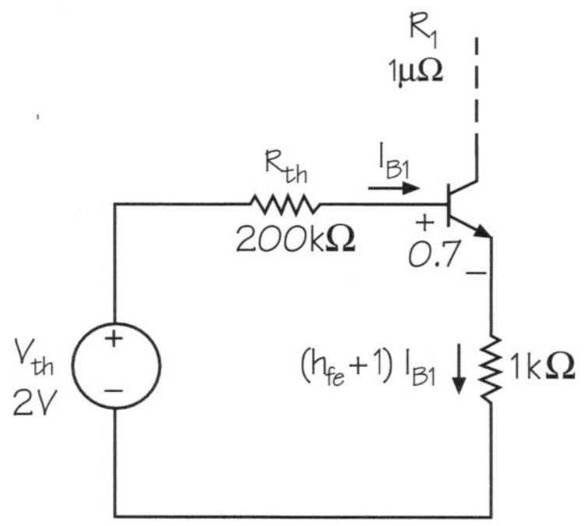

Fig. S6.10a

For the C_E stage:

$$V_{Th} = 10\left(\frac{250}{25 + 1000}\right) = 2V$$

$$R_{Th} = 1000 // 250 = 200K$$

KVL (See Fig. S6.10a) around the loop gives:

$$2 - 200\, I_{B1} - 0.7 - 101\, I_{B1} = 0$$

From which $I_{B1} = 4.32\mu A$

$$I_{C1} = h_{fe} I_{B1} = 100 \times 4.32\mu A = 0.432mA$$

$$h_{ie1} = \frac{26mV}{I_{B1}} = \frac{26mV}{4.32\mu A} = 6020\Omega = 6k\Omega$$

For the CC stage:

$$I_1 \approx I_{C1} = 4.32mA$$

The voltage at the collector of Q_1 is:

$$V_{C1} = 10 - 10k\Omega \times 0.432mA$$

$$V_{C1} = 5.68V$$

Then:

$$I_{E2} = \frac{5.68 - 0.7}{1k\Omega} = 4.98mA$$

$$I_{B2} = \frac{I_{E2}}{h_{fe} + 1} = \frac{4.98}{101} = 49.3\mu A$$

$$h_{ie2} = \frac{26mV}{49.3\mu S} = 0.53k\Omega$$

Also from the given data,

$$\frac{1}{h_{oe}} \text{ (for CE)} = \frac{1}{2.9\mu S} = 345k\Omega$$

and $\frac{1}{h_{oe}}$ (for CC) = 30kΩ

These values are very large and can be replaced by an open-circuit approximation in the ac model. The low-frequency model is shown in Fig. S6.10b.

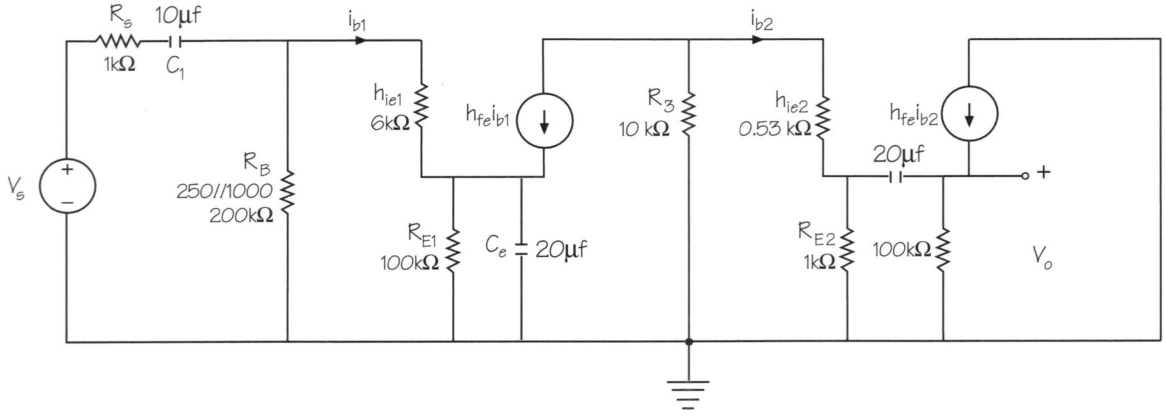

Fig. S6.10b

For the CE amplifier:

The Thevenin resistance seen by the capacitor C_1 [see Fig. S6.10c] is:

$$R_{C1} = (6 // 200) + 1 = 6.83\text{k}\Omega$$

The R-C frequency response is given by the relation:

$$f = \frac{1}{2\pi RC}$$

Therefore the R-C frequency response due to the capacitor C_1 is:

$$f_{(C1)} = \frac{1}{\qquad\qquad\qquad} = 2.33\text{Hz}$$

The Thevenin resistance seen by the capacitor, C_e (see Fig. 6.10d):

$$R_{Ce} = R_{E1} // \left[\frac{h_{ei1}}{h_{fe}+1} + \frac{R_B // R_S}{h_{fe}+1}\right]$$

$$= 1 // \left[\frac{6}{101} + \frac{200 // 1}{101}\right] = 65\Omega$$

The frequency response due to the capacitor C_e is therefore:

$$f_{(Ce)} = \frac{1}{\qquad\qquad\qquad} = 123\text{ Hz}$$

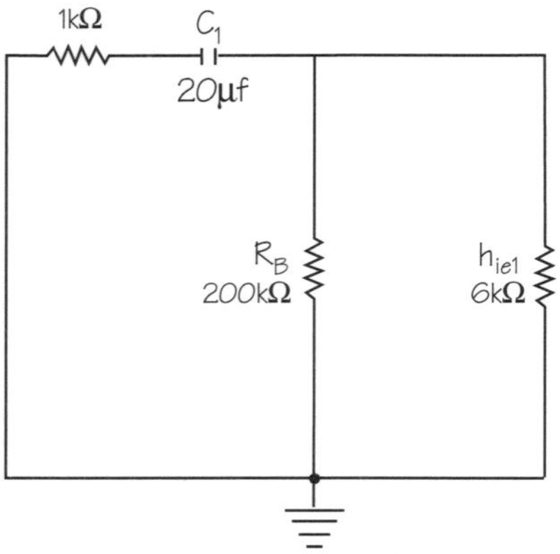

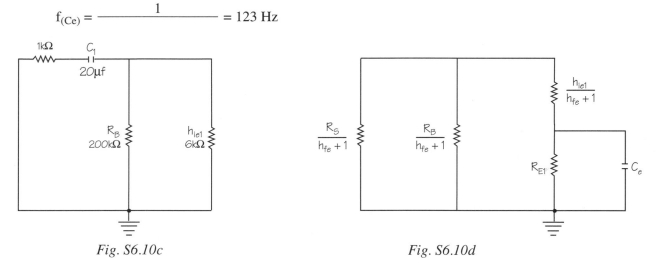

Fig. S6.10c

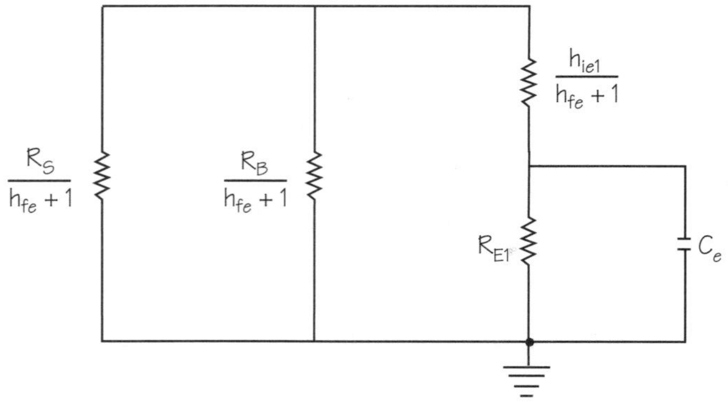

Fig. S6.10d

For the CC stage, the Thevenin resistance seen by the capacitor C2 (see Fig. S6.10e):

$$R_{C2} = R_L + R_{E2} \,//\, \left(\frac{h_{ie2} + R_3}{h_{fe} + 1}\right)$$

$$= 0.1 + 1 \,//\, \left(\frac{0.53 + 10}{101}\right) = 194\Omega$$

Then $f_{C2} = \frac{1}{\qquad\qquad} = 41Mz.$

The lower cutoff frequency is the highest amonly the low-frequency response. Therefore the lower cutoff frequency is $f_{LO} = 123Hz$.
The Bode plot is shown in Fig. S6.10f.

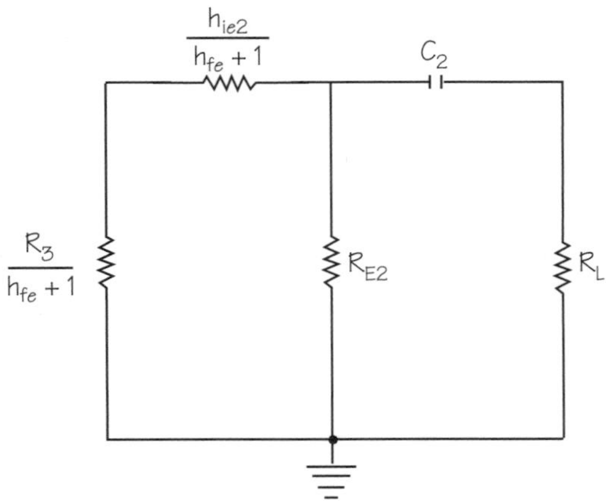

Fig. S6.10e

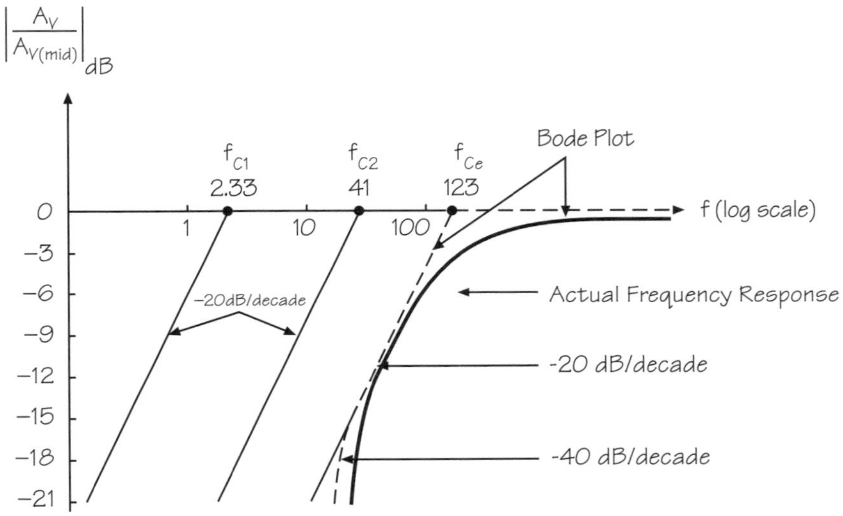

Fig. S6.10f (not scaled)

(CE-to-CC cascade amplifier)

11. Consider the worst case, in which transistor Q_1 is saturated. Assume that $V_{CE(sat)} = 0.2V$ (as a typical value), and $V_{BE} = 0.7V$ for the transistor to be on.
Since $V_{CE2} = V_{CE1} + V_{(BE)2}$
Therefore $V_{CE2} = 0.2 + 0.7 = 0.9V$
This value is much higher than the voltage required to bring Q_2 into saturation. Therefore, even if Q1 is saturated, Q_2 will never be saturated.
(Darlington pair)

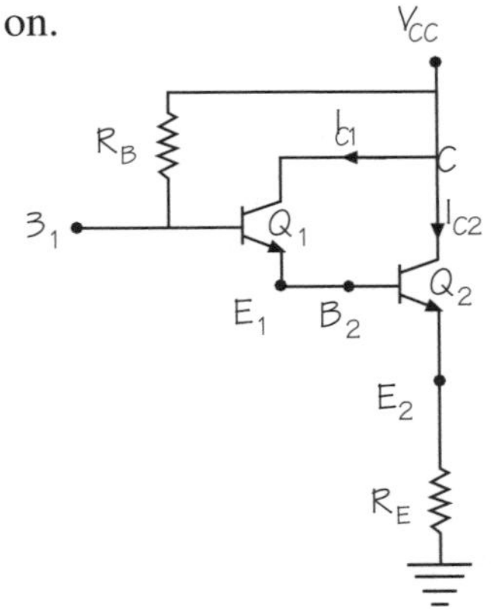

Fig. S6.11

12. To prove that $\beta_D \approx \beta_1\beta_2$ for Darlington pair, we have to draw the small-signal ac model for the circuit. The ac model is shown in Fig. S6.12a.
As shown in Fig.S6.12a

$$i_{e1} = i_{b2} = (\beta_1 + 1)\, i_{b1}$$

Since $\beta >> 1$
Therefore $i_{e1} \simeq \beta_1 i_{b1} = i_{b2}$
Also $i_{C2} = \beta_2 i_{b2} = \beta_2\beta_1 i_{b1}$

$$A_i = \frac{i_o}{i_{in}} = \frac{i_{C2}}{i_{b1}} = \frac{\beta_2\beta_1 i_{b1}}{i_{b1}} = \beta_1\beta_2$$

Recall A_i as β_D
Then $\beta_D \approx \beta_1\beta_2$ **(Darlington pair)**

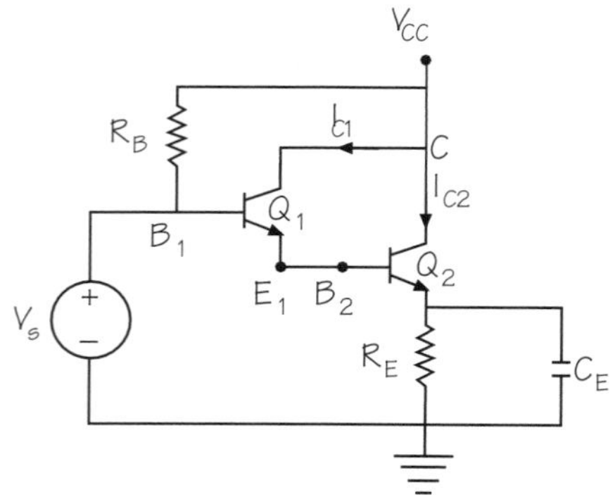

Fig. S6.12

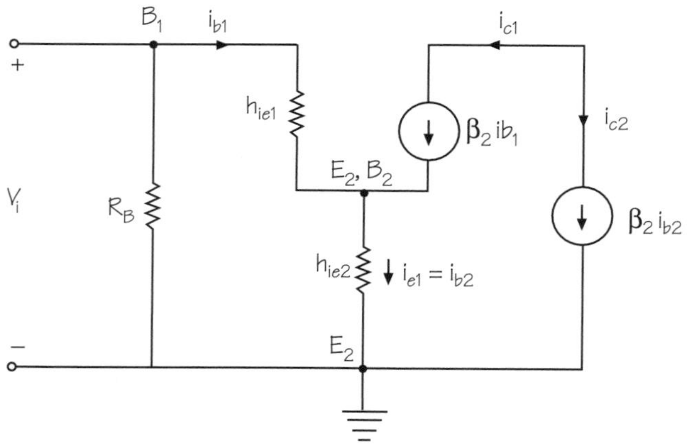

Fig. S12a

13. The small ac signal model is shown in Fig. S6.13a.

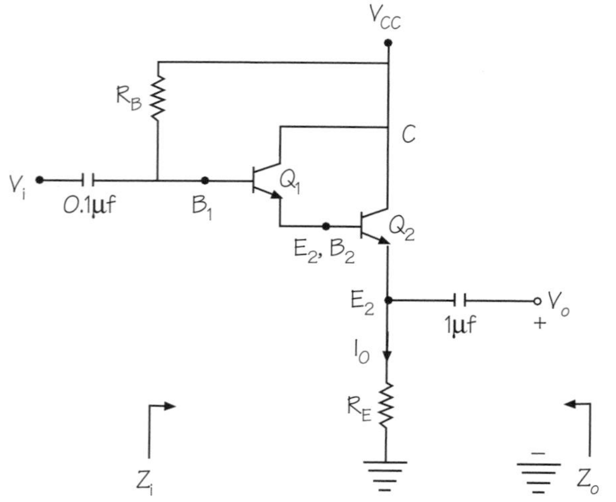

Fig. S6.13

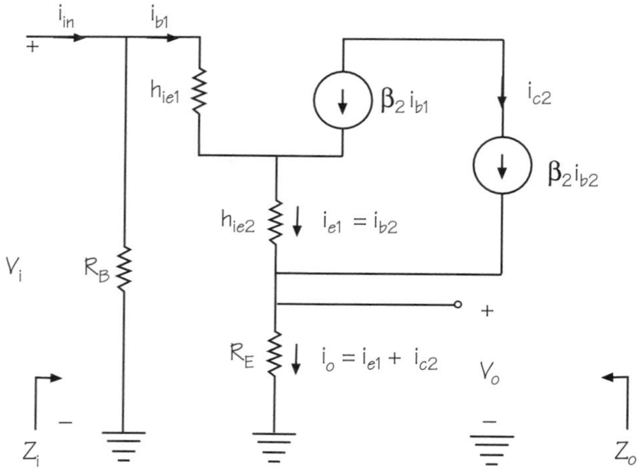

Fig. S6.13a

a) Since $i_{e1} \simeq \beta_1 i_{b1} = i_{b2}$

and $i_o = i_{e1} + i_{c2}$

$= \beta_1 i_{b1} + \beta_2 i_{b2}$

$= \beta_1 i_{b1} + \beta_2 \beta_1 i_{b1}$

$= i_{b1}(1 + \beta)$ $[\beta_1 = \beta_2 = \beta]$

$i_o \approx i_{b1}\beta^2$

Therefore, the input impedance $Z_i = R_B // [h_{ie1} + \beta h_{ie2} + \beta^2 R_E]$

Because $h_{ie1} = h_{ie2} = h_{ie}$

$$Z_i = \frac{R_B[h_{ie}(1 + \beta) + \beta^2 R_E]}{R_B + h_{ie}(1 + \beta) + \beta^2 R_E}$$

$$Z_i = \frac{R_B[h_{ie}\,\beta + \beta^2 R_E]}{R_B + h_{ie}\beta + \beta^2{}_R E}$$

Z_o is simply $= R_E$

b) $V_i = i_{b1}h_{ie1} + i_{b2}h_{ie2} + i_o R_E$

$= i_{b1}h_{ie} + \beta i_{b1}h_{ie} + \beta^2 R_e i_{b1}$

$V_i \simeq i_{b1}\,[h_{ie}\beta + \beta^2 R_E]$

$V_o = i_{b1}\beta^2 R_E$

The voltage gain $A_V = \dfrac{V_o}{V_i} = \dfrac{\beta^2 R_E}{h_{ie}\beta + \beta^2 R_E}$

$$A_V = \frac{\beta R_E}{h_{ie} + \beta R_E}$$

c) $$i_{in} = \frac{i_{b1}[R_B + \beta h_{ie} + \beta^2 R_E]}{R_B}$$

$i_o = \beta^2 R_e i_{b1}$

Therefore, the current gain of the circuit is:

$$A_i = \frac{i_o}{i_{in}} = \frac{\beta^2 R_E R_B}{R_B + \beta h_{ie} + \beta^2 R_E}$$

(Darlington pair)

14. a) Transistor Q_1 supplies the current of Q_2 with signal current $i_{b1}\beta_1$. Transistor Q_2 acts as a current follower and passes this current on to its collector terminal.
Notice that R_1 and h_{ie2} are replaced by short circuits in the ac equivalent model because both of their terminals are connected to ground.

b) To find h_{ie}, use the dc analysis.
Using a voltage divider principle and neglecting the base currents of both transistors:

$$V_{B1} = \frac{18 \times 5}{7 + 5.8 + 4.8} = 5V$$

$$I_{E1} = \frac{5 - 0.7}{1k\Omega} = 4.4mA$$

$$I_{B1} = \frac{I_{E1}}{\beta + 1} = \frac{4.4}{201} = 0.022mA$$

$$h_{ie} = \frac{26mV}{I_{B1}} = 1.184k\Omega$$

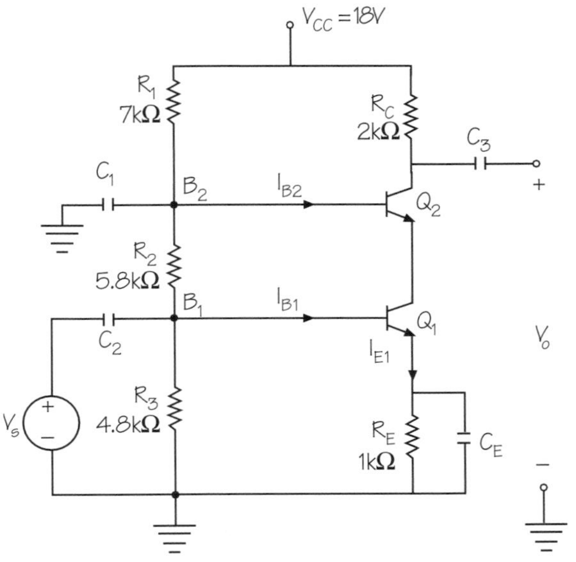

Fig. S6.14

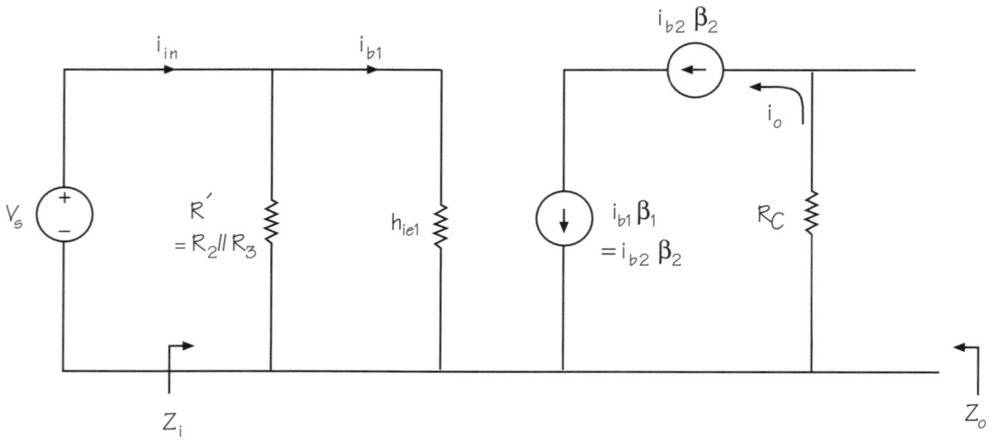

Fig. S6.14a

$$Z_i = R' \,//\, h_{ie1} = R_2 \,//\, R_3 \,//\, h_{ie1}$$
$$Z_i = 4.8 \,//\, 5.8 \,//\, 1.184$$
$$Z_i = 0.816 k\Omega$$

and

$$Z_o = R_C = 2k\Omega$$
$$A_V = \frac{V_o}{V_i} = \frac{-i_{b1}\beta R_C}{i_{b1}h_{ie1}} = -\frac{\beta R_C}{h_{ie1}}$$
$$A_V = \frac{-200 \times 2}{1.184} = -378$$
$$A_i = \frac{i_o}{i_{in}} = \frac{i_o}{i_{b1}} \cdot \frac{i_{b1}}{i_{in}} = \frac{\beta R'}{R' + h_{ie}} = \frac{200(4.8 \,//\, 5.8)}{4.8 \,//\, 5.8 + 1.184} = 138$$

(Cascade amplifier)

15. a) Clearly from Fig. S6.15

$$I_E = I_{E1} + I_{E2} \qquad \text{(Eqn. 1)}$$

Since $I_{C1} = \alpha I_{E1}$

and $I_{C2} = \alpha I_{E2}$ (Eqn. 2)

Where $\alpha = \dfrac{\beta}{\beta + 1}$

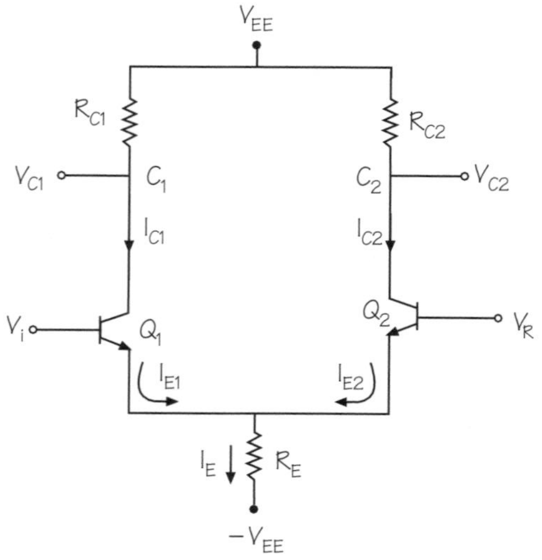

Fig. S6.15

Then $I_{C1} + I_{C2} = \alpha(I_{E1} + I_{E2}) = \alpha I_E$ (Eqn. 3)

Take the case in which $\Delta V = V_i - V_R$

Then $\Delta V = V_{BE1} - V_{BE2}$ (Eqn. 4)

From the diode equation

$$I = I_s[e^{(V_{\beta E1}/V_T)} - 1] \approx I_s e^{(V_{\beta E}/V_T)} \quad \text{(Eqn. 5)}$$

$$I_{C1} = I_s e^{(V_{\beta E2}/V_T)} \quad \text{(Eqn. 6a)}$$

and

$$I_{C2} = I_s e^{(V_{\beta E2}/V_T)} \quad \text{(Eqn. 6b)}$$

$$I_{C1} \backslash I_{C2} = e^{(V_{\beta E1} - V_{\beta E2}/V_T)} = e^{\frac{V_i - V_R}{V_T}} = e^{\frac{\Delta V}{V_T}} \quad \text{(Eqn. 7)}$$

Also,

$$V_{C1} = V_{CC} - I_{C1}R_{C1} \quad \text{(Eqn. 8)}$$

and $V_{C2} = V_{CC} - I_{C2}R_{C2}$ (Eqn. 9)

From Eq. 7, if $V_1 = V_R$, then $\Delta V = 0$, and $I_{C1} = I_{C2}$ (Eqn. 10)

Substituting Eq. 10 into Eqs. 8 and 9, respectively, results in:

$V_{C1} = V_{C2}$ (This is the quiescent point of the circuit).

b) If $V_i - V_R = 120$ mV

Then $\dfrac{I_{C1}}{I_{C2}} = e^{(120/V_T)}$ (Eqn. 11)

at room temperature, $V_T = 26$mV

Equation (11) gives:

$$\frac{I_{C1}}{I_{C2}} = e^{(120/26)} = 101$$

or $I_{C1} = 101\, I_{C2}$ (Eqn. 12)

Since in Eqs. 8 and 9, V_{CC}, R_{C1}, and R_{C2} are all constants, we conclude from those equations and equation 12 that for the case at which $V_i > V_R$, V_{C1} drops below the operating (quiescent) point and V_{C2} rises above the operating point.

In other words, transistor Q_1 is ON and transistor Q_2 is OFF.

For the case $V_i - V_e = -\Delta V = -120$mV,

$$I_{C1} = \frac{1}{101} I_{C2}$$

which means that transistor Q_1 is OFF and transistor Q_2 is ON.

(Differential amplifier)

16. For $V_i = V_R$

$$V_{C1} = V_{C2} \text{ and } I_{C1} = I_{C2}$$

$$V_E = V_i - V_{BE1} = V_R - V_{BE2} = 1 - 0.7 = 0.3\text{V}$$

$$I_E = \frac{V_E - V_{EE}}{R_E} = \frac{0.3 - (-5)}{2} = 2.65\text{mA}$$

Since Q_1 and Q_2 are identical, then $I_{E1} = I_{E2} = \dfrac{I_E}{2} = 1.33$mA

$$I_{C1} = \propto I_{E1} = \frac{\beta}{\beta + 1} I_{E1}$$

$$I_{C1} = \frac{50}{51} \times 1.33 = 1.3\text{mA} = I_{C2}$$

$$V_{C1} = V_{CC} - I_{C1}R_{C1} = 5 - 1.3\text{mA} \times 1\text{k}\Omega = 3.7\text{V} = V_{C2}$$

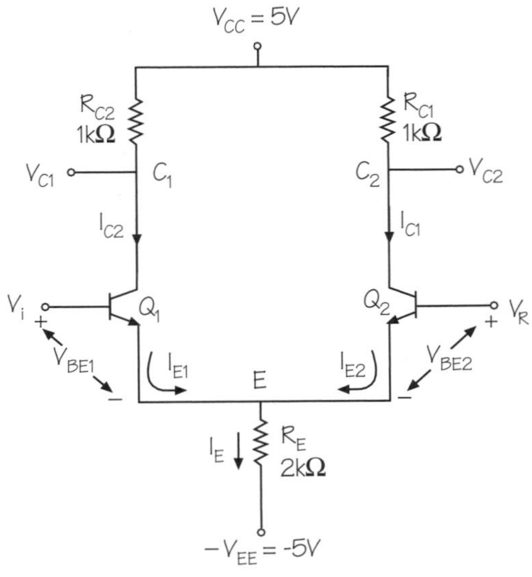

Fig. S6.16

For $V_i = V_R \mp 120$ mV

a) $V_i = V_R + 120$

$I_{C1} = 101\ I_{C2}$

Since $I_{C1} + I_{C2} = \propto I_E$

$$101\ I_{C2} + I_{C2} = \frac{50}{51} \times 2.65$$

$I_{C2} = 25.5\mu A$

and $I_{C1} = 101 \times 25.5 = 2.57mA$

$V_{C1} = V_{CC} - I_{C1}R_{C1}$

$V_{C1} = 5 - 2.57mA \times 1k\Omega = 2.43V$

and $V_{C2} = 5 - 25.5 \times 10^{-3}mA \times 1k\Omega \approx 5V$

b) For the case $V_i = V_R - 120$, by following the same procedure above you will find that:

$I_{C1} = 25.5\mu A$, and $V_{C1} \approx 5V$

$I_{C2} = 2.57mA$, and $V_{C2} = 2.43V$

As you can see from the above results of V_{C1} and V_{C2} that for $V_i = V_R + 120mV$, transistor Q2 is in the cutoff state, while transistor Q1 is at ON state (active region). For $V_i = V_R - 120mV$ the situation is reversed.

$$I_E = \frac{I_{C1} + I_{C2}}{\propto} = 2.65mA \text{ as before.}$$

c) $$I_E = 2.65 \propto = 2.65 \times \frac{\beta}{\beta + 1}$$

If β changes by 10%, i.e. $\beta = 50 \pm 10\% \times 50$

$$I_E = 2.65 \times \frac{55}{56} = 2.6mA$$

or $$I_E = 2.65 \times \frac{45}{46} = 2.592mA$$

which means that the change in I_E is insignificant with the change of β. **(Differential amplifier)**

17. Because both transistors are identical,

$i_{b1} = i_{b2} = i_b$,

$h_{ie1} = h_{ie2} = h_{ie}$

and $\beta_1 = \beta_2 = \beta$

Apply KVL for a look containing both inputs as shown in Fig. S6.17b. Notice that R_E has been omitted in this figure since, in most practical cases, $(\beta + 1)R_E >> h_{ie}$.

KVL gives:

$V_{i1} - 2i_b h_{ie} - V_{i2} = 0$

$V_{i1} - V_{i2} = 2i_b h_{ie}$

By definition of the difference amplifier:

$V_d = V_{i1} - V_{i2} = 2i_b h_{ie}$

$V_o = i_C R_C = \beta i_b R_C$

The voltage gain $A_{vd} = \dfrac{\beta R_C}{2h_{ie}}$

(Differential amplifier)

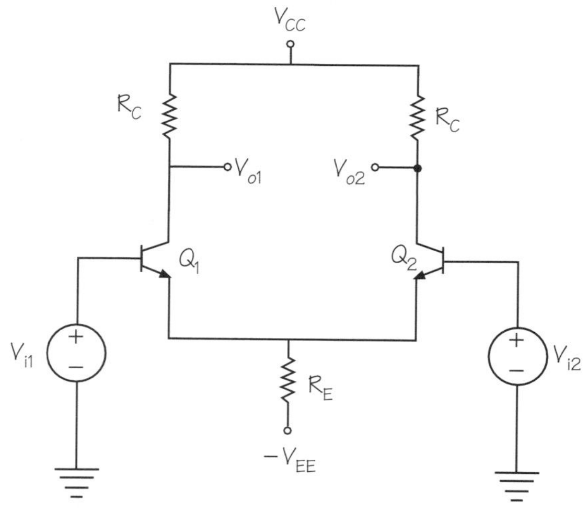

Fig. S6.17

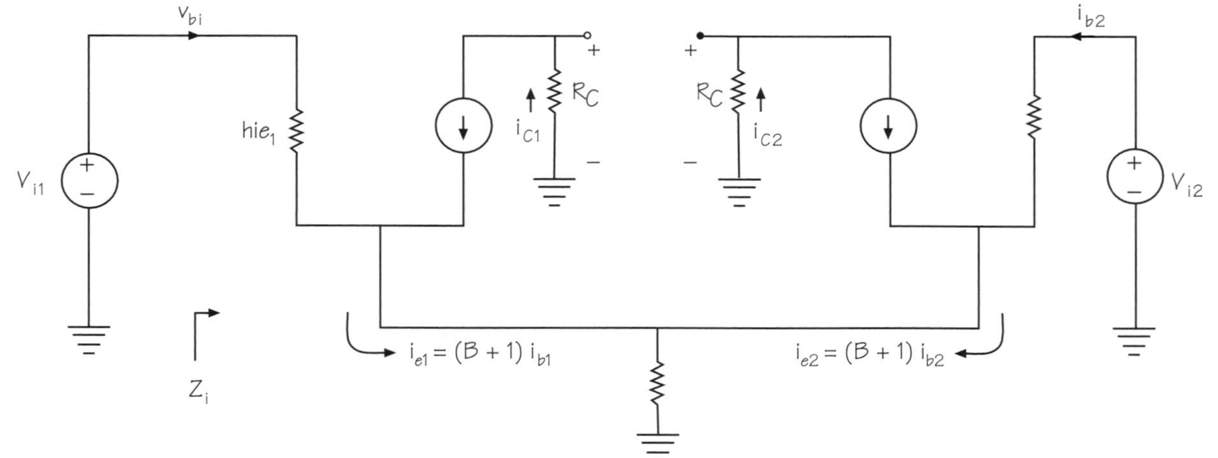

Fig. S6.17a

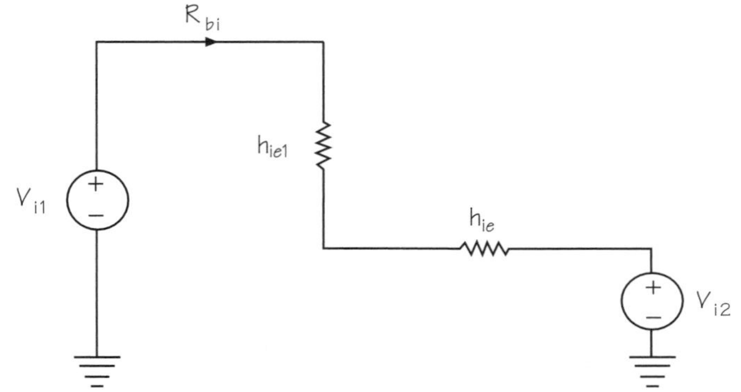

Fig. S6.17b

18. Take the loop shown in Fig. S6.18b and apply KVL:

$$V_i = i_b h_{ie} - 2i_b(\beta + 1)R_E = 0$$

$$i_b = \frac{v_i}{h_{ie} + 2(\beta + 1)R_E} \simeq \frac{V_i}{h_{ie} + 2\beta R_E}$$

$$V_o = -i_C R_C = -\beta i_b R_C$$

$$= \frac{-\beta R_C V_i}{h_{ie} + 2\beta R_E}$$

$$\frac{V_o}{V_i} = \frac{-\beta R_C}{h_{ie} + 2\beta R_E} \triangleq A_C \quad \text{[common-mode voltage gain]}$$

For $2\beta R_E >> h_{ie}$

$$A_C \simeq \frac{-R_C}{2R_E}$$

(Common mode differential amplifier)

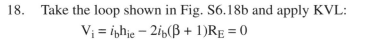

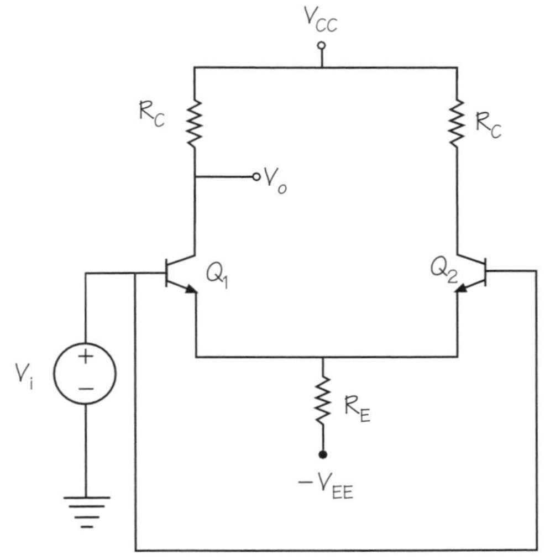

Fig. S6.18

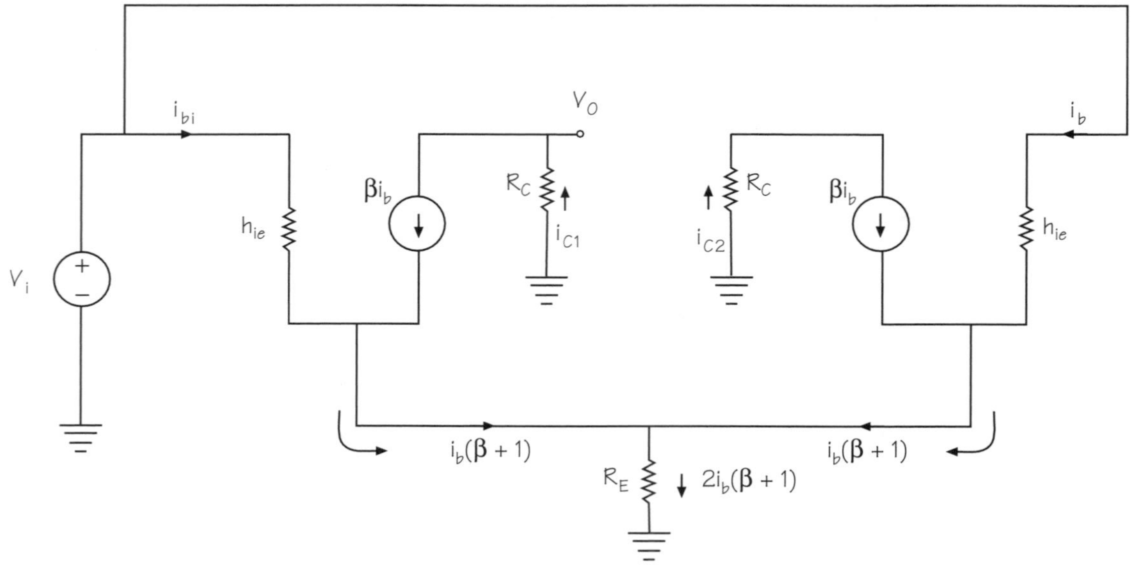

Fig. S6.18a

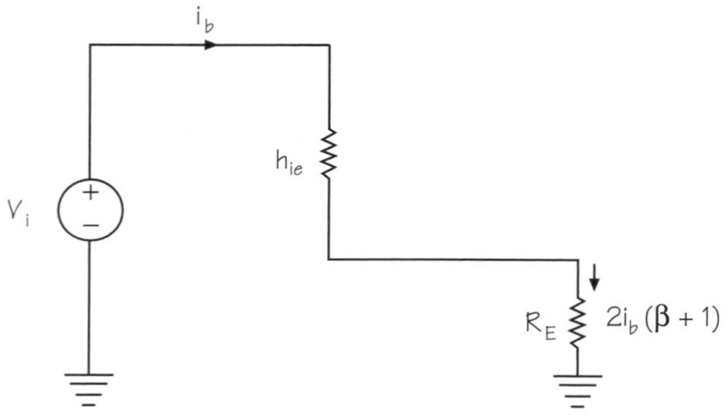

Fig. S6.18b

19. a) Since the base of transistor Q_1 is shorted out to its collector, therefore $V_{BC1} = 0$

Since the transistors are identical, then

$$V_{BE1} = V_{BE2},\ I_{B1} = I_{B2} \text{ and } I_{C1} = I_{C2} = Io$$

$$I = I_{C1} + 2I_{B1} = I_{C1} + \frac{2I_{CI}}{\beta}$$

$$I = I_{CI}\left(1 + \frac{2}{\beta}\right)$$

Because the emitters are at ground potential, then I is given by

$$I = \frac{V_{CC} - V_{BE}}{R}$$

Therefore, $I_{C1}\left(1 + \dfrac{2}{\beta}\right) = \dfrac{V_{CC} - V_{BE}}{R}$

$$I_{C1} = \left(\frac{\beta}{\beta + 2}\right)\left(\frac{V_{CC} - V_{BE}}{R}\right) = I_{C2} = I_o$$

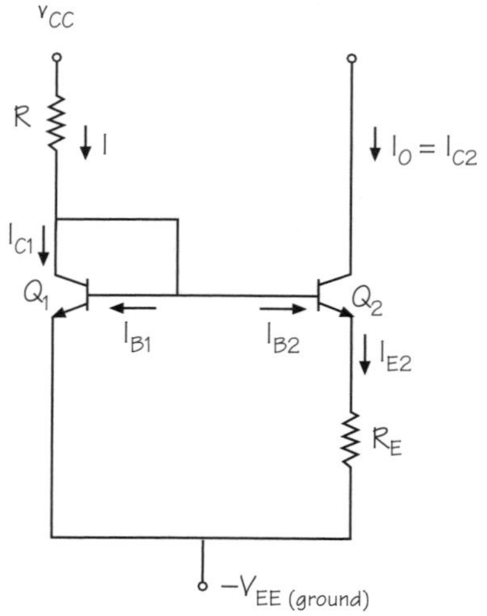

Fig. S6.19

b) $I_o = \frac{100}{102}\left(\frac{5-0.7}{2.5}\right) = 1.686\text{mA}$

c) For 10% change in β

i) $\beta = 90$

$$I_o = \frac{90}{92}\left(\frac{5-0.7}{2.5}\right) = 1.683\text{mA}$$

ii) $\beta = 110$

$$I_o = \frac{110}{112}\left(\frac{5-0.7}{2.5}\right) = 1.689\text{mA}$$

The above results show that the change in I_o due to a 10% change in is only ±0.003mA, or about 0.18% of the original value. Comparing these results with those obtained from problem 6.16, we notice that a similar change in β caused I_E to change ±0.05mA, or about 1.9%. This shows that the Widlar current source circuit provides almost a constant current source despite the change of β due to temperature variations.
(Widlar current source)

Grade Yourself

Circle the numbers of the questions you missed. Then fill in the total incorrect for each topic. If you answered more than three questions incorrectly, you need to focus on that topic. If a topic has less than three questions and you had at least one wrong, we suggest you study that topic also. Read your textbook, a review book, or ask your teacher for help.

Subject: Compound Configurations

Topic	Question Numbers	Number Incorrect
Cascade amplifier	1, 2, 3, 4, 5, 14	
JFETs cascade amplifier	6	
JFET and BJT cascade amplifier	7	
CE-to-CB cascade amplifier	8	
Differential amplifier	9, 15, 16, 17	
CE-to-CC cascade amplifier	10	
Darlington pair	11, 12, 13	
Common mode differential amplifier	18	
Widlar current source	19	

Power Amplifiers

7

Brief Yourself

Practical amplifiers such as those used in public-address or stereo systems have three amplification stages: the input stage, the intermediate stage, and the power amplifier stage. The input stage is a low-noise amplifier whose main purpose is to amplify the small-input signal to a certain level of low noise. The intermediate stage is designed to give the system a good frequency response. The frequency-response range of a typical home stereo system ranges from 50 Hz to 25 Khz. A power-amplifier stage boosts the signal so that it can adequately drive a load such as a loudspeaker system or the cathode ray tube of an oscilloscope, etc. Power amplifiers such as class A, class B, class AB, and other classes have the capability of delivering large-load current at moderate voltages and thus can deliver large amounts of power. The classification has evolved to describe amplifier operation, depending on the type of biasing employed. In a class-A power amplifier, the operating point (Q-point) is near the center of the load line of the I_C versus V_{CE} characteristics. Such selection of the Q-point results in a power amplifier that operates in a rather inefficient manner. The efficiency can be considerably improved by using a class-B power amplifier. In such a class, the Q-point is moved down the load line so that the dc current drain is very low. The problem that arises here is the distortion in the output signal, since the negative portions of the input sinusoidal current variation would be cut off. The latter problem can be solved by using a push-pull class-B arrangement. Class-AB operation leads to efficiencies intermediate between class A and B.

Test Yourself

1. The circuit shown in Fig. P7.1 is a series-fed class-A amplifier.
   a) Calculate the input power, output power, and efficiency of the amplifier circuit for input sinusoidal voltage that results in a base current of 10mA maximum.
   b) Calculate the maximum efficiency of the amplifier.
2. The circuit shown in Fig. P7.2 is an inductively coupled class-A amplifier. Consider that the

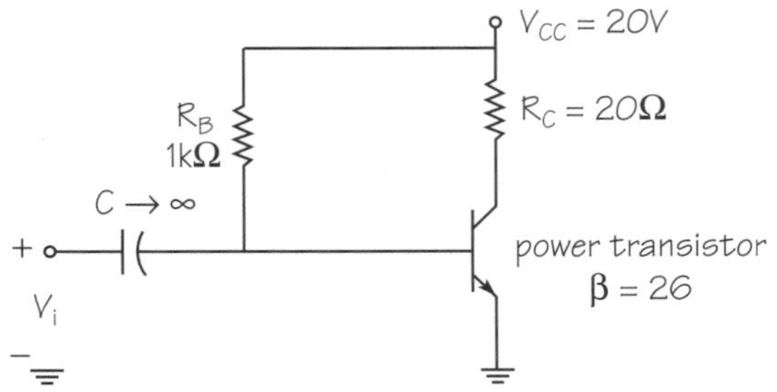

Fig. P7.1

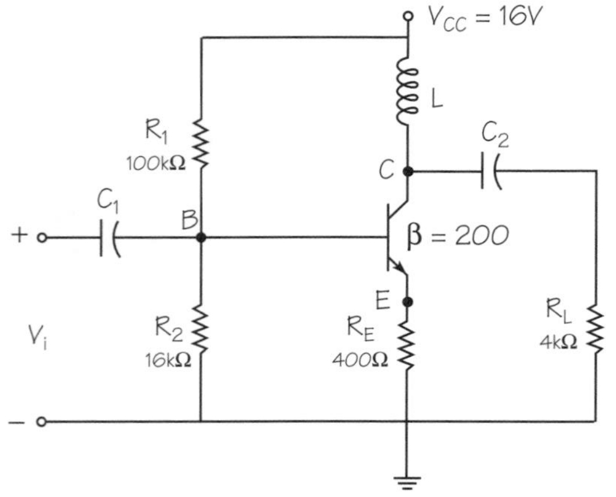

Fig. P7.2

inductor is selected so that it approximates an open circuit for the ac input but a short circuit for the dc. Determine:

a) the maximum output power.

b) the power dissipated in the transistor.

c) the amplifier efficiency.

3. The circuit in Fig. P7.3 is a transformer-coupled class-A amplifier. The transformer has a transformer ratio of a = 5:1, and the dc resistance of the primary coil is 40Ω.

   a) Draw the dc and ac load lines.

   b) Determine the efficiency of the amplifier.

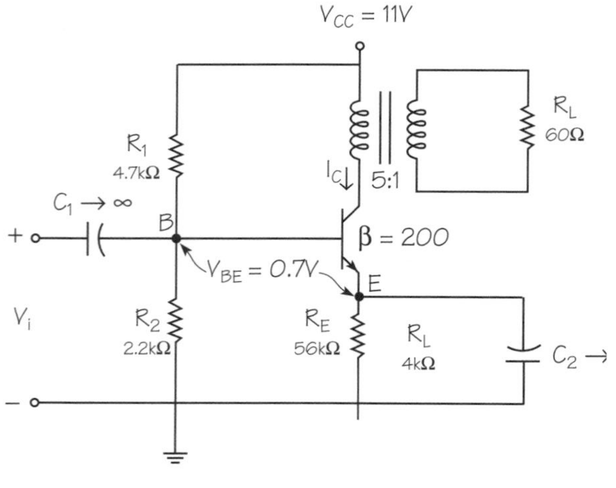

Fig. P7.3

4. *i)* Design a transformer-coupled emitter follower power amplifier if the input impedance Z_{in} = 2kΩ. (see Fig. P7.4).

   ii) Find the following:

   a) the overall current gain

   b) the output power

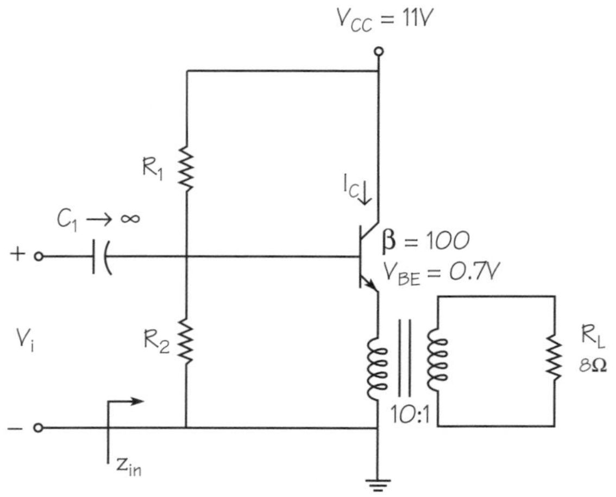

Fig. P7.4

c) maximum undistorted voltage output swing

d) amplifier efficiency

e) maximum efficiency

5. A class-B push-pull amplifier must deliver an output of 1/2W to an 8Ω speaker. The available supply is 18V. Assuming a sinusoidal input signal, determine:

   a) the transformer ration.

   b) the maximum power dissipated in the transistor.

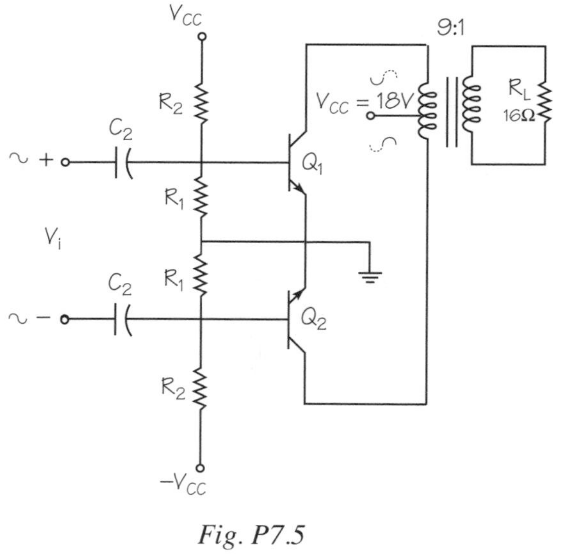

Fig. P7.5

6. A class-B push-pull amplifier can be designed without the use of a coupling transformer, as shown in Fig. P7.6a. This arrangement is known as "complementary symmetry class-B power amplifier," where two transistors, one pnp, and one npn with symmetrical characteristics are used. Further, a single power

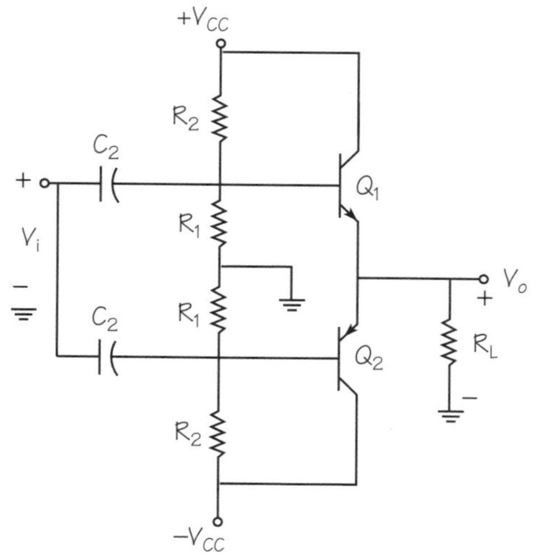

Fig. P7.6a

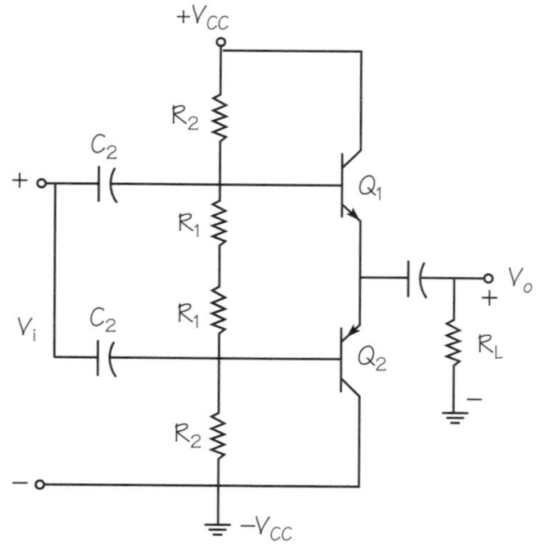

Fig. P7.6b

supply can be used by isolating the load, R_L, by a capacitor, C_1, as shown in Fig. P7.6b.
In the circuit of Fig. P7.6b, $V_{CC} = 12V$, $\beta = 60$, $C_1 = 500$ µf, $R_L = 8\Omega$, and the mid-frequency current gain $A_i = 23$. Consider that the value of each one of the capacitors C_2 is large enough so that it can be replaced by a short circuit at the signal frequency. Neglect the values of h_{ie}. Determine:

a) the values of R_1 and R_2.

b) the maximum power dissipated by each transistor.

c) the lower half-power frequency of the amplifier.

7. The complementary symmetry class-B power amplifier of problem P7.6 can be further modified — to improve circuit operation — by replacing the two resistors R_1 by two diodes D_1 and D_2, as shown in Fig. P7.7. This circuit is called "diode compensated complementary symmetry circuit." Design a complementary-symmetry diode-compensated class-B amplifier to drive a 4Ω load with 1W power for a frequency range of 20 to 20,000 Hz. Use npn and pnp matched transistors, each having $\beta = 100$ and $V_{BE} = \pm 0.7V$ with equivalent characteristic diodes having forward resistances, $R_f = 50\Omega$. Let $V_{CC} = 12V$. Determine C_1, R_2, the mid-frequency input impedance [Z_{in}], the maximum power dissipated in each transistor, and the total dc power dissipation.

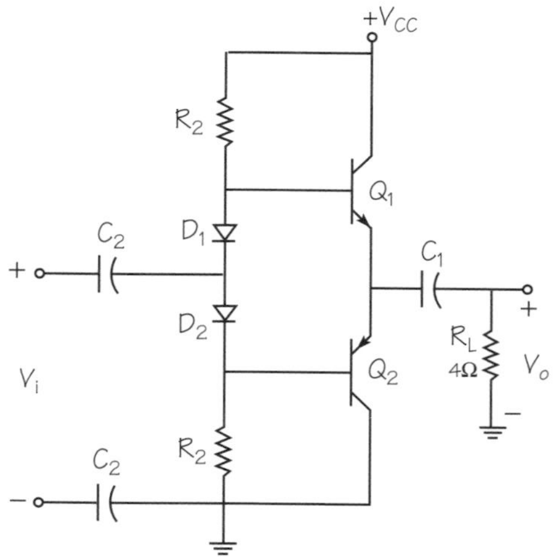

Fig. P7.7

8. For the push-pull class-AB complementary amplifier shown in Fig. P7.8, the input voltage $V_i = 6V$ (rms). Assuming an ideal amplifier:

a) calculate the input power, the output power, power handled by each transistor and the circuit efficiency.

b) calculate the maximum input power, maximum output power, input voltage for maximum operation, maximum efficiency, and the power dissipated by the output transistors.

c) determine the maximum power dissipated by the output transistors and the input voltage at which this occurs.

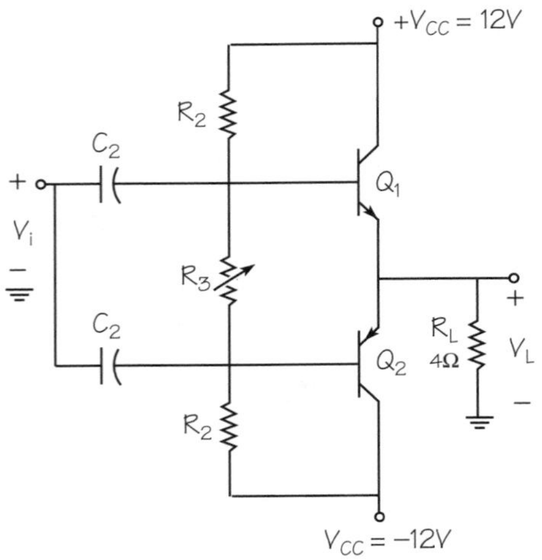

Fig. P7.8

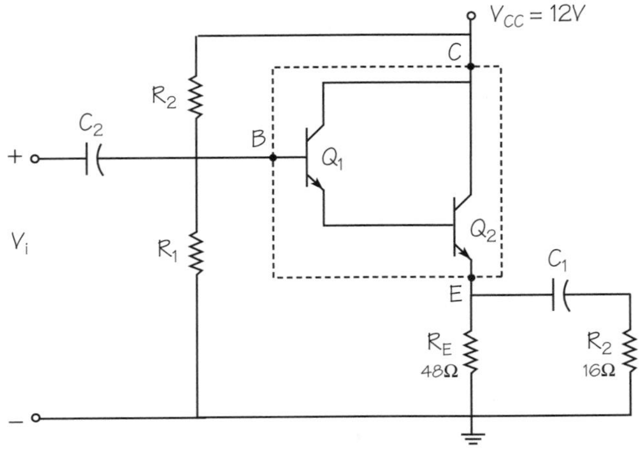

Fig. P7.9

9. The circuit shown in Fig. P7.9 represents a Darlington pair class-A amplifier. The circuit parameters are: $\beta_1 = \beta_2 = \beta = 100$, $V_{BE} = 1.4V$, $V_{CC} = 12V$, $R_L = 16\Omega$, $R_E = 48\Omega$. The input impedance of the circuit $[Z_{in}] = 2k\Omega$. Ignore h_{ie} for the transistors. Determine:
   a) R_1 and R_2.
   b) C_1 if the lower cutoff frequency $f_L = 50Hz$.
   c) the output power.

Check Yourself

1.

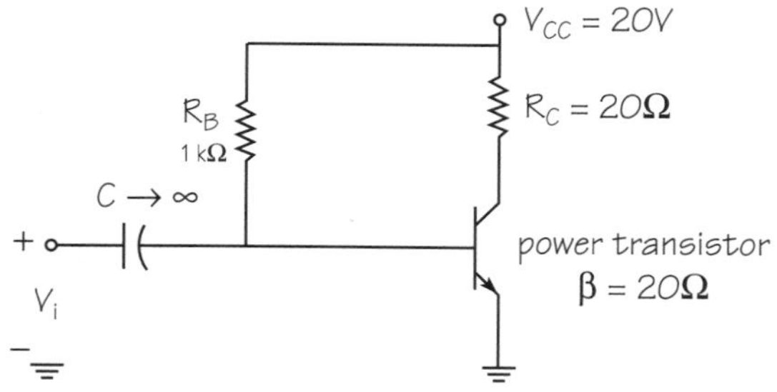

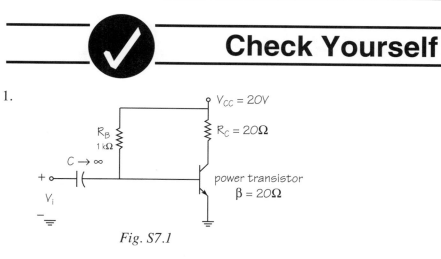

Fig. S7.1

a) For maximum possible swing, the collector current at the operating point is:

$$I_{CQ} = \frac{V_{CC}}{R_{ac} + R_{dc}}$$

where R_{ac} is the equivalent ac resistance of the load, and R_{dc} is its dc resistance.
In this particular problem $R_{ac} = R_{dc} = 20\Omega$.

Then $I_{CQ} = \frac{20}{20 + 20} = 0.5A$

Notice that I_{CQ} can also be found by direct dc analysis.

$$I_{CQ} = \beta I_B = \beta\left[\frac{V_{CC} - V_{BE}}{R_B}\right]$$

$$= 26\left[\frac{20 - 0.7}{1k\Omega}\right] = 0.5A$$

P_i (dc) $= V_{CC}I_{CQ} = 20 \times 0.5 = 10W$

Since I_B (max) $= 10mA$

Then I_C (max) $= \beta I_B$ (max) $= 26 \times 10 = 260mA = 0.26A$

$$P_o(ac) = I_C^2(rms)R_C = \frac{I_C^2(max)}{2}R_C$$

$$P_o(ac) = \frac{(0.26)^2 \times 20}{2} = 0.676W$$

$$\eta = \frac{P_o(ac)}{P_i(dc)} \times 100\%, \qquad \eta = \frac{0.676}{10} \times 100\% = 6.76$$

b) P_i (dc) $= 10W$

Notice that the input dc power remains the same regardless of the change in the input signal.
The peak (maximum) voltage swing of V_{CE} is:

$$V_{(peak)} = 1/2\ V_{CC}$$

and the peak value of the current swing

$$I_C(peak) = \frac{V_{CC}}{2R_C}$$

$$\text{max. } P_o(ac) = V\ (rms)\ I_C\ (rms) = \frac{1}{2}V_{(peak)}\ I_{C\ (peak)} = \frac{1}{2}\left[\frac{V_{CC}}{2} \cdot \frac{V_{CC}}{2R_C}\right] = \frac{V_{CC}^2}{8R_C} = \frac{(12)^2}{8 \times 20} = 2.5W$$

$$\text{max. efficiency } \eta = \frac{2.5}{10} \times 100\% = 25\%$$

This result is always true for a class-A power amplifier. **(Class-A power amplifier)**

2.

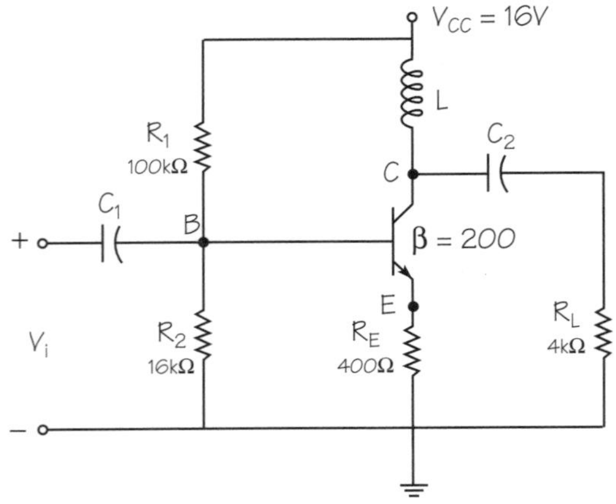

Figure S7.2

a) First we have to find I_{CQ}. There are two approaches:

i) Using regular dc analysis:
Since $\beta R_E = 200 \times 0.4k\Omega = 80k\Omega$
and $10R_2 = 10 \times 16 = 160k\Omega$
Then $\beta R_E < 10R_2$ and the conditions to find V_B by approximation method is not satisfied. An exact analysis must be used. The Thevenin equivalent circuit is found as follows:

$$R_{Th} = R_1 \,//\, R_2 = \frac{R_1R_2}{R_1 + R_2} = \frac{100 \times 16}{116} = 13.8k\Omega$$

$$V_{Th} = \frac{V_{CC}R_2}{R_1 + R_2} = \frac{16 \times 16}{116} = 2.21V$$

$$I_{BQ} = \frac{V_{TH} - V_{BE}}{R_{Th} + \beta R_E} = \frac{2.21 - 0.7}{13.8 + 200 \times 0.4} = 16.1\mu A$$

$$I_{CQ} = \beta I_{BQ} = 200 \times 16.1\mu = 3.22mA$$

ii) By using approximation formula for maximum swing:

$$I_{CQ} = \frac{V_{CC}}{R_{ac} + R_{dc}}$$

where $R_{ac} = R_L \,//\, Z_{inductor} + R_E$
Under the given condition $Z_{inductor} = \infty$
Therefore, $R_{ac} = R_L + R_E = 4000 + 400 = 4400\Omega$
and $R_{dc} = R_E = 400\Omega$

Then $I_{CQ} = \dfrac{16}{4400 + 400} = 3.33mA$

The output power = I_C^2 (rms) R_L
$P_{out} = 1/2\ I_{CQ}^2R_L$
$P_{out} = 1/2 \times (3.22)^2 \times 4k\Omega = 20.74mW$
In fact, the above result did not take into account the maximum swing near cutoff and saturation regions. To account for the distortion near these regions, about 5% of the maximum current has to be eliminated.

b) The power dissipated in the transistor is:

$$\begin{aligned} P_{transistor} &= I_{CQ}V_{CEQ} \\ &= I_{CQ}[V_{CC} - I_ER_E] \\ &= I_{CQ}[V_{CC} - (\beta + 1)I_BR_E] \\ &= 3.22[16 - 201 \times 16.1 \times 10^{-6} \times 400] \end{aligned}$$

$$P_{transistor} = 47.35mW$$

c) $P_{ac} = I_{CQ}V_{CC}$

$= 3.22 \times 16 = 51.52\text{mW}$

$$\eta = \frac{P_o(ac)}{P_i(dc)} \times 100\%$$

$$\eta = \frac{20.74}{51.52} \times 100\% = 40.25\%$$

(Inductively coupled class-A power ampifier)

3.

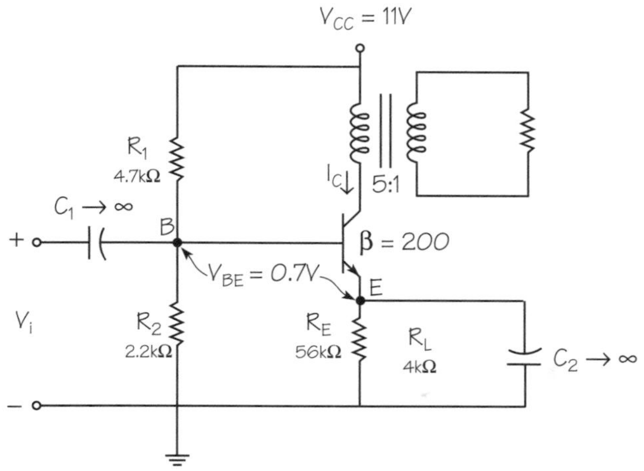

Figure S7.3

a) To find I_{CQ}:

$\beta R_E = 200 \times 0.56 = 112k\Omega$

$10R_2 = 22k\Omega$

$\beta R_E > 10R_2$

Approximation method to find V_B is satisfied.

$$V_B = \frac{V_{CC}R_2}{R_1 + R_2} = \frac{11 \times 2.2}{4.7 + 2.2} = 3.5V$$

$$I_E = \frac{V_B - V_{BE}}{R_E} = \frac{3.5 - 0.7}{560} = 5mA$$

$\therefore\ I_{CQ} \approx I_E = 5mA$

$V_{CEQ} = V_{CC} - I_{CQ}(R_{primary} + R_E)$

$= 11 - 5 \times 10^{-3}(40 + 560) = 8V$

To draw the load lines on the $I_C - V_{CE}$ characteristics:

i) Mark the Q point. This point is located at $I_{CQ} = 5mA$ and $V_{CEQ} = 8V$. The dc and ac load lines must pass through the Q point.

ii) The dc load line:

Since $V_{CE} = V_{CC} - I_C R_{dc}$

Here $R_{dc} = R_{primary} + R_E$

then at $I_C = 0$, $V_{CE} = V_{CC} = 11V$

The dc line is the line that passes through V_{CC} and the Q point.

iii) The ac load line:

Choose a point (V'_{CC}) on the V_{CE} axis such that

$$V'_{CC} = V_{CEQ} + I_{CQ}R_{ac}$$

where R_{ac} is the load resistance as seen at the primary coil.

$$R_{ac} = a^2R_L = 25 \times 60 = 1500\Omega$$

Therefore $V'_{CC} = 8 + 5 \times 10^{-3} \times 1500 = 15.5V$

The ac load line is the line that passes through V'_{CC} and the Q point (see Fig. S7.3b)

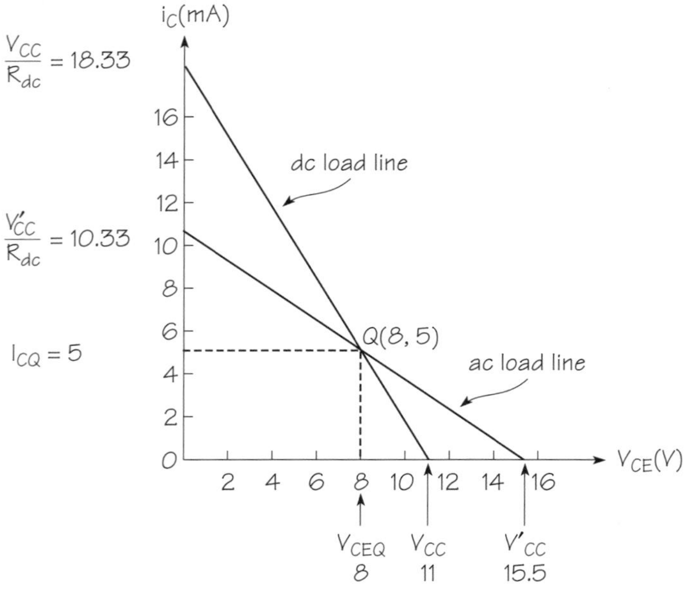

Figure S7.3b

b) The input power (taking into account the power dissipated in the biasing circuit) is given by:

$$P_{i(d)} = V_{CC}I_{CQ} + \frac{V_{CC}^2}{R_1 + R_2}$$

$$P_{i(d)} = 11 \times 5 + \frac{(11)^2}{(4.7 + 2.2)} = 72.54\text{mW}$$

$$P_o = 1/2\ I_L^2R_L$$

where I_L is the peak load current.
Since I_L is the current in the secondary coil,

and $a = \frac{I_{secondary}}{I_{primary}} = \frac{I_L}{I_{CQ}}$

Then $I_L = aI_{CQ}$

Therefore, $P_o = 1/2\ (aI_{CQ})^2R_L = 1/2 \times (5 \times 5 \times 10^{-3})^2 60$
$= 18.75\text{mW}$

$$\eta = \frac{P_o}{P_i} \times 100\%$$

$$\eta = \frac{18.75}{72.54} \times 100\% = 25.8$$

Note: To get a more accurate result for the output power you must take into account the distortion in the output signal caused by the saturation and cutoff regions. A maximum undistorted amplitude of I_L is about 95% of its peak value.

Then $P_o = 1/2\ (0.95\ a\ I_{CQ})^2R_L = 16.9\text{mW}$

The efficiency in this case is:
$\eta = 23.3\%$

(Transformer-coupled class-A power amplifier)

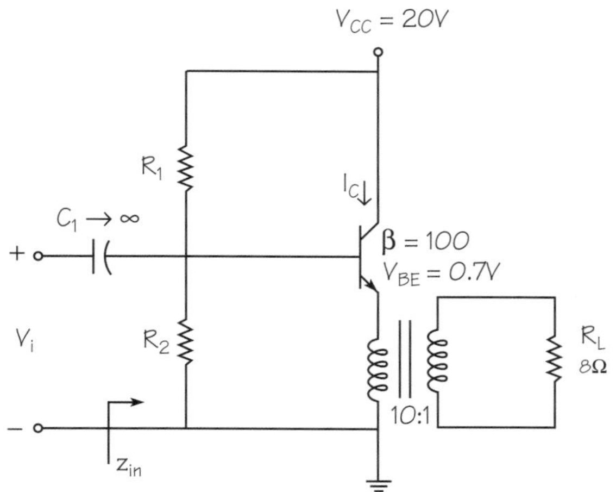

Fig. S7.4a

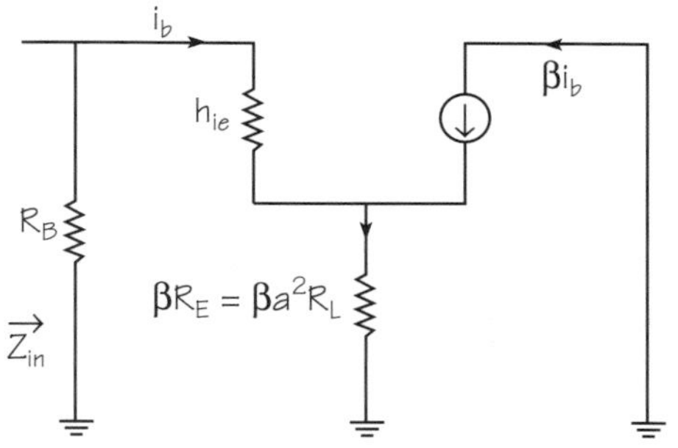

Fig. S7.4b

4. *i*) For the design part, one has to find R_1 and R_2.
From the ac small-signal analysis (see Fig. S7.4b)

$$Z_{in} = R_B \,//\, [h_{ie} + \beta R_E]$$

where $R_B = R_1 \,//\, R_2$, and R_E is the reflected resistance of the load as seen at the primary coil.
$R_E = a^2 R_L$

Therefore, $Z_{in} = \dfrac{R_B[h_{ie} + \beta a^2 R_L]}{R_B + h_{ie} + \beta a^2 R_L}$

To find h_{ie} $\quad I_{CQ} = \dfrac{V_{CC}}{R_{ac} + R_{dc}}$

where R_{dc} is the resistance of the primary coil. If we neglect R_{dc}, then:

$$I_{CQ} = \frac{V_{CC}}{R_{ac}} = \frac{V_{CC}}{a^2 R_L} = \frac{20}{(10)^2 \times 8} = 25\text{mA}$$

$$h_{ie} = \frac{26\text{mV}}{I_B} = \frac{26}{\frac{I_{CQ}}{\beta}} = \frac{26}{\frac{25}{100}} = 104\Omega$$

This value of $h_{ie} << \beta R_E$ and can be neglected.

Then $Z_{in} = \dfrac{R_B[a^2 \beta R_L]}{R_B + a^2 \beta R_L}$

$$2\text{k}\Omega = \frac{R_B[100 \times 100 \times 8]}{R_B + 100 \times 100 \times 8}$$

$$R_B \simeq 2\text{k}\Omega$$

From the dc analysis of the circuit:

$$V_B = I_B R_B + V_{BE} = \frac{V_{CC}}{R_1} R_B$$

$$V_B = \frac{I_{CQ}}{\beta} + V_{BE} = \frac{25 \times 2}{100} + 0.7 = 1.2\text{V}$$

Then $R_1 = \dfrac{V_{CC} R_B}{V_B} = \dfrac{20 \times 2}{1.2} = 33.34\Omega$

Since $R_B = R_1 \,//\, R_2 = \dfrac{R_1 R_2}{R_1 + R_2}$

$$2 = \frac{\frac{100}{3} R_2}{\frac{100}{3} + R_2} \qquad \text{and} \qquad R_2 = 2.13\text{k}\Omega$$

ii) a) The current gain of the transistor is:

$$A_i = \frac{\beta R_B}{R_B + h_{ie} + \beta R_E} = \frac{\beta R_B}{R_B + \beta R_E}$$

$$A_i = \frac{100 \times 2}{2 + 100 \times 0.8} = 2.44$$

Since the current gain of the transformer is equal to its transformer ratio [a], then: the overall current gain of the circuit is aA_i.

The overall current gain = 10 × 2.44 = 24.4.

b) The output power (power delivered to the load)

$$P_{out} = P_L = I_L{}^2{}_{(rms)}R_L = 1/2\ I_L{}^2{}_{(max)}R_L$$

But $I_L = I_{secondary\ coil} = aI_{primary} = aI_{CQ}$

By taking into account the distortion parts near the cutoff and saturation regions, then:

$$I_L = 0.95I_{L(max)} = 0.95aI_{CQ}$$

$$P_o = 1/2\ (0.95aI_{CQ})^2R_L$$

$$= 1/2\ (0.95 \times 10 \times 25 \times 10^{-3})^2 \times 8$$

$$P_o = 225.5\text{mW}$$

c) Maximum peak-to-peak undistorted voltage:

$$V_{o(p\text{-}k)} = I_{L(P-P)}R_L = 2I_{L(P)}R_L$$

$$= 2 \times aI_{CQ(P)} \times R_L$$

$$= 2 \times 10 \times .05 \times 25\text{m} \times 8$$

$$= 3.8\text{V}$$

d) To find the efficiency, we must find the input power delivered to the circuit:

$$P_{i(dc)} = V_{CC}I_{CQ} + \frac{V_{CC}{}^2}{R_1 + R_2} = 20 \times 0.025 + \frac{(20)^2}{\qquad\qquad} = 511.3\text{mW}$$

$$\eta = \frac{P_o}{P_{in}} \times 100\%$$

$$\eta = \frac{225.6}{511.3} \times 100\% = 44\%$$

e) Maximum input power = $V_{CC}I_{CQ}$

$$= V_{CC} \cdot \frac{V_{CC}}{a^2R_L} = \frac{V_{CC}{}^2}{a^2R_L}$$

Maximum output power = $1/2\ I_L{}^2{}_{(max)}R_L$

$$= 1/2\ (aI_{CQ})^2R_L = 1/2 \frac{V_{CC}{}^2}{a^2R_L}$$

$$\text{max. } \eta = \frac{1}{2} \frac{\frac{V_{CC}{}^2}{a^2R_L}}{\frac{V_{CC}{}^2}{a^2R_L}} \times 100\% = 50\%$$

(Transfer-coupled emitter-fallover power amplifier)

5. a) The output power (power dissipated in the load):

$$P_o = \frac{V_o{}^2(\text{rms})}{R_L} \quad \text{or} \quad V_o = \sqrt{P_oR_L}$$

$$V_o = \sqrt{\frac{1}{2} \times 8} = 2\text{V}$$

But the rms value of the voltage is related to the peak value by the relation

$$V_{ms} = \frac{V_p}{\sqrt{2}} \quad \text{or} \quad V_p = \sqrt{2} = V_{rms}$$

Thus $V_p = 2\sqrt{2}$ volt

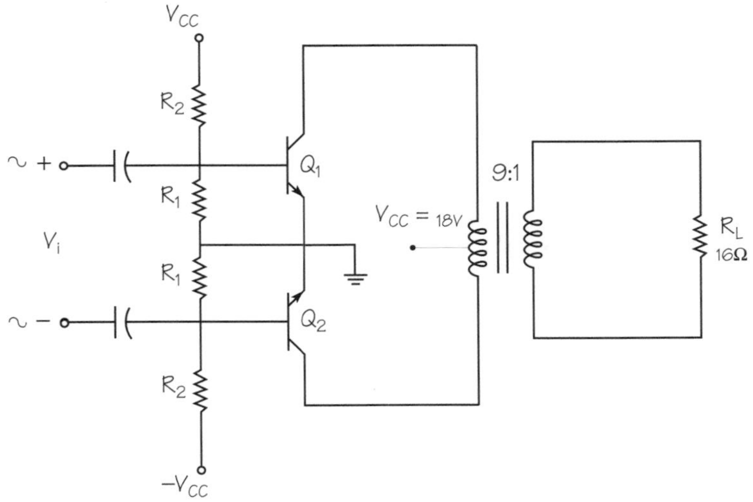

Fig. S7.5

The peak input voltage to each half of the transformer's primary:

$$V_{input}(peak) \approx V_{CC} = 18V$$

The transformer ratio of one-half of the primary to the secondary is:

$$a' = \frac{N_1}{N_2} = \frac{V_{in}(peak)}{V_o(peak)} = \frac{18}{2\sqrt{2}} = 6.364$$

The transformer ratio of the whole primary coil to the secondary coil is:

$$a = 2a' = 12.73$$

b) To calculate the maximum power dissipated in the transistors, let us analyze the circuit by considering a single transistor, as shown in Fig S7.5b.

The average dc collector current in each transistor, assuming sinusoidal input, is given by:

$$I_{dc} = \frac{I_{C(max)}}{\pi}\int_0^{\pi} \sin \omega t \, dt$$

$$I_{dc} = \frac{2I_{C(max)}}{\pi}$$

The input power from the supply is given approximately by:

$$P_{in(dc)} = V_{CC}I_{dc} = \frac{2V_{CC}I_{C(max)}}{\pi}$$

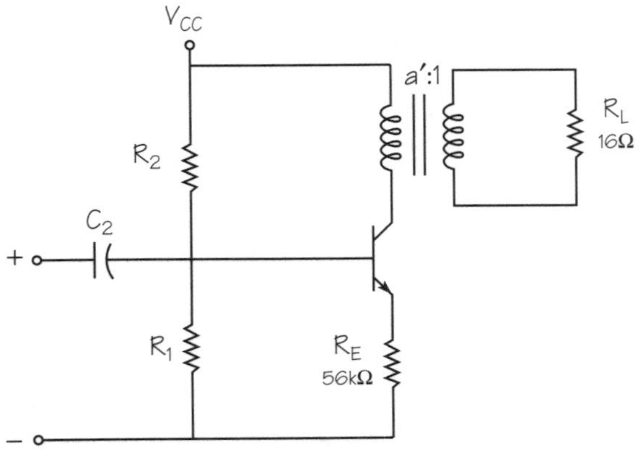

Fig. S7.5b

The ac output power

$$P_{o(ac)} = 1/2\, I_{C(max)}^2 R'_L$$

Where R'_L is the effective value of the load R_L as seen at the primary coil of the transformer.

$$R'_L = a^2 R_L$$

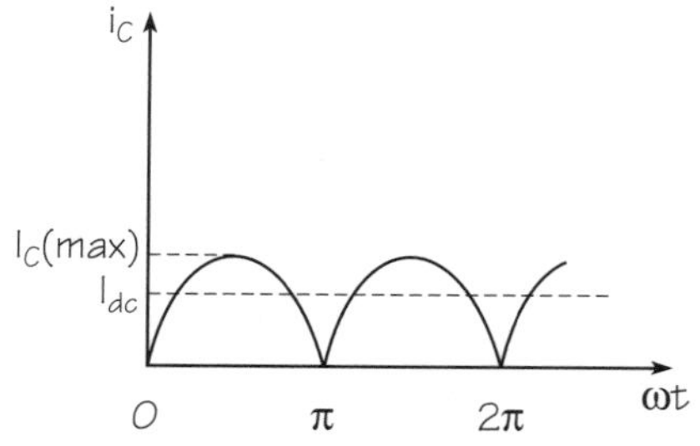

Fig. S7.5c

The dissipation in the transistors is the difference between the power input to the collector circuit and the power delivered to the load.

$$P_{transistors} = \frac{2V_{CC}I_{C(max)}}{\pi} - \frac{1}{2}I_{C(max)}^2 R'_L$$

Since the power is shared equally between the two transistors, the power dissipated by a single transistor is

$$P_{transistors} = \frac{1}{2}\left[\frac{2V_{CC}I_{C(max)}}{\pi} - \frac{1}{2}I_{C(max)}^2 R'_L\right]$$

The maximum power dissipated by a single transistor is found by differentiating the above equation with respect to $I_{C(max)}$. Thus,

$$\frac{dI_P}{dI_{C(max)}} = 0 = \frac{1}{2}\left[\frac{2V_{CC}}{\pi} - I_{C(max)}R'_L\right]$$

from which $I_{C(max)} = \dfrac{2V_{CC}}{\pi R'_L}$

Therefore, the maximum power dissipated by each transistor is:

$$\text{max. } P_{transistor} = \frac{V_{CC}^2}{\pi^2 R'_L} = \frac{V_{CC}^2}{\pi^2 a^2 R_L} = \frac{(18)^2}{\pi^2 \times 25 \times 16} = 50.66\text{mW}$$

Notice that for a direct couple of the load, a = 1 and the maximum power dissipated in each transistor will be:

$$\frac{V_{CC}^2}{\pi^2 R_L}$$

(Class-B push-pull amplifier)

6. a) To find the current gain A_i, we first draw the mid-frequency ac model of the amplifier. This model is shown in Fig. S7.6b.

By using a current divider rule:

$$i_b = \frac{i_{in}R_B}{R_B + (\beta + 1)R_1}$$

where $R_B = R_2 \,//\, R_2 = \dfrac{R_2}{2}$

Notice that the two input capacitors short-circuited both resistors, R_1, for the ac operations.
Since $\beta + 1 \approx \beta$, then:

$$i_b = \frac{i_n R_B}{R_B + \beta R_L}$$

But $\quad i_b = \dfrac{i_o}{\beta}$

Therefore, $i_o = \dfrac{i_{in}\beta R_B}{R_B + \beta R_L}$

$$A_i = \frac{i_o}{i_{in}} = \frac{\beta R_B}{R_B + \beta R_L}$$

$$23 = \frac{60R_B}{R_B + 60 \times 8}$$

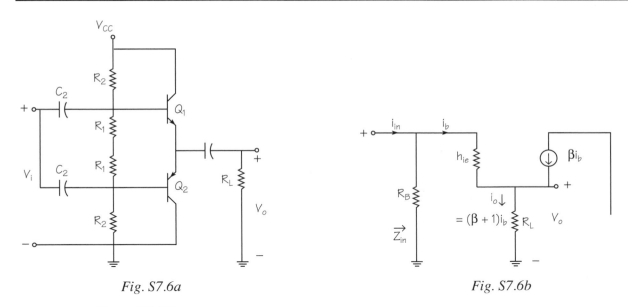

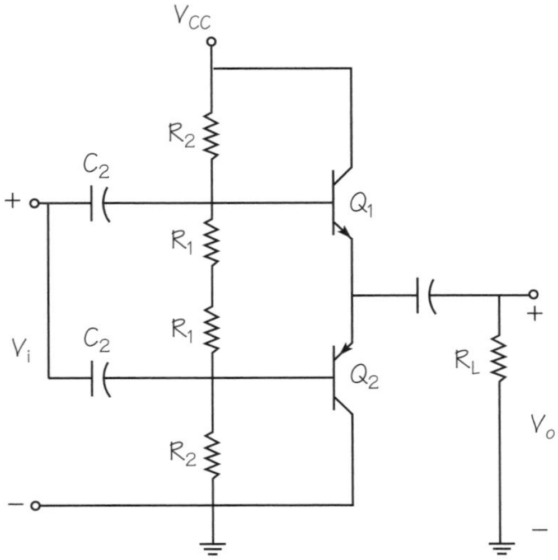

Fig. S7.6a

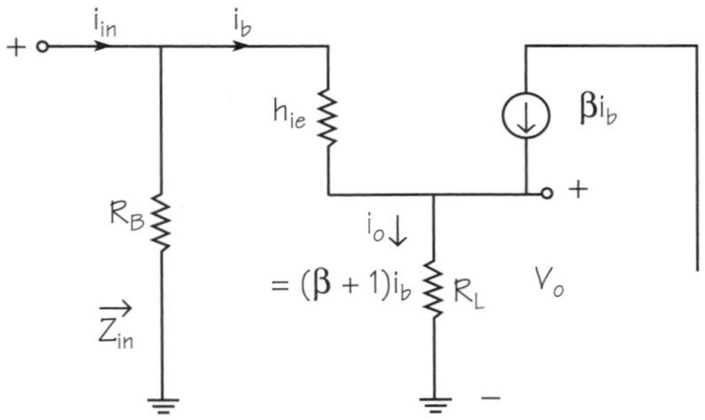

Fig. S7.6b

or $\quad R_B = 298.4\Omega$

$$R_2 = 2R_B \simeq 597\Omega$$

R_1 is determined from the dc analysis of the circuit. By taking a loop containing both R_1 and the base-emitter of both transistors, then:

$$V_{CC} \cdot 2R_1/2(R_1 + R_2) = 2V_{BE}$$

or $\quad R_1 = \dfrac{2V_{BE}R_2}{V_{CC} - 2V_{BE}}$

Assuming silicon transistors with $V_{BE} = 0.7V$

$$R_1 = \frac{2 \times 0.7 \times 597}{12 - 1.4} = 79\Omega$$

b) $\quad I_{dc} = \dfrac{I_c(\max)}{\pi}$

Notice that the average dc value of the collector current, I_{dc}, is one-half of the value obtained in problem P7.5. The reason is that in one-half of the input cycle, the current flows through the upper transistor into the capacitor and the load resistor. The energy is stored in $R_L - C_1$ circuit. The second transistor is cut off. During the second half of the cycle, the energy is released from the capacitor and the upper transistor is cut off.

$$P_{in}(dc) = V_{CC}I_{dc} = \frac{V_{CC}I_{C(\max)}}{\pi}$$

By following the same steps as in problem P7.5 for determining the maximum power dissipated in each transistor, then:

$$\text{max. } P_{transistor} = \frac{V_{CC}^2}{2\pi^2 R_L} = \frac{(12)^2}{4\pi^2 \times 8} = 1.842\text{mW}$$

c) The lower half (or the 3 dB) power frequency is determined from the following relations:

$$R_L = X_{C1} = \frac{1}{\omega C_1}$$

Then $\quad \omega = \dfrac{1}{R_L C_1}$

The above relation is derived from the fact that at the lower half-power frequency, the output power drops to one-half of the power at mid-range frequency, and that the voltage across R_L equals the voltage across C_1.

Since $\omega = 2\pi f$, then:

$$f = \frac{1}{2\pi R_L C_1} = \frac{1}{\qquad\qquad} = 40\text{Hz}$$

This is the lowest frequency that can be effectively produced by the amplifier.

(Complementary symmetrical class-B push-pull amplifier)

7.

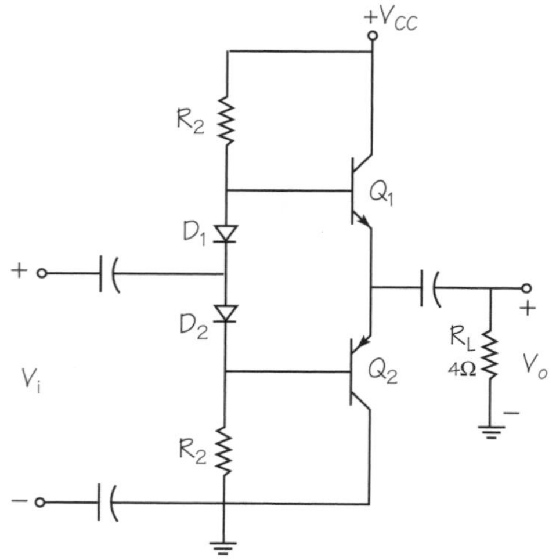

Fig. S7.7a

The output ac power $P_{o(ac)} = \dfrac{I_C^2(\max)R_2}{2} = 1\text{W}$

Then $I_{C(\max)} = \sqrt{\dfrac{2}{R_L}} = \sqrt{\dfrac{2}{4}} = 0.707\text{A}$

and the maximum base current, $I_{B(\max)} = \dfrac{I_{C(\max)}}{\beta}$

$$I_{B(\max)} = \frac{0.707}{100} = 7.07\text{mA}$$

The lower frequency, 20Hz, represents the half-power frequency; then:

$$C_1 = \frac{1}{2\pi f_{low} R_L} = \frac{1}{2\pi \times 20 \times 4} = 1989.4\mu\text{f}$$

One may choose a capacitor of 2000μf without a significant error. Therefore:

$$C_1 = 2000\mu\text{f}$$

At mid-range frequency, C_1 is replaced by a short circuit. The voltage across the load in this case is:

$$V_L = (\beta + 1)i_b R_L \approx i_c R_L$$
$$V_L = 0.707 \times 4 = 2.83 \text{ volt}$$

Notice that the output voltage is taken out of the emitter of Q_1. Therefore, transistor Q_1 circuit's along with the load resistor represent an emitter follower amplifier having a voltage gain of unity. Then:

$$V_{R2} = V_L = 2.83\text{V}$$

The diodes' current, I_d, can be determined from the dc biasing condition by neglecting the base current. By taking a loop containing the two resistors R_2 and the base-emitter of the two transistors:

$$I_D = \frac{V_{CC} - 2V_{BE}}{2R_2}$$

The ac components of the currents at the mid-frequency range are shown in Fig. S7.7b.

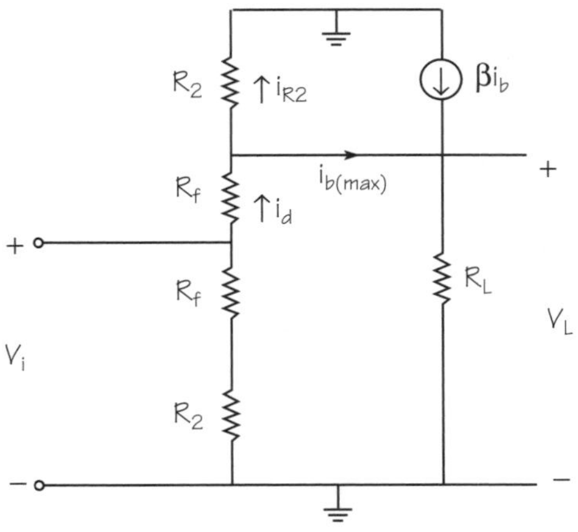

Fig. S7.7b

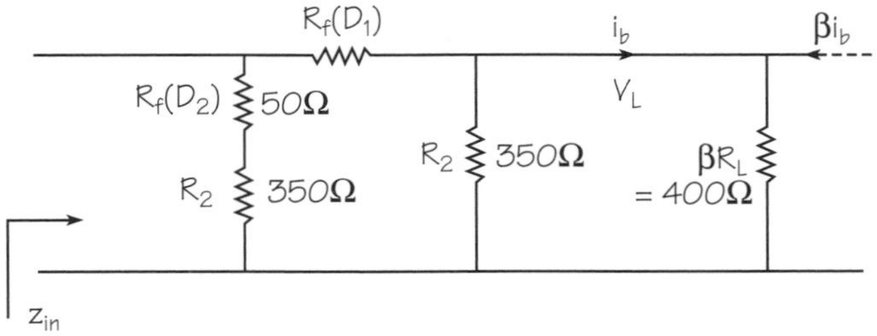

Fig. S7.7c

The peak (max) value of the ac diodes' current:

$$i_{dp} = i_{b(max)} = i_{R2}$$
$$= i_{b(max)} + \frac{V_{R2}}{R_2}$$
$$i_{dp} = i_{dp(max)} + \frac{V_L}{R_2}$$

To keep the diodes operating in the linear operation of forward mode, the dc component of the current has to be greater than the negative peak of the ac component. The minimum requirement of such condition is:

$$I_D = i_{dp}$$

Therefore, $\dfrac{V_{CC} - 2V_{BE}}{2R_2} = i_{b(max)} + \dfrac{V_L}{R_2}$

from which $R_2 = \dfrac{\dfrac{V_{CC}}{2} - V_{BE} - V_L}{i_{b(max)}}$

$$R_2 = \frac{6 - 0.7 - 2.83}{7.07\text{mA}} = 350\Omega$$

To find the input impedance, we draw the input ac equivalent circuit in Fig. S7.7b:

$$Z_{in} = [R_f + R_2] \,//\, [R_f + R_2 \,//\, \beta R_L]$$
$$= [50 + 350] \,//\, [50 + (350 \,//\, 400)]$$
$$Z_{in} = 149\Omega$$

Since one transistor conducts at each half-cycle of the input (see S7.6), then:

$$\max P_{transistor} = \frac{V_{CC}^2}{4\pi^2 R_L} = \frac{(12)^2}{4\pi^2 \times 4} = 0.912\text{W}$$

The power delivered to the transistor:

$$P_{i(dc)[transistor]} = V_{CC} I_{dc} = \frac{V_{CC} I_{C(max)}}{\pi}$$

The total dc power to the amplifier is the sum of the power delivered to the transistor and the power to the bias and compensation circuit.

$$P_{i(total)} = \frac{V_{CC} I_{C(max)}}{\pi} + \frac{V_{CC} I_C}{2(R_2 + R_f)}$$

where $I_{C(max)} = \dfrac{V_{CC}}{2R_L}$

Then $P_{i(total)} = \dfrac{V_{CC}^2}{2\pi R_L} + \dfrac{V_{CC}I_C}{2(R_2 + R_f)}$

$$P_{i(total)} = \frac{(12)^2}{2\pi \times 4} + \frac{(12)^2}{2(350 + 50)} = 5.91 \text{ W}$$

(Diode-compensated complementary-symmetry power amplifier)

8.

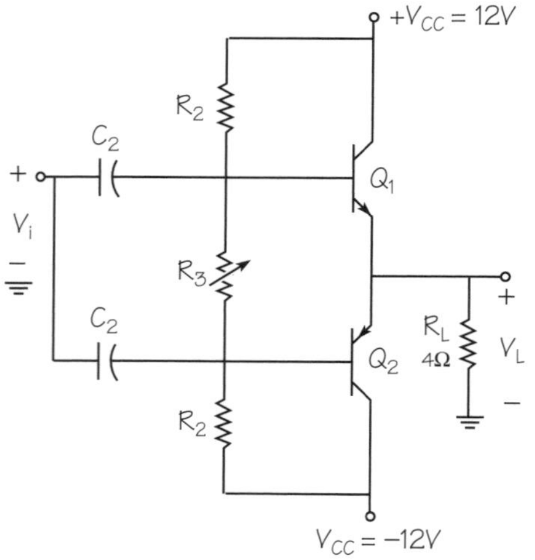

Fig. S7.8

a) Since $V_{i(rms)} = \dfrac{V_{i(peak)}}{\sqrt{2}}$

Then $V_{i(peak)} = \sqrt{2}V_{i(rms)} = 6\sqrt{2} = 8.5\text{V}$

For an ideal EF amplifier, the voltage gain is unity.

Therefore, $V_L = V_{i\,(peak)} = 8.5\text{V}$

The ac output power delivered to the load:

$$P_{o(ac)} = \frac{V_L^2}{2R_L} = \frac{(6\sqrt{2})^2}{2 \times 4} = 9\text{W}$$

The load peak current:

$$I_{L(peak)} = \frac{V_{L(peak)}}{R_L} = \frac{8.5}{4} = 2.12\text{A}$$

The average dc current:

$$I_{dc} = \frac{2I_{L(peak)}}{\pi} = \frac{2 \times 2.125}{\pi}$$

$$I_{dc} = 1.35\text{A}$$

$$P_{i(dc)} = V_{CC}I_{dc} = 12 \times 1.35 = 16.2\text{W}$$

The power dissipated by both transistors is the difference between the input power and the output power. Then

$$P_{transistors} = P_{i(dc)} - P_{o(ac)}$$

$$P_{transistors} = 16.2 - 9 = 7.2\text{W}$$

The power dissipated in each transistor $= \dfrac{7.2}{2} = 3.6\text{W}$.

The efficiency

$$\eta = P_{o(ac)}/P_{i(dc)} \times 100\%$$

$$\eta = (9/16.2) \times 100\% = 55.54\%$$

b) The maximum input power

$$\max P_{i(dc)} = \frac{2V_{CC}^2}{\pi R_L} = \frac{2 \times (12)^2}{4\pi} = 22.92$$

and the maximum output ac power

$$\max P_{o(ac)} = \frac{2V_{CC}^2}{\pi R_L} = \frac{(12)^2}{2 \times 4} = 18W$$

$$\max \eta = \frac{\dfrac{V_{CC}^2}{2R_L}}{\dfrac{2V_{CC}^2}{\pi R_L}} = \frac{\pi}{4} \times 100\% = 78.5\%$$

This is the maximum efficiency for a class-B or class-AB push-pull amplifier.
The maximum voltage required to achieve maximum efficiency is $V_{L(peak)} = V_{CC} = 12V$.
The power dissipated in each transistor is:

$$P_{transistor} = 1/2\ (P_{i(dc)} - P_{o(ac)})$$
$$= 1/2\ [22.92 - 18] = 2.46W$$

c) The maximum power dissipated by each transistor is:

$$\max P_{transistor} = \frac{1}{2}\left[\frac{2V_{CC}^2}{\pi R_L}\right] = \frac{V_{CC}^2}{\pi R_L} = \frac{(12)^2}{\pi^2} \times 4 = 3.65$$

(Push-pull class-AB power amplifier)

9.

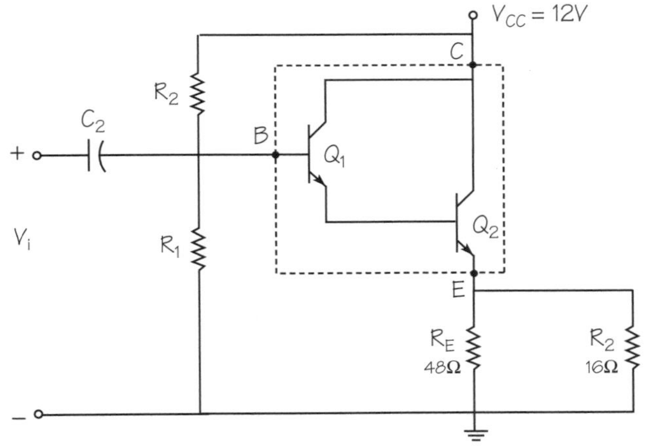

Fig. S7.9a

a) From problem P6.13 with $h_{ie} = 0$ (see Fig. S7.9b)

$$Z_{in} = \beta^2 R_L (R_E \,//\, R_L)/R_B + \beta^2 (R_E \,//\, R_L)$$

Where $\beta^2 = \beta_1 \beta_2 = 10{,}000$
and $R_B = R_1 \,//\, R_2$

$$\text{Then } 2k\Omega = \frac{10{,}000 R_B (48 \,//\, 16)}{R_B + 10{,}000(48 \,//\, 16)} = \frac{120{,}000 R_B}{R_B + 120{,}000} \quad \therefore R_B \approx 2k\Omega$$

$$I_{CQ} = \frac{V_{CC}}{R_{ac} + R_{dc}} = \frac{V_{CC}}{R_E \,//\, R_L + R_E}$$

$$I_{CQ} = \frac{12}{12 + 48} = 200mA$$

To find R_1 and R_2 we use the dc analysis for the circuit in Fig. S7.9a. The Thevenin equivalent circuit is shown in Fig. S7.9c.

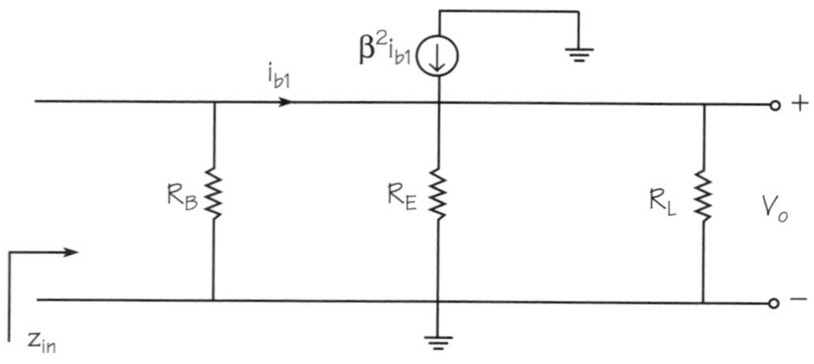

Fig. S7.9b

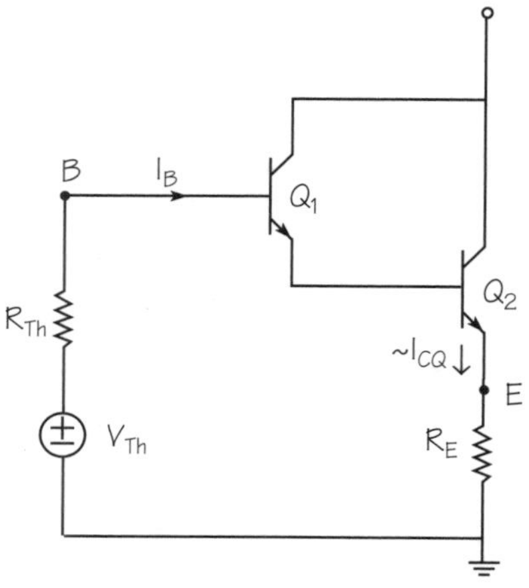

Fig. S7.9c

$$R_{Th} = R_1 \,//\, R_2 = R_B$$

$$V_{Th} = \frac{V_{CC}R_1}{R_1 + R_2}$$

By multiplying the numerator and the denominator of the last equation by R_2:

$$V_{Th} = \frac{V_{CC}R}{R_2}B$$

$$I_B = \frac{V_{Th} - V_{BE}}{R_B + \beta^2 R_E}$$

Since $I_{CQ} = \beta^2 I_B$

Then $I_{CQ} = \dfrac{\beta^2[V_{Th} - V_{BE}]}{R_B + \beta^2 R_E}$

and $V_{Th} = V_{BE} + I_{CQ}\left[\dfrac{R_B}{\beta^2} + R_E\right]$

$$V_{Th} = 1.4 + \left(\frac{2k}{10{,}000} + 48\right) \times 0.2 = 11\text{V}$$

Then $R_2 = \dfrac{V_{CC}R_B}{V_{Th}} = \dfrac{12 \times 2}{11} = 2.18\text{k}\Omega$

but $R_B = R_1 \,//\, R_2 = \dfrac{R_1 R_2}{R_1 + R_2}$

Then $R_1 = \dfrac{R_2 R_B}{R_2 + R_B} = \dfrac{2.18 \times 2}{2.18 - 2} = 24\text{k}\Omega$

b) To find C_1 notice that the capacitor will discharge through the total resistance of:

$R_L + Z_0 \approx R_E // \dfrac{R_B}{\beta^2} \approx 0$ Then

$$C_1 \approx \frac{1}{2\pi f R_2} = \frac{1}{2\pi(50)(16)} = 198\mu\text{f}$$

c) The output power $P_o = \dfrac{1}{2}\left(\dfrac{I_{CQ}}{2}\right)^2 R_L$

$$P_o = \frac{1}{2}\left(\frac{0.2}{2}\right)^2 \times 16 = 0.08\text{W}$$

(Darlington-pair class-A amplifier)

Grade Yourself

Circle the numbers of the questions you missed. Then fill in the total incorrect for each topic. If you answered more than three questions incorrectly, you need to focus on that topic. If a topic has less than three questions and you had at least one wrong, we suggest you study that topic also. Read your textbook, a review book, or ask your teacher for help.

Subject: Power Amplifiers

Topic	Question Numbers	Number Incorrect
Class-A power amplifier	1	
Inductively coupled class-A power amplifier	2	
Transformer-coupled class-A power amplifier	3	
Transfer-coupled emitter-fallover power amplifier	4	
Class-B push-pull amplifier	5	
Complementary symmetrical class-B push-pull amplifier	6	
Diode-compensated complementary-symmetry power amplifier	7	
Push-pull class-AB power amplifier	8	
Darlington-pair class-A amplifier	9	

Operational Amplifiers

8

Brief Yourself

The operational amplifier, or op-amp, is one of the basic building blocks for constructing analog electronic systems. Originally, the op-amp was used to perform mathematical operations in analog computers. Examples of such operations include summing, integrating, and other mathematical operations. The op-amp can also perform many other signal processings including amplification, analog filtering, buffering, phase inversion, and rectification.

An op-amp is characterized by very high input impedance, and large open-circuit voltage gain as well as low output impedance. Futhermore, it has two inputs, both of which are used during its operation. The inputs are differentiated as inverting input (or the minus " – "), and the noninverting input (or the plus " + "). These terminologies are so designated because the polarity of the output voltage and the inverting input voltage are of opposite signs, whereas the ouput and noninverting input voltages have the same polarity. Because of the high-input impedance of the op-amp, it can be reasonably assumed that the current I_i drawn by the amplifier's input terminals is negligible. Thus, the potential at the (–) and the (+) terminals is taken to be the same. In particular, if one of the terminals is at ground, then the other terminal is considered to be ground potential. But since the current is approximately zero, the input terminal, which is not directly connected to ground, is referred to as virtual ground.

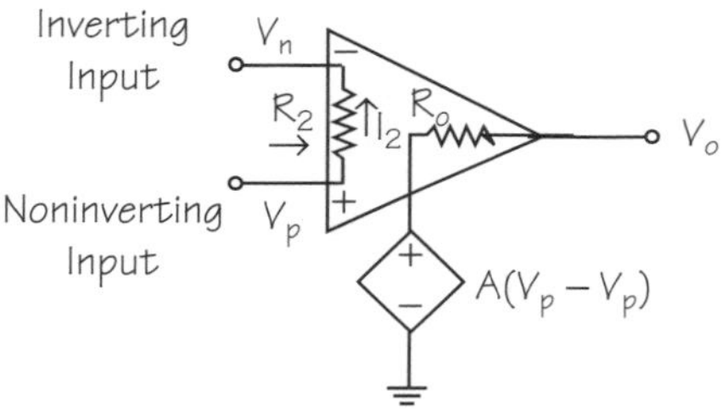

The output voltage of the amplifier is proportional to the difference in the input voltages at the noninverting and the inverting terminals. The constant of proportionality is the open-loop gain (or the differential gain), A. Thus, the output voltage,

$$v_o = A\,(v_p - v_n) = A\,v_d$$

Here, v_p and v_n are the voltages at the noninverting and the inverting terminals, respectively, and v_d is the difference between them. A practical op-amp cannot be described by the above equation, because, in general, the output depends not only upon the difference signal vd of the two signals, but also upon the average level, called the *common-mode signal* v_{cm}, where

$$v_{cm} = 1/2\,(v_p + v_n).$$

Test Yourself

1. Prove that the output voltage for an ideal open-loop op. amp. is given by:

$$\upsilon_o = -\frac{AR_2}{R_1 + R_2}\upsilon_i$$

where A is the open-loop voltage gain.

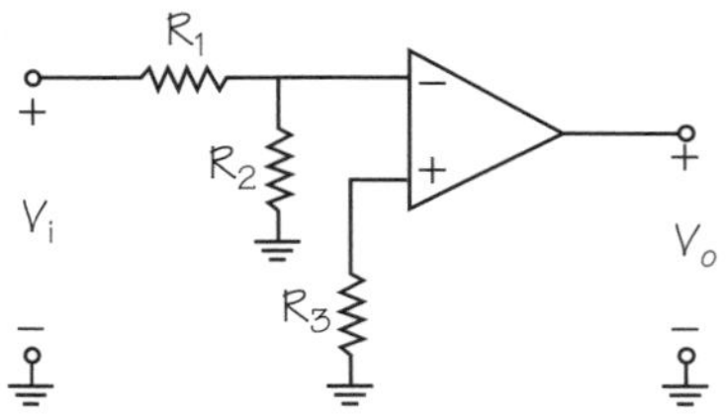

Fig. P8.1

2. Assume that the ideal op. amp. in the circuit shown in Fig. P8.2 is operating in the linear region.

   a) Draw the equivalent circuit.

   b) Show that $\upsilon_o = \frac{R_1 + R_f}{R_1}\upsilon_i$.

   c) What happens if $R_1 \Rightarrow \infty$ and $R_f \Rightarrow 0$?

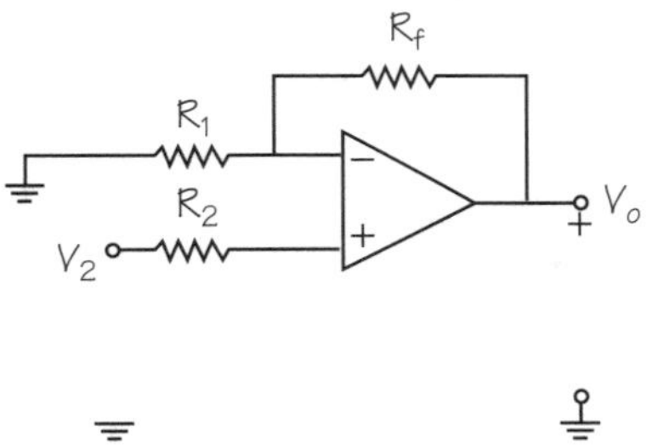

Fig. P8.2

3. Show that the output voltage, υ_o, for the ideal op. amp. shown in Fig. P8.3 is given by:

$$\upsilon_o = \left(1 + \frac{R_f}{R_a}\right)\upsilon_b - \frac{R_f}{R_a}\upsilon_a$$

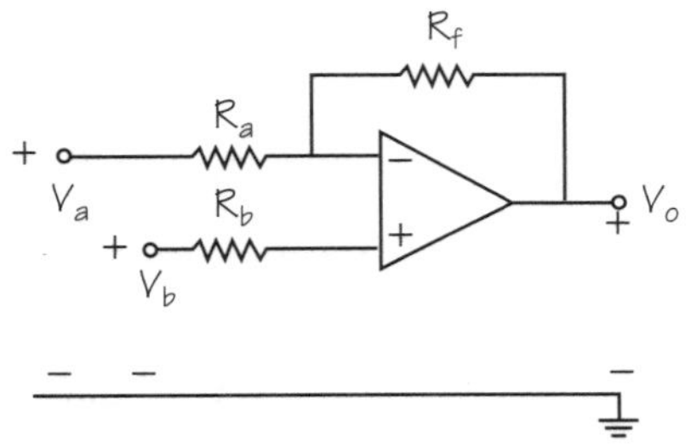

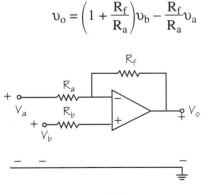

Fig. P8.3

4. Fig. P8.4 represents a weighted differencing op. amp. circuit. Show that the output voltage is given by:

$$\upsilon_o = \left(1 + \frac{R_f}{R_a}\right)\left(\frac{R_2}{R_1 + R_2}\right)\upsilon_b - \frac{R_f}{R_a}\upsilon_a$$

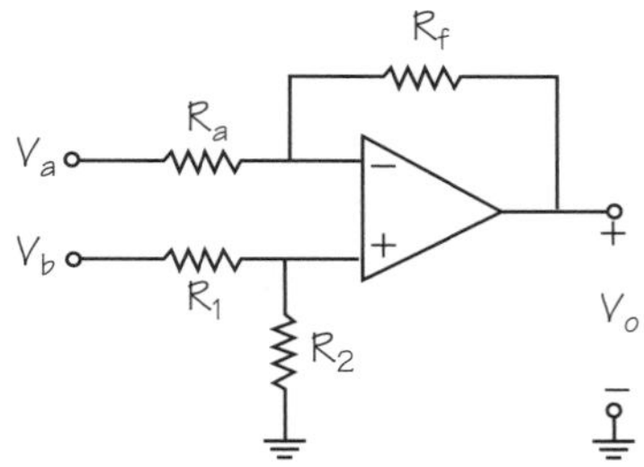

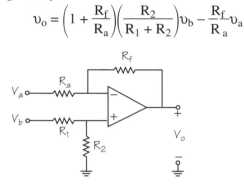

Fig. P8.4

5. For the sign switcher op. amp. shown in Fig. P8.5 with $R = R_f$, show that

   a) $\upsilon_o = \upsilon_i$ if R_1 is connected to υ_i.

   b) $\upsilon_o = -\frac{R_f}{R}\upsilon_i$ if R_1 is connected to the ground.

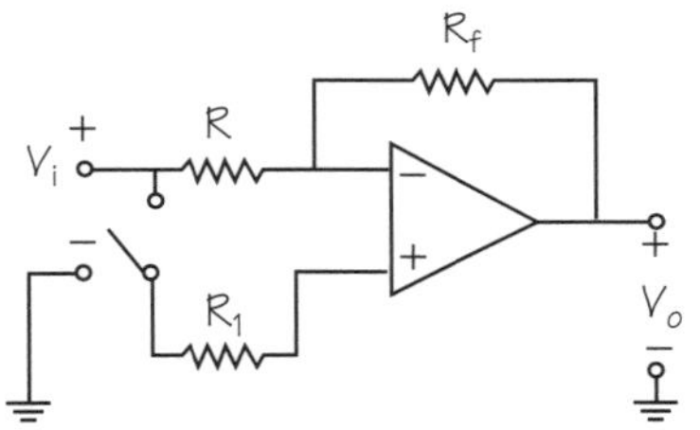

Fig. P8.5

6. In the circuit of Fig. P8.6, $R_1 = 100k\Omega$, $R_f = 10\ M\Omega$, the input resistance $R_i = 100M\Omega$, the output resistance $R_o = 100\Omega$ and the voltage gain $A = 10^5$.

   a) Determine υ_o if $\upsilon_i = 5 \sin \omega t$.

   b) What happens if $R_i \to \infty$ and $R_o \to 0$?

   c) What happens if $R_i \to \infty$ and $R_f \to 0$?

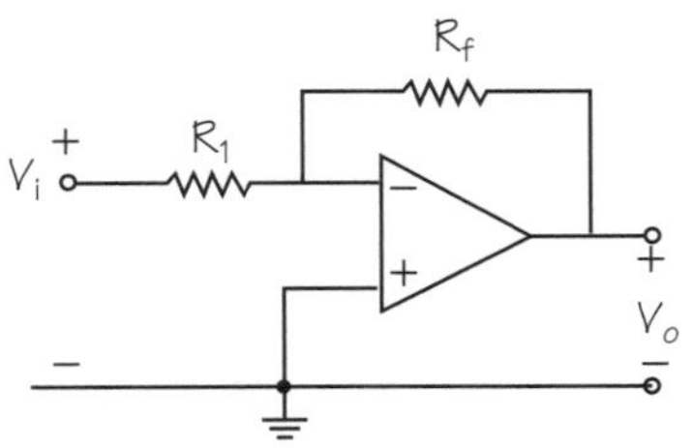

Fig. P8.6

7. For the op. amp circuit shown in Fig. P8.7, show that:

$$v_s = v_o\left[1+\left(\frac{1}{R_L}-\frac{AR_i - R_L}{R_L(AR_i + R_o)}\right)(R_s + R_i)\right]$$

where R_i and R_o are the open-loop input and output resistances, respectively. A is the open-loop voltage gain.

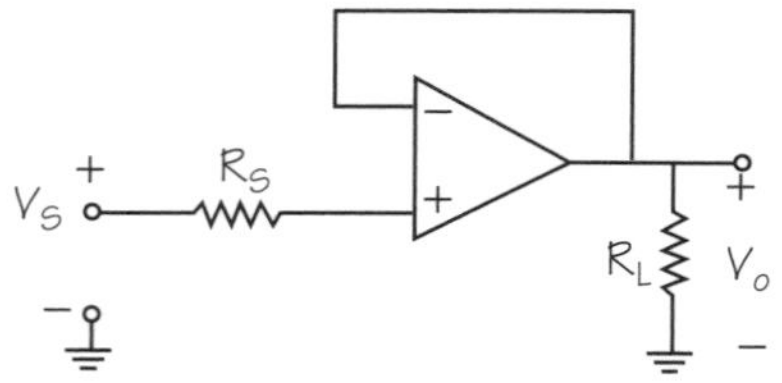

Fig. P8.7

8. Show that the output resistance of the non-ideal op. amp. circuit of Fig. P8.8 is given by

$$R_{out} \approx \frac{R_o}{A}\left(1+\frac{R_F}{R_1}\right)$$

[R_o and A are as defined in problem 8.7.]

Hint: Assume that the common-mode resistance R_{cm} is large enough and can be replaced by an open-circuit approximation.

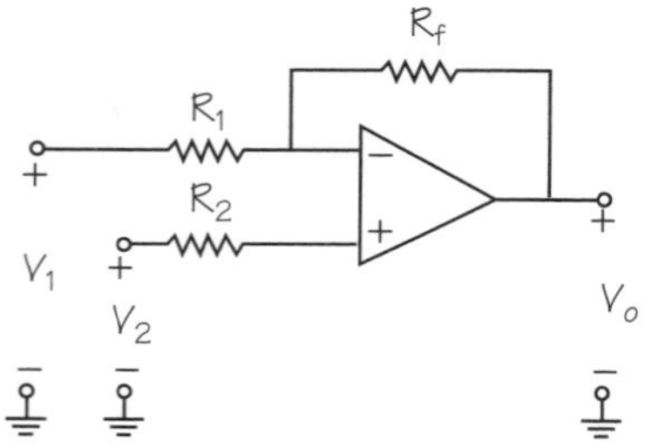

Fig. P8.8

9. Find the output resistance, R_{out}, of the non-ideal op. amp. circuit of Fig. P8.9.

Hint: In this problem, the common-mode resistance cannot be approximated by an open circuit.

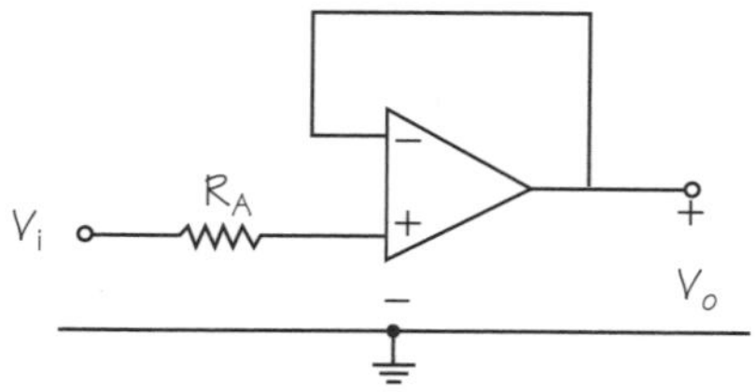

Fig. P8.9

10. Prove that the input resistance, R_{in} of the non-ideal op. amp. circuit of Fig. P8.10 is given by:

$$R_{in} = 2R_{cm}//\frac{AR_i}{1+\frac{R'_f}{R'_A}}$$

where

$$R'_f = R_f + R_o$$
$$R'_A = R_A//2R_{cm}$$

$2R_{cm}$ is taken as the common-mode resistance.
Hint: Consider that $R_L >> R_o$ and $2R_{cm}$ is large enough.

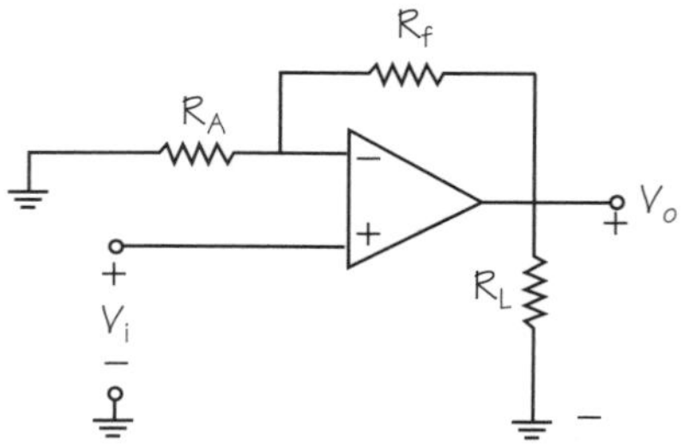

Fig. P8.10

11. The circuit shown in Fig. P8.11 is called "dual inverted weighted summer." Prove that the output voltage $v_o = -(v_a + 10\,v_b)$.
[assume ideal amplifier]

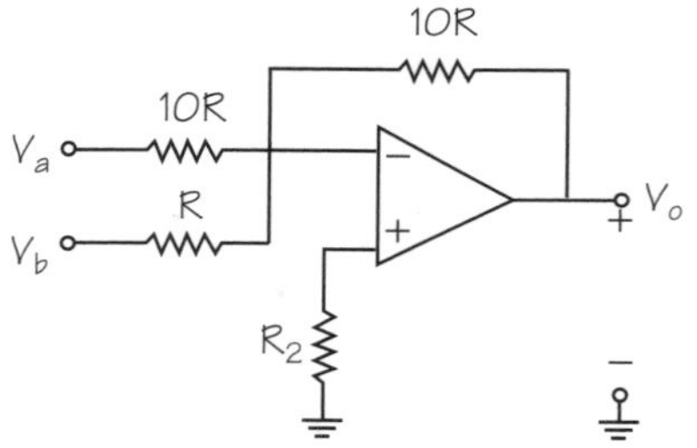

Fig. P8.11

12. For the weighted summer circuit shown in Fig. P8.12, show that:

$$v_0 = \frac{1}{11}\left(1+\frac{R_f}{R_a}\right)(10v_1 + v_2)$$

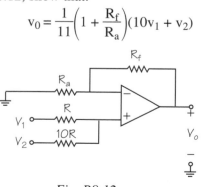

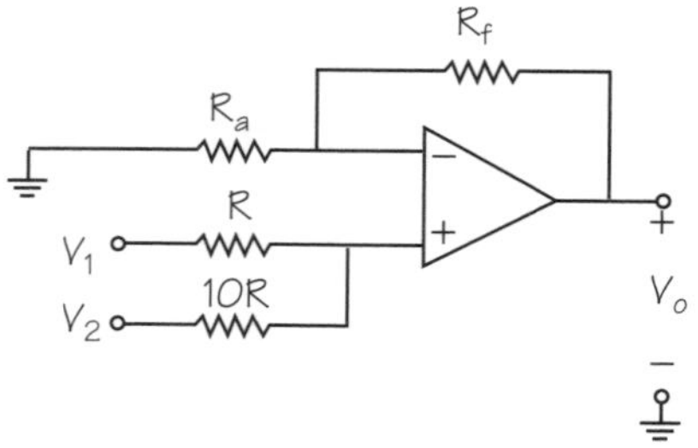

Fig. P8.12

13. For the non-inverting integrator shown in Fig. P8.13, show that:

$$v_o(t) = \frac{2}{RC}\int_o^t v_i(\tau)d\tau$$

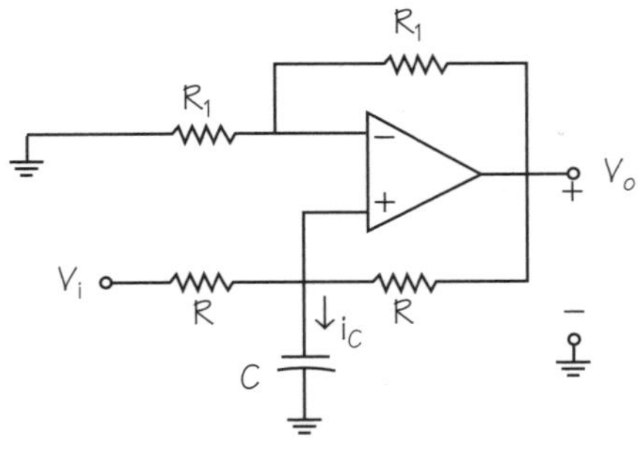

Fig. P8.13

14. If υ_i in the circuit shown in Fig. P8.14 is given by $\upsilon_i = V_m \sin \omega t$, shown that the output voltage v_o is:

$$v_o = -\omega RCV_m \cos \omega t$$

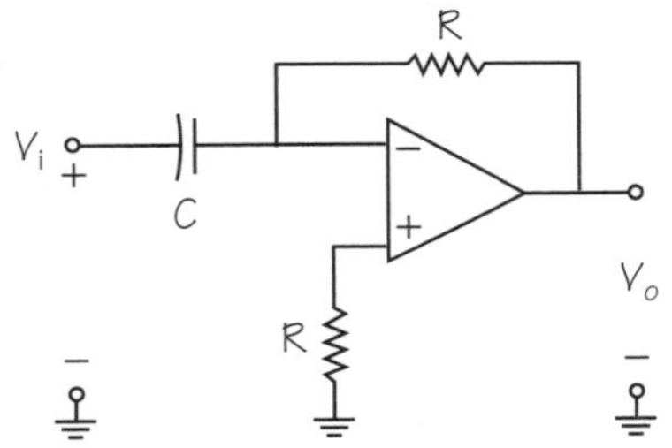

Fig. P8.14

15. For the differencing differentiator shown in Fig. P8.15, show that:

$$v_o = \frac{d}{dt}[v_2(t) - v_1(t)]$$

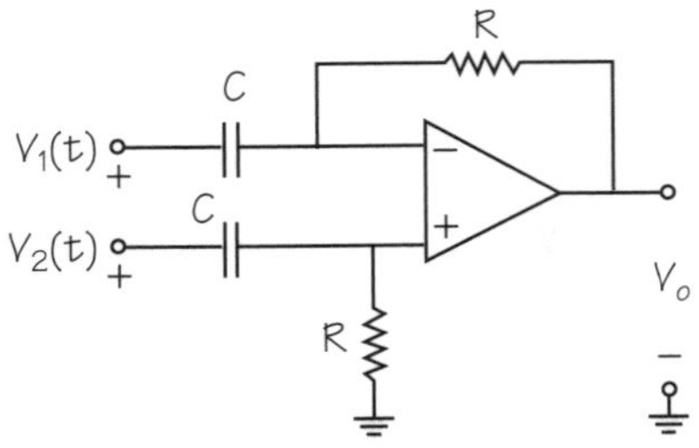

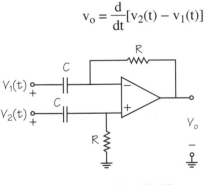

Fig. P8.15

16. For the logarithmic amplifier circuit shown in Fig. P8.16, given that:

$$I_C = I_s e^{V_{BE}/V_T}, \text{ show that}$$

$$V_o = -V_T \ln\left(\frac{V_i}{I_s R}\right)$$

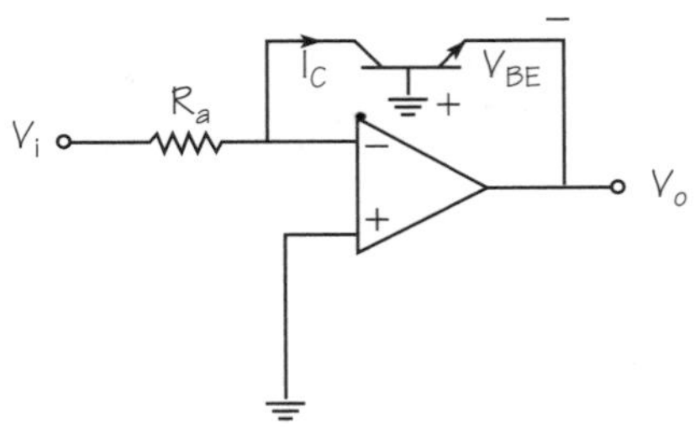

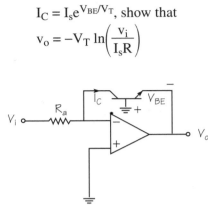

Fig. P8.16

17. The circuit of Fig. P8.17 is called the "exponentator." For the collector current $I_C \approx I_e = I_s e^{q\upsilon_i/kT}$, show that:

$$\upsilon_o = -RI_s e^{q\upsilon_i/kT}$$

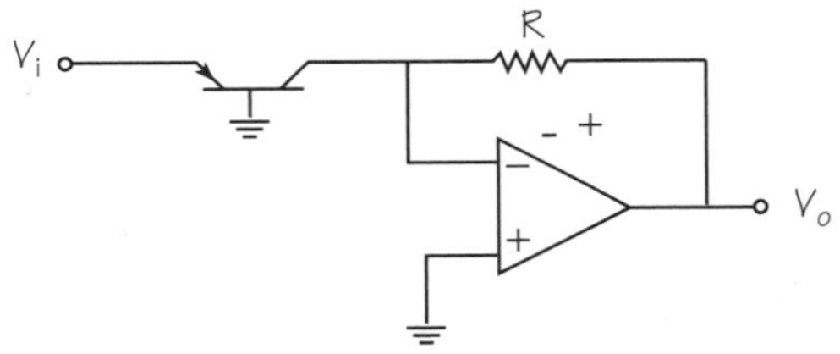

Fig. P8.17

18. Fig. P8.18 shows a simplified model of the op. amp., giving only the important quantities that relate to the slew rate [SR]. The two important quantities are the capacitor, C, and the current, i_1, which is equal to the controlled source, $G_m\upsilon_i$.

a) Determine an expression for the slew rate of the amplifier.

b) Determine the frequency at which the voltage gain, $\frac{\upsilon_o}{\upsilon_i}$, is unity.

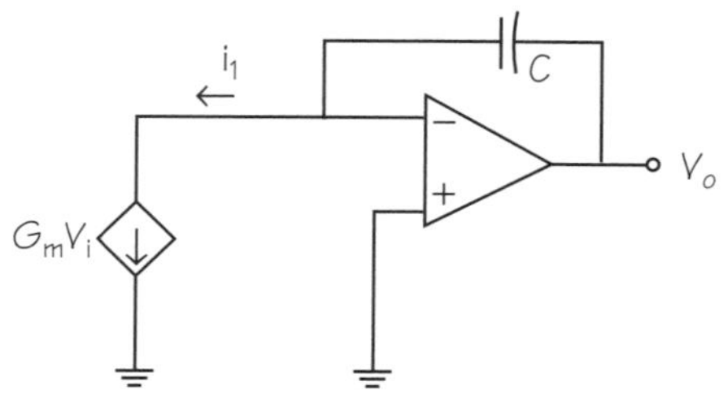

Fig. P8.18

19. The circuit shown in Fig. P8.19 is a voltage regulator. The op-amp compares the Zener-diode voltage with the feedback voltage from sensing resistors R_1 and R_2. Transistor Q is to maintain the output voltage at constant level. Show that:

$$V_o = \left(1 + \frac{R_1}{R_2}\right)V_Z$$

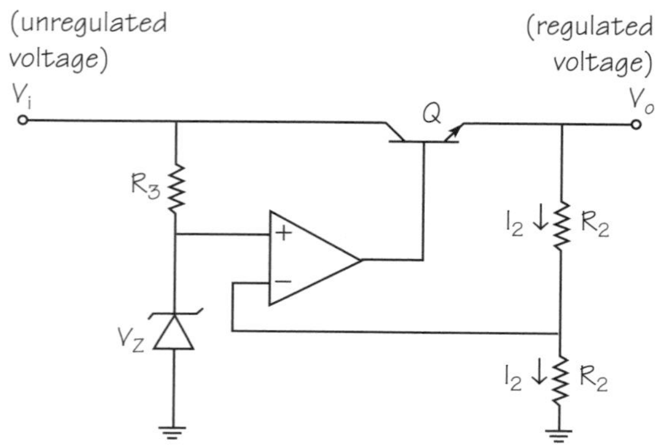

Fig. P8.19

20. The circuit of Fig. P. 8.20 is an inverting half-wave rectifier. Neglect the forward resistance of the diodes and assume that the built-in voltage for each diode is 0.7V. Find a relation between the input voltage and the output voltage.

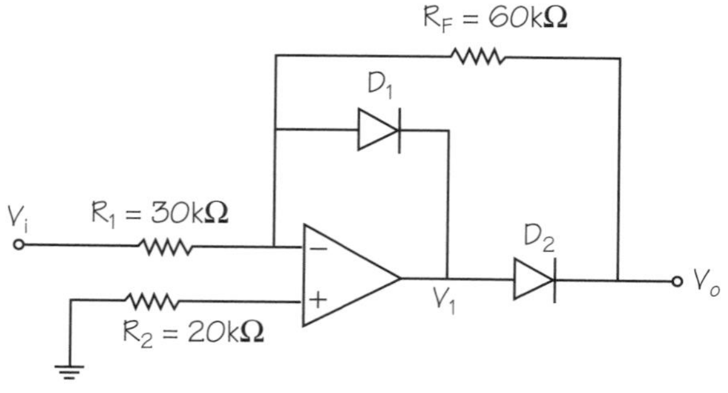

Fig. P8.20

21. a) For the low-pass filter circuit shown in Fig. P8.21, find the transfer function (voltage gain ratio, V_o/V_i).
b) Plot the Bode plot for the transfer function.

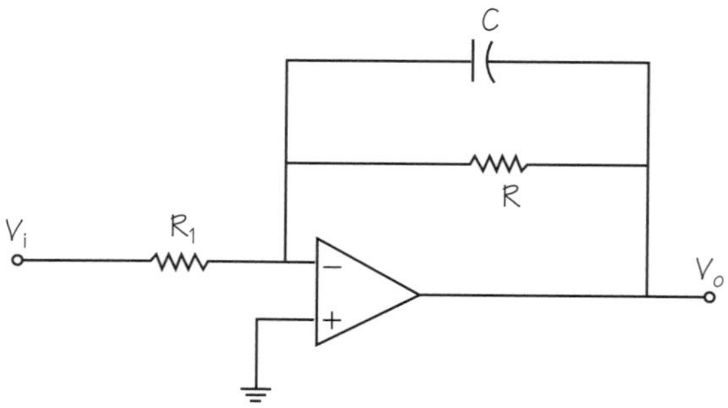

Fig. P8.21

22. Design a first-order active low-pass filter with a dc gain of 10 and a corner frequency of 1kHz, using the circuit shown in Fig. P8.22. Choose R such that $R = R_F // R_1$. (This will achieve what is called the "bias-current balance.")

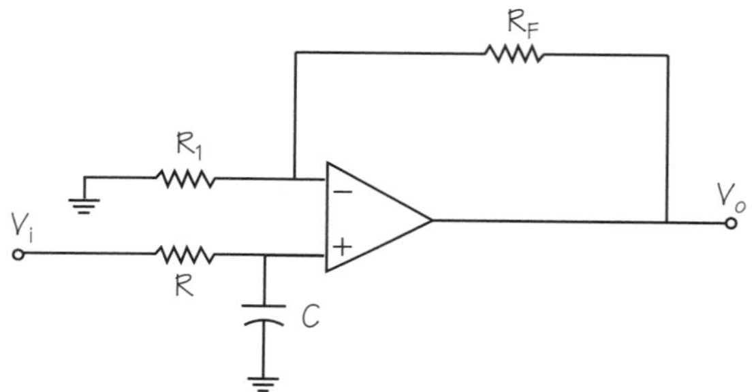

Fig. P8.22

23. a) Show that the circuit shown in Fig. P8.23 is a high-pass filter.
b) Given that C = 0.01μf, the high-frequency

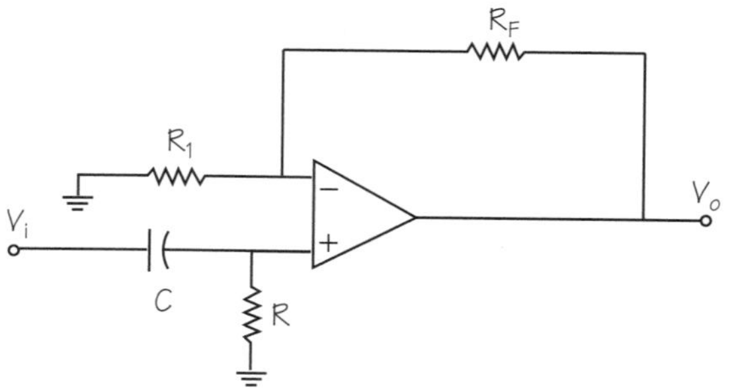

Fig. P8.23

gain, is 10 and the corner frequency is 1Khz. Determine R, R_1, and R_F, assuming that $R = R_F // R_1$.

c) Sketch the Bode plot.

24. What is the dc gain and the corner frequency of the circuit shown in Fig. P8.24? What type of circuit is this?

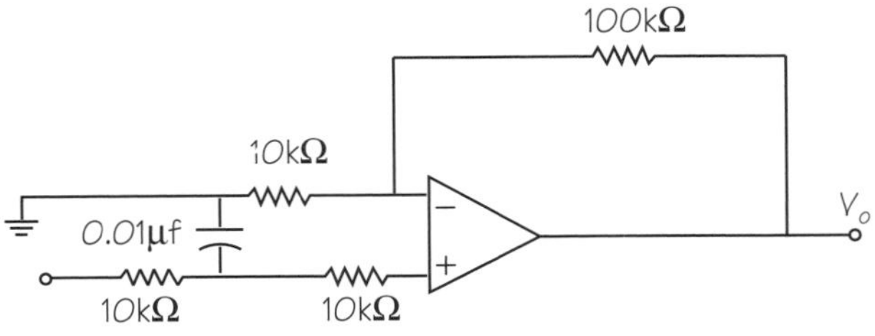

Fig. P8.24

25. Show that the transfer function (voltage-gain ratio, V_o/V_i) for the circuit shown in Fig. P8.25 is given by:

$$\frac{V_o}{V_i} = -\frac{(s+4)^2}{s(s+20)^2}$$

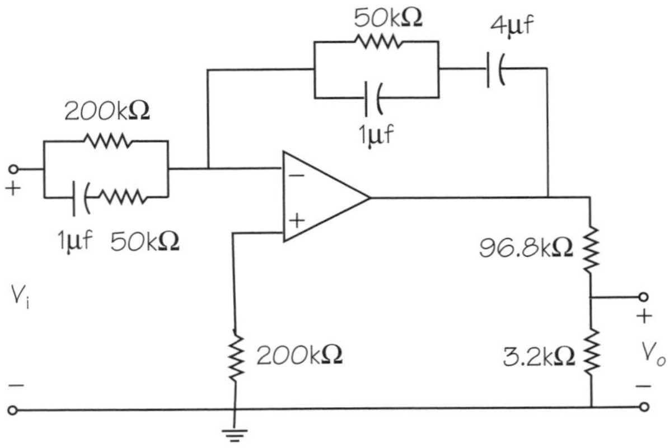

Fig. P8.25

Check Yourself

1. The equivalent circuit of Fig. S8.1a is shown in Fig. S8.1b.

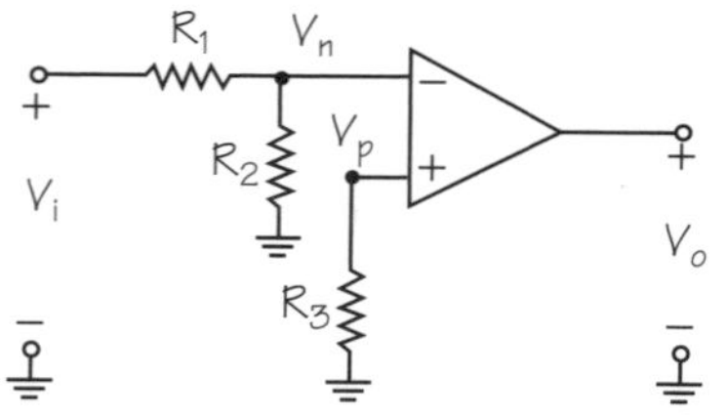

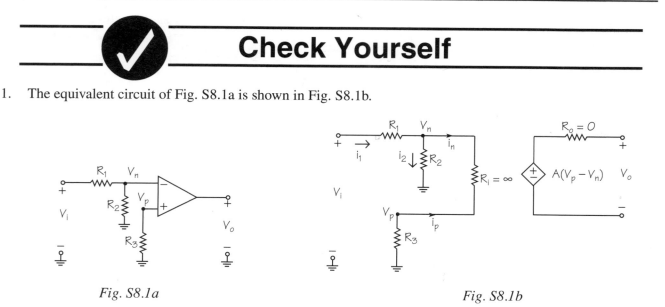

Fig. S8.1a

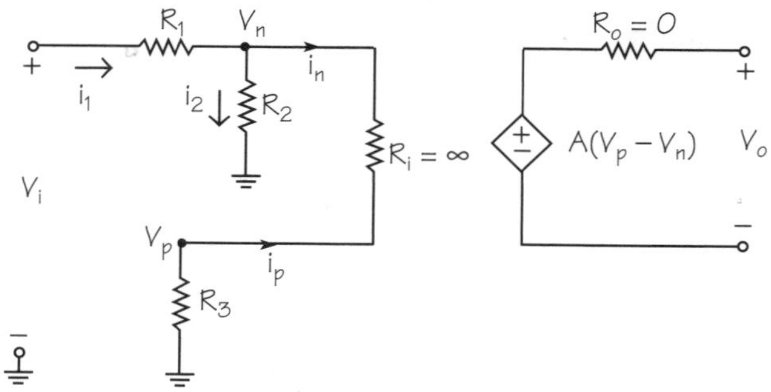

Fig. S8.1b

For an ideal op-amp, the input resistance $R_i = \infty$ and the output resistance $R_o = 0$. Since $R_i = \infty$, thus the input current is zero.

$$i_n = i_p = 0$$

Thus $i_1 = i_2$

By using voltage divider,

$$\upsilon_n = \frac{\upsilon_i R_2}{R_1 + R_2} \quad \text{(Eqn. 1.1)}$$

For the output circuit,

$$\upsilon_o = A(\upsilon_p - \upsilon_n) = -A\upsilon_n \; \{\text{since } V_p \text{ is virtually grounded and equal to zero}\} \quad \text{(Eqn. 1.2)}$$

Here A is the open-loop voltage gain.

Equations 1.1 and 1.2 give:

$$\upsilon_o = -\frac{AR_2}{R_1 + R_2}\upsilon_i$$

(Inverting operational amplifiers)

2. a) The equivalent circuit of Fig. S8.2a is shown in Fig. S8.2b.

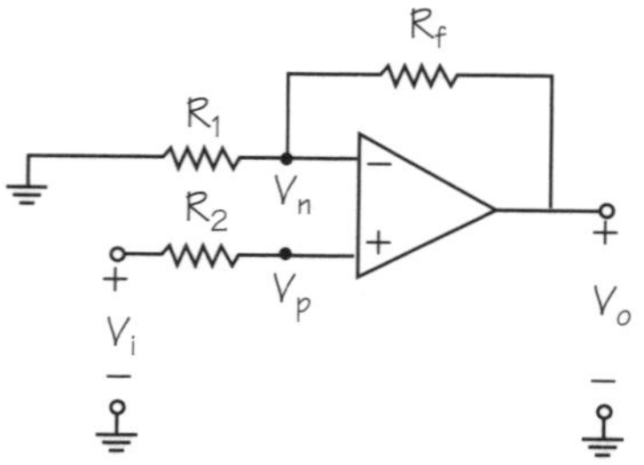

Fig. S8.2a

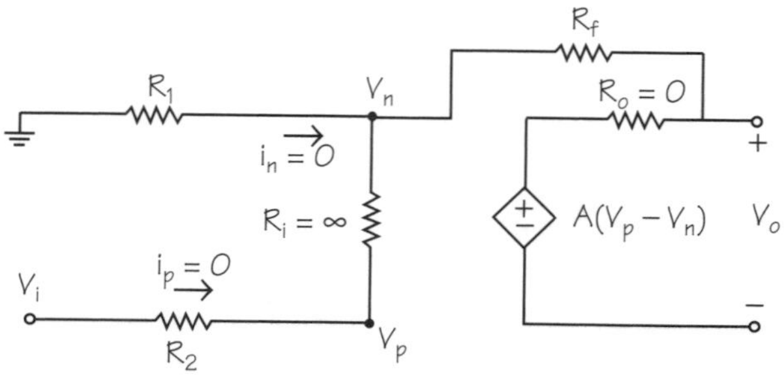

Fig. S8.2b

By using node-voltage analysis at the inverting node, υ_n, the current balance is:

$$\frac{\upsilon_n}{R_1} + \frac{\upsilon_n - \upsilon_o}{R_f} = 0 \quad \text{(Eqn. 2.1)}$$

For an ideal op-amp, $\upsilon_n = \upsilon_p$ (Eqn. 2.2)
Since $i_p = 0$, then $\upsilon_p = \upsilon_i$ (Eqn. 2.3)
Equations 2.1, 2.2, and 2.3 give

$$\frac{\upsilon_i}{R_1} + \frac{\upsilon_i - \upsilon_o}{R_f} = 0$$

or $$\upsilon_i\left[\frac{1}{R_1} + \frac{1}{R_f}\right] = \frac{\upsilon_o}{R_f}$$

from which

$$\upsilon_o = \left[\frac{R_1 + R_f}{R_1}\right]\upsilon_i = \upsilon_i\left[1 + \frac{R_f}{R_1}\right]$$

b) From the result of part a, if $R_f = 0$, $R_1 = \infty$, then:

$$\upsilon_o = \upsilon_i$$

The op-amp becomes a unity voltage gain, i.e., $\frac{\upsilon_o}{\upsilon_i} = 1$

(Non-inverting operational amplifiers with feedback)

3. At node υ_n, nodal voltage analysis gives:

$$\frac{\upsilon_n - \upsilon_a}{R_a} + \frac{\upsilon_n - \upsilon_o}{R_f} = 0 \qquad \text{(Eqn. 3.1)}$$

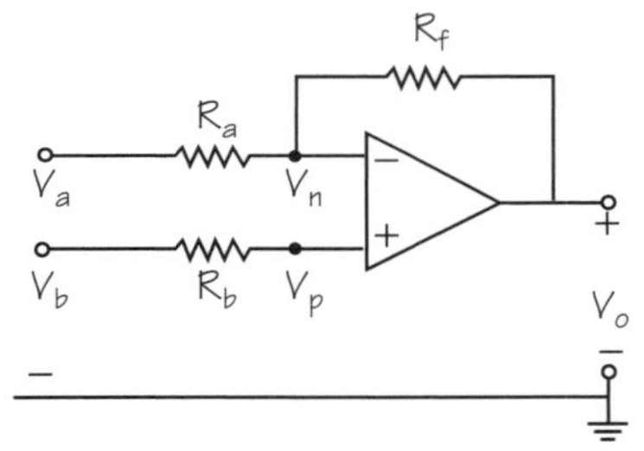

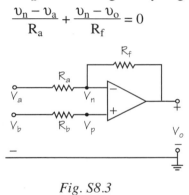

Fig. S8.3

As indicated in problem S8.2, for an ideal op-amp

$$\upsilon_n = \upsilon_P = \upsilon_b \qquad \text{(Eqn. 3.2)}$$

Equations 3.1 and 3.2 result in:

$$\frac{\upsilon_b - \upsilon_a}{R_a} + \frac{\upsilon_b - \upsilon_o}{R_f} = 0 \qquad \text{(Eqn. 3.3)}$$

By simplifying Equation 3.3 for υ_o:

$$\upsilon_o = \left(1 + \frac{R_f}{R_a}\right)\upsilon_b - \frac{R_f}{R_a}\upsilon_a.$$

(Dual-input operational amplifiers)

4. At node υ_n, the node voltage gives:

$$\frac{\upsilon_n - \upsilon_a}{R_a} + \frac{\upsilon_n - \upsilon_o}{R_f} = 0 \qquad \text{(Eqn. 4.1)}$$

Since we have an ideal op-amp, then:

$$\upsilon_n = \upsilon_P \qquad \text{(Eqn. 4.2)}$$

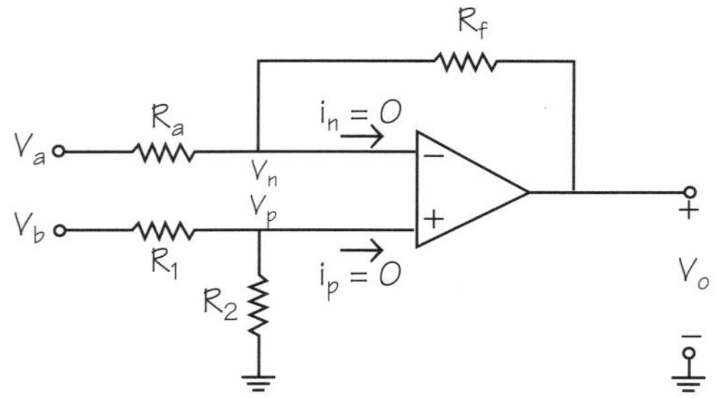

Fig. S8.4

Equations 4.1 and 4.2 result in:

$$\frac{\upsilon_P - \upsilon_a}{R_a} + \frac{\upsilon_p - \upsilon_o}{R_f} = 0 \qquad \text{(Eqn. 4.3)}$$

The voltage at node υ_P is found by using voltage divider. Therefore:

$$\upsilon_p = \frac{\upsilon_b R_2}{R_1 + R_2} \qquad \text{(Eqn. 4.4)}$$

Put equation 4.4 into equation 4.3 and solve for υ_o, resulting in:

$$\upsilon_o = \left(1 + \frac{R_f}{R_a}\right)\left(\frac{R_2}{R_1 + R_2}\right)\upsilon_b - \frac{R_f}{R_a}\upsilon_a$$

(Weighted-differencing operational amplifiers)

5. a) With R_1 connected to the ground, the op-amp is an inverting amplifier. At node υ_n, we write the node equation as:

$$\frac{\upsilon_n - \upsilon_i}{R} + \frac{\upsilon_n - \upsilon_o}{R_f} = 0 \qquad \text{(Eqn. 5.1)}$$

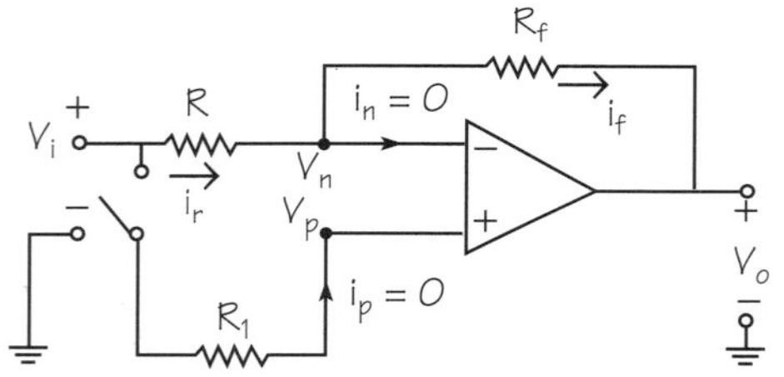

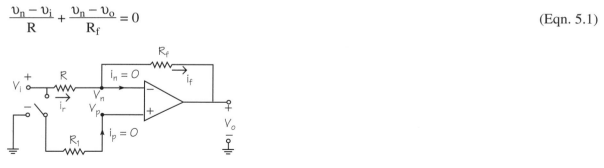

Figure S8.5

Since the op-amp is ideal, then:

$$\upsilon_n = \upsilon_p \qquad \text{(Eqn. 5.2)}$$

But $i_p = 0$; therefore, $\upsilon_p = 0$ (Eqn. 5.3)

$\therefore \quad \upsilon_n = \upsilon_P = 0$ [This is called virtual ground] (Eqn. 5.4)

Equations 5.1 and 5.4 result in:

$$\frac{0 - \upsilon_i}{R} + \frac{0 - \upsilon_0}{R_f} = 0$$

$$\upsilon_o = -\frac{R_f}{R}\upsilon_i = \upsilon_i \text{ under given condition that } R = R_F$$

b) With R_i connected to υ_i

$$\upsilon_n = \upsilon_p = \upsilon_i \qquad \text{(Eqn. 5.5)}$$

Equations 5.5 and 5.1 result in:

$$\frac{\upsilon_i - \upsilon_o}{R_f} = 0$$

or $\upsilon_i = \upsilon_o$

(Sign-switcher operational amplifiers)

6. a) The equivalent circuit of Fig. S8.6a is shown in Fig. S8.6b, where R_i is the input resistance of the op-amp and R_o is its output resistance and A is the open-loop voltage gain. Since υ_p is connected directly to the ground, then $\upsilon_p = 0$

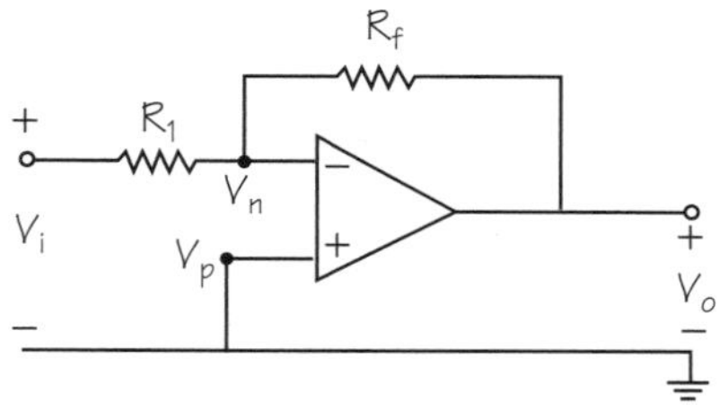

Fig. S8.6a

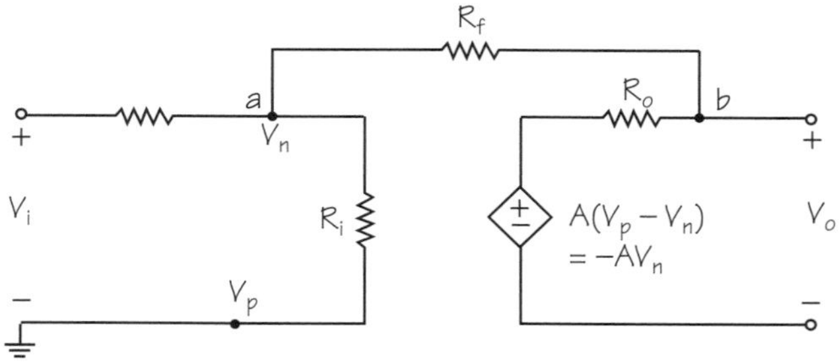

Fig. S8.6b

At node a, the node-voltage analysis gives us:

$$\frac{\upsilon_n - \upsilon_i}{R_1} + \frac{\upsilon_n}{R_i} + \frac{\upsilon_n - \upsilon_o}{R_f} = 0 \qquad \text{(Eqn. 6.1)}$$

At node b, node-voltage equation is:

$$\frac{\upsilon_o - \upsilon_n}{R_f} + \frac{\upsilon_o + A\upsilon_n}{R_o} = 0 \qquad \text{(Eqn. 6.2)}$$

Rearranging equations 1 and 2 results in:

$$\left[\frac{1}{R_1} + \frac{1}{R_i} + \frac{1}{R_f}\right]\upsilon_n - \frac{\upsilon_o}{R_f} = \frac{\upsilon_i}{R_1} \qquad \text{(Eqn. 6.3)}$$

and

$$\left[\frac{A}{R_o} - \frac{1}{R_f}\right]\upsilon_n + \left(\frac{1}{R_f} + \frac{1}{R_o}\right)\upsilon_o = 0 \qquad \text{(Eqn. 6.4)}$$

Solve for υ_o from equations 6.3 and 6.4:

$$\upsilon_o = \left[\frac{\frac{R_o}{R_f} - A}{\frac{R_1}{R_2}\left(1 + A + \frac{R_o}{R_i}\right) + \left(\frac{R_1}{R_i} + 1\right) + \frac{R_o}{R_f}}\right]\upsilon_i \qquad \text{(Eqn. 6.5)}$$

Equation 6.5 is the exact solution for υ_o, However, because $R_o << R_2$ and $A >> 1$, equation 6.5 can be simplified by approximation to become:

$$\upsilon_o = \frac{-A\upsilon_i}{A\frac{R_1}{R_f} + \left(\frac{R_1}{R_i} + 1\right)} \qquad \text{(Eqn. 6.6)}$$

$$\upsilon_o = \frac{-10^5\upsilon_i}{10^5 \times \frac{10^5}{10^7} + \left(\frac{10^5}{10^7} + 1\right)} = -100\upsilon_i$$

Since $\upsilon_i = 5 \sin \omega t$

$\therefore \quad \upsilon_o = -500 \sin \omega t$ volt.

b) If $R_i \to \infty$, $R_o \to 0$, equation 6.5 becomes

$$v_o = \frac{-Av_i}{\frac{R_1}{R_f}(1+A)} \qquad \text{(Eqn. 6.7)}$$

Since A >> 1, Eqn. 6.7 becomes

$$v_o = -A\frac{R_f}{R_1} \qquad \text{(Eqn. 6.8)}$$

(Non-ideal inverting operational amplifiers)

7. Fig. S8.7b is the equivalent circuit of Fig. S8.7a.

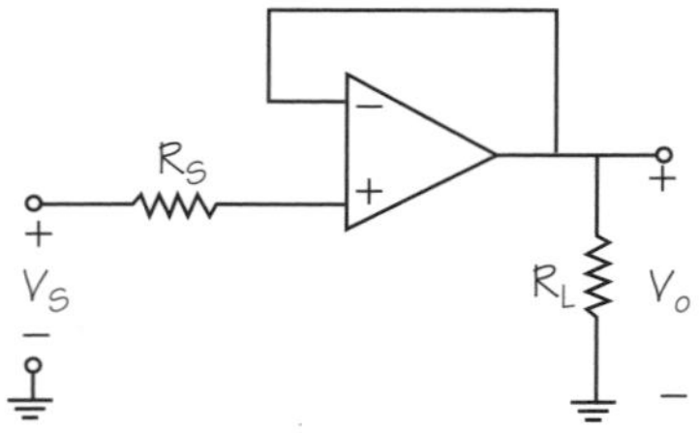

Fig. S8.7a

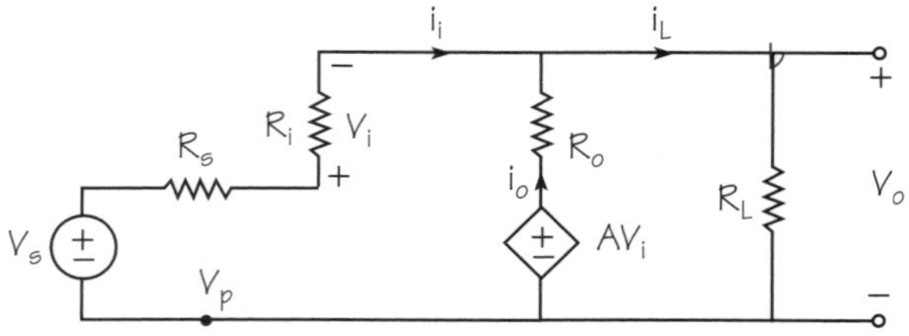

Fig. S8.7b

By applying KVL around the outer loop of the circuit in Fig. S8.7b:

$$v_s = i_i(R_S + R_i) + v_o \qquad \text{(Eqn. 7.1)}$$

$$i_i = \frac{v_i}{R_i} \qquad \text{(Eqn. 7.2)}$$

Also, KVL around the loop containing the dependent voltage source (Av_i), R_o and R_L gives:

$$v_o = Av_i - i_oR_o \qquad \text{(Eqn. 7.3)}$$

Equations 7.2 and 7.3 result in:

$$v_o = Ai_iR_i - i_oR_o \qquad \text{(Eqn. 7.4)}$$

By KCL

$$i_i = i_L - i_o \qquad \text{(Eqn. 7.5)}$$

where $i_L = \dfrac{v_o}{R_L}$ (Eqn. 7.6)

Equations 7.4, 7.5, and 7.6 give:

$$v_o = A\left[\frac{v_o}{R_L} - i_o\right]R_i - i_oR_o$$

from which

$$i_o = \frac{v_o\left[A\frac{R_i}{R_L} - 1\right]}{AR_i + R_o} \qquad \text{(Eqn. 7.7)}$$

Combining equations 7.5, 7.6, and 7.7 gives:

$$i_i = \frac{v_o}{R_L} - \frac{v_o\left(A\frac{R_i}{R_L} - 1\right)}{AR_i + R_o}$$

$$i_i = \upsilon_o\left[\frac{1}{R_L} - \frac{AR_i - R_L}{R_L(AR_i + R_o)}\right] \quad \text{(Eqn. 7.8)}$$

Equations 7.1 and 7.8 give:

$$\upsilon_s = \upsilon_o\left[\frac{1}{R_L} - \frac{AR_i - R_L}{R_L(AR_i + R_o)}\right](R_s + R_i) + \upsilon_o$$

or $$\upsilon_s = \upsilon_o\left[1 + \left(\frac{1}{R_L} - \frac{AR_i - R_L}{R_L(AR_i + R_o)}\right)(R_s + R_i)\right] \quad \text{(Eqn. 7.9)}$$

In fact, equation 7.9 can be simplified further using the following facts:

$R_i >> 1, A >> 1$

∴ $AR_i >>> R_o$

If $AR_i >> R_L$

Then $\upsilon_s = \upsilon_o\left[\frac{1}{R_L} - \left(\frac{AR_i}{R_L AR_i}\right)(R_s + R_i)\right]$

or $$\upsilon_s = \upsilon_o\left[\frac{1}{R_L} - \frac{R_s + R_i}{R_L}\right] \quad \text{(Eqn. 7.10)}$$

(A buffer-non-ideal operational amplifier)

8. The equivalent circuit to Fig. S8.8a is drawn in Fig. S8.8b.

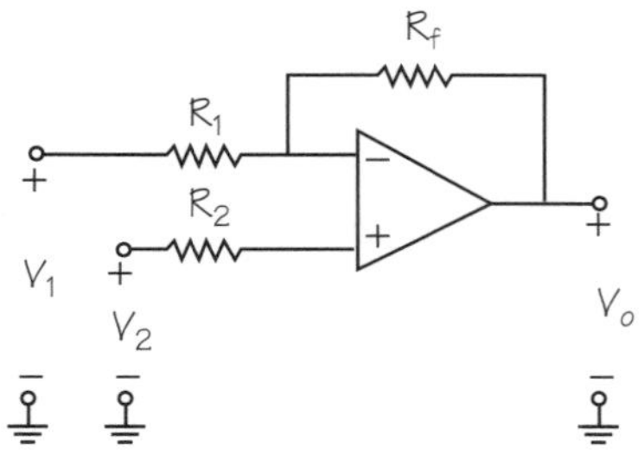

Fig. S8.8a

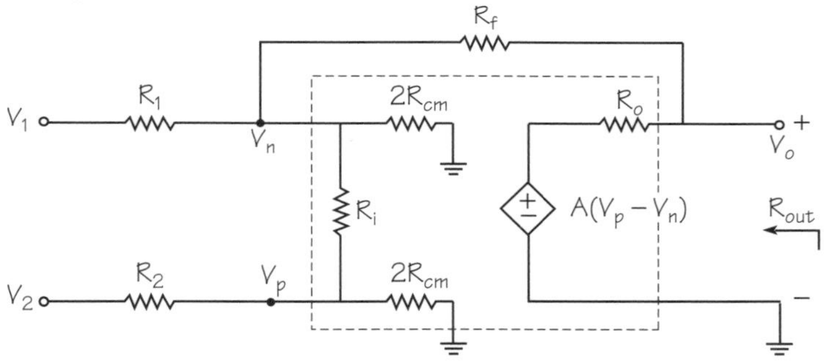

Fig. S8.8b

In the equivalent circuit:

$2R_{cm}$: is the common mode resistance which is taken as $2R_{cm}$ to simplify the solution.

R_i: the open-loop input resistance

R_o: the open-loop output resistance

R_{out}: the output resistance of the circuit

First we find the Thevenin equivalent circuit for the portion of the op-amp circuit shown in the box enclosed by the dashed line.

Since this circuit has only dependent source, the Thevenin equivalent voltage is zero and the Thevenin short-circuit current is also zero. Therefore, the circuit is equivalent to a single resistance. The Thevenin resistance of such circuit is found by applying a test voltage source, υ_T, to the open-circuit terminals. The test-voltage source produces a test current, i_T. The Thevenin resistance is then

$$R_{Th} = \frac{\upsilon_T}{i_T} = R_{out} \quad \text{(Eqn. 8.1)}$$

The procedure of applying a test source is shown in Fig. S8.8c. Fig. S8.8c is simplified in Fig. S8.8d.

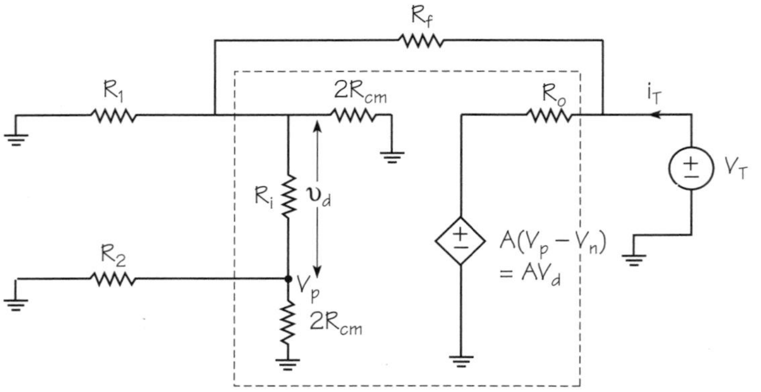

Fig. S8.8c

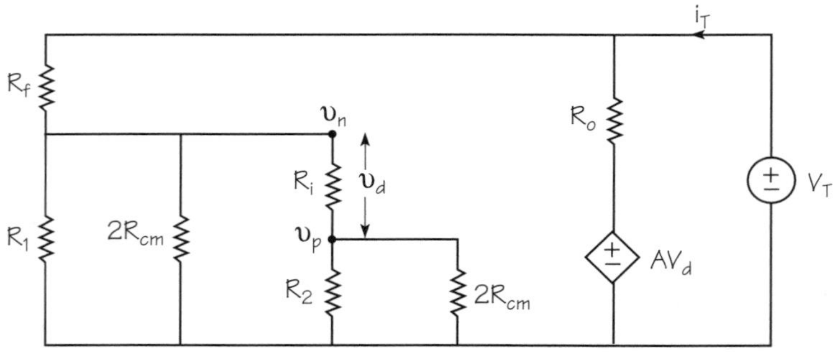

Fig. S8.8d

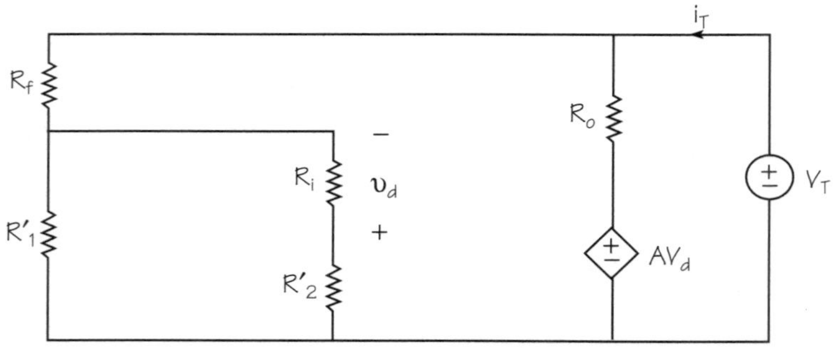

Fig. S8.8e

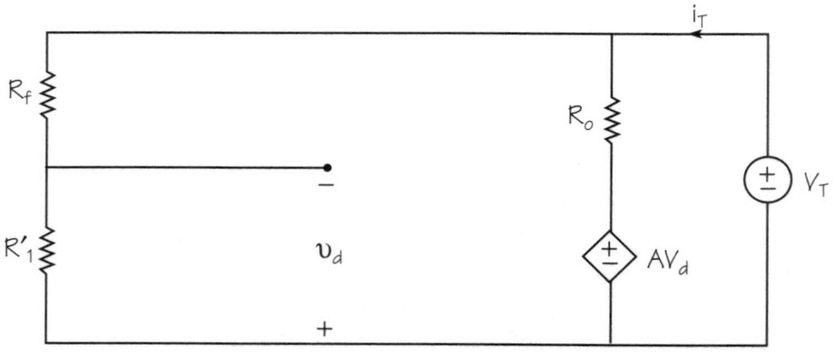

Fig. S8.8f

Fig. S8.8d is further simplified to combine R_1 and $2R_{cm}$ and R_2 and $2R_{cm}$ into their equivalent resistors R'_1 and R'_2, as shown in Fig. S8.8e.

$$R'_1 = R_1 || 2R_{cm} \quad \text{(Eqn. 8.2)}$$
$$R'_2 = R_2 || 2R_{cm} \quad \text{(Eqn. 8.3)}$$

We make the assumption that:

$$R'_1 << (R'_1 + R_i), \text{ and} \quad \text{(Eqn. 8.4)}$$
$$R_0 << R'_1 || (R_i + R'_2), \quad \text{(Eqn. 8.5)}$$

The circuit in Fig. S8.8e is approximated in the circuit of Fig. S8.8f. Notice that $(R_i + R'_2)$ are replaced by an open circuit.

The input voltage, υ_d, is found from Fig. S8.8f using voltage divider ratio.

$$\upsilon_d = -\frac{R'_1 \upsilon_T}{R_f + R'_1} \quad \text{(Eqn. 8.6)}$$

In the loop containing υ_T, R_o, and $A\upsilon_d$, KVL gives:

$$i_T R_o = \upsilon_T - A\upsilon_d \quad \text{(Eqn. 8.7)}$$

Equations 8.6 and 8.7 will give:

$$i_T R_o = \upsilon_T + \frac{AR'_1 \upsilon_T}{R_F + R'_1}$$
$$= \upsilon_T \left[1 + \frac{AR'_1}{R_f + R'_1}\right]$$
$$R_{out} = \frac{\upsilon_T}{i_T} = \frac{R_o}{1 + R'_1 A/(R_f + R'_1)} \quad \text{(Eqn. 8.8)}$$

Typical value of $R_o \approx 1\Omega$.
In most cases $2R_{cm}$ is so large; then:

$$R'_1 = R_1 \quad \text{and} \quad R'_2 = R_2$$

Therefore, equation 8.8 is simplified as:

$$R_{out} = \frac{R_o}{1 + \dfrac{AR_1}{R_f + R_1}} = \frac{R_o}{A}\left[1 + \frac{R_f}{R_1}\right]$$

(Non-ideal operational amplifiers)

9. If we compare Fig. S8.9a with Fig. S8.8a, we notice that R_1 is relaced by an open circuit, i.e., $R_1 \to \infty$ and R_f is replaced by a short circuit. R_2 is renamed as R_A
R'_1 of Fig. S8.8e becomes

$$R'_1 = \infty // 2R_{cm} = 2R_{cm} \quad \text{(Eqn. 9.1)}$$

The equivalent circuit is shown in Fig. S8.9b.

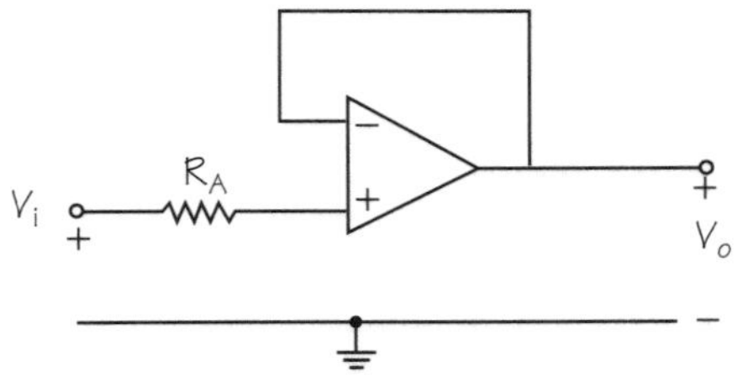

Fig. S8.9a

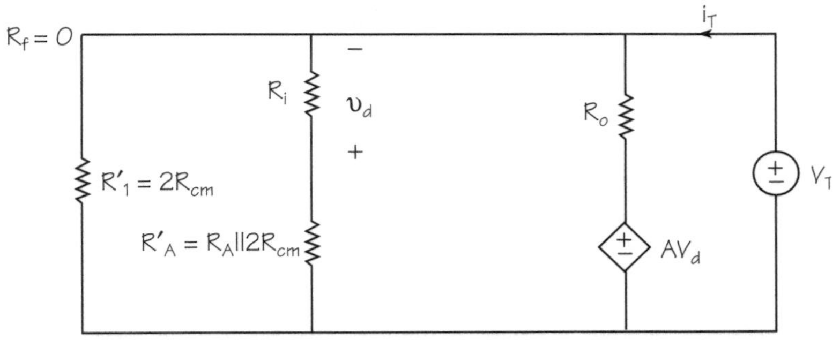

Fig. S8.9b

Notice that equation 8.8 of problem P8.8 cannot be used, since we are not sure that the inequalities leading to the simplification of Fig. S8.8e apply in this case. That is, the necessary simplification is:

$$2R_{cm} << [R_A // (2R_{cm} + R_i)] \qquad \text{(Eqn. 9.2)}$$

Without this simplification, the circuit takes the form shown in Fig. S8.9b. Using voltage divider:

$$\upsilon_d = -\frac{R_i \upsilon_T}{R_i + R'_A} \qquad \text{(Eqn. 9.3)}$$

If we assume that:

$$R_o << [R_i + R'_A] << R'_1 \qquad \text{(Eqn. 9.4)}$$

Then $R_o i_T = \upsilon_T - A\upsilon_d$

$$R_o i_T = \upsilon_T + \frac{AR_i \upsilon_T}{R_i + R'_A} = \upsilon_T\left[1 + \frac{AR_i}{R_i + R'_A}\right]$$

Since $R_{out} = \dfrac{\upsilon_T}{i_T}$

Then $R_{out} = \dfrac{R_o}{1 + R_i A/(R_i + R'_A)}$

(Non-inverting operational amplifiers with shorted feedback)

10. The equivalent circuit is shown in Fig. S8.10b, where $\upsilon_d = \upsilon_p - \upsilon_n$ and R_{in} is the input resistance of the circuit. Other parameters on the figure are as defined before. By considering that $R_L >> R_o$, the load resistance R_L can be replaced by an open-circuit approximation. Accordingly, R_o and R_f are in series connection. The circuit of Fig. S8.10b is now reduced to the circuit shown in Fig. S8.10C.

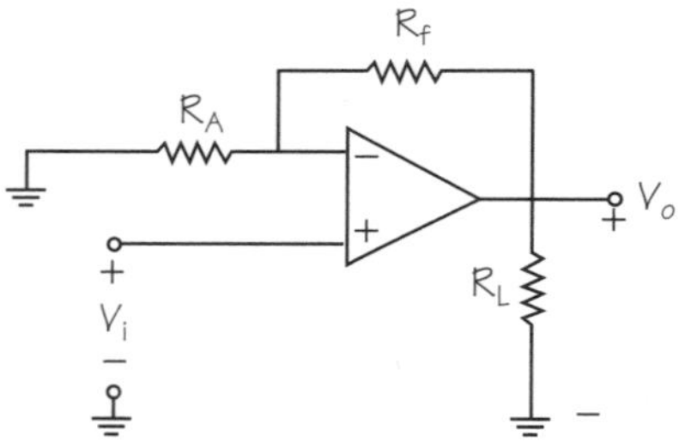

Fig. S8.10a

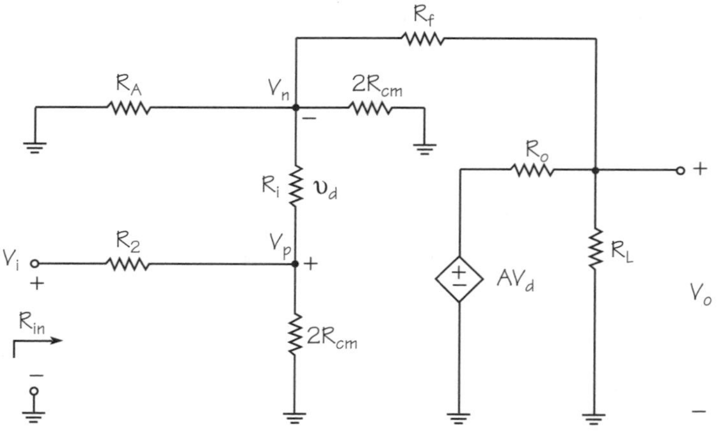

Fig. S8.10b

Again, since the circuit has only one dependent voltage source, we find R_{in} by inserting a test voltage source at the input terminals and follow the same technique of problem P8.9's solution; i.e., $R_{Th} = \upsilon_T / i_T$.

First, we find the Thevenin equivalent of the circuit enclosed by the dashed curve.

Here, the Thevenin equivalent resistance is $R'_f // R'_A$, and the Thevenin voltage is found by using voltage divider as:

$$\upsilon'_{Th} = \left(\frac{R'_A}{R'_A + R'_f}\right) A\upsilon_d$$

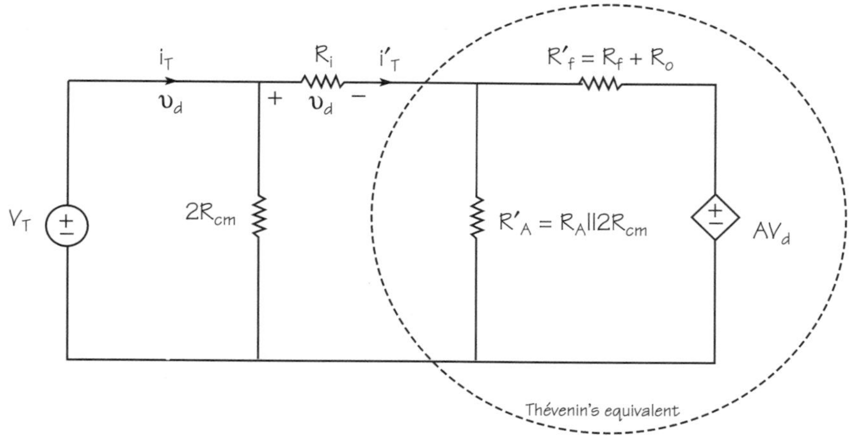

Fig. S8.10c

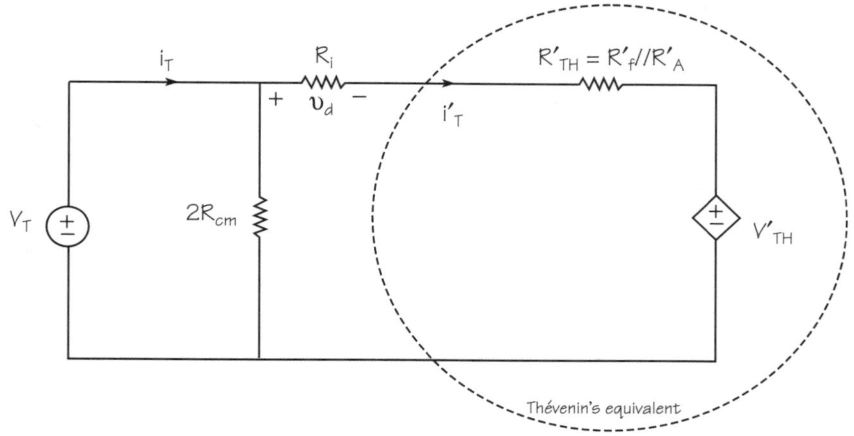

Fig. S8.10d

The circuit of Fig. S8.10C is then reduced to the circuit shown in Fig. S8.10d.
By applying KVL around the outer loop of the circuit shown in Fig. S8.10d, we get:

$$\upsilon_T = (R_i + R'_{Th})i'_T + V'_{Th}$$

$$\upsilon_T = (R_i + R'_A \| R'_f)i'_T + \left(\frac{R'_A}{R'_A + R'_f}\right)A\upsilon_D$$

since $\upsilon_d = R_i \cdot i'_T$

Therefore $\upsilon_T = (R_i + R'_A \| R'_f)i'_T + \left(\frac{AR'_A R_i i'_T}{R'_A + R'_f}\right)$

The resistance to the right of $2R_{cm}$ is given by:

$$\frac{\upsilon_T}{i'_T} = (R'_A \| R'_f) + \left(1 + \frac{R'_A A}{R'_A + R'_f}\right)R_i$$

Finally, the input resistance is calculated from the circuit of Fig. S8.10e as:

$$R_{in} = 2R_{cm} \| \left[(R'_A \| R'_f) + \left(1 + \frac{R'_A A}{R'_A + R'_f}\right) R_i \right]$$

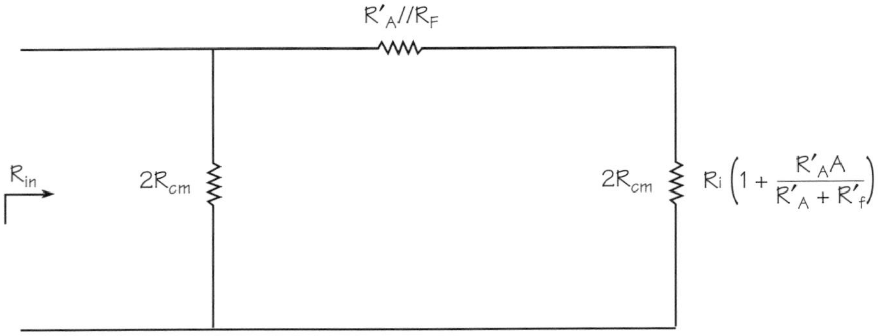

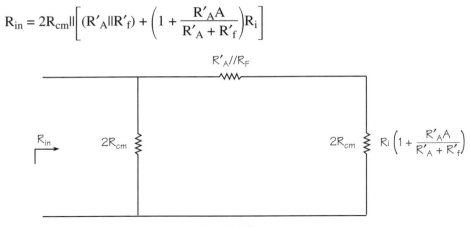

Fig. S8.10e

(Input resistance for non-ideal operational amplifiers)

11. At node υ_n, the node-voltage equation gives:

$$\frac{\upsilon_n - \upsilon_a}{10R} = \frac{\upsilon_n - \upsilon_b}{R} + \frac{\upsilon_n - \upsilon_o}{10R} = 0 \qquad \text{(Eqn. 11.1)}$$

For ideal op-amp, $\upsilon_n = \upsilon_p$ (Eqn. 11.2)

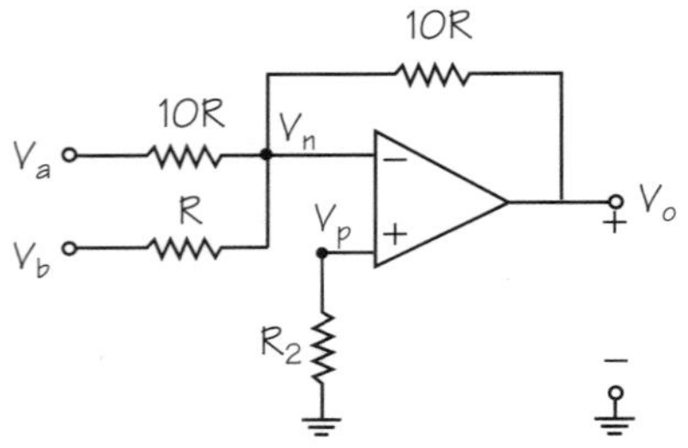

Fig. S8.11

Since there is no current in R_2, this will cause $\upsilon_p = 0$ [virtually grounded]

Thus $\upsilon_n = \upsilon_p = 0$ (Eqn. 11.3)

Equations 11.1 and 11.3 give:

$$-\frac{10\upsilon a}{10R} - \frac{\upsilon_b}{R} = \frac{\upsilon_o}{10R} \qquad \text{(Eqn. 11.4)}$$

Solve for υ_o from equation 11.4 results in:

$$\upsilon_o = -(\upsilon_a + 10\upsilon_b)$$

(Dual-inverted weighted summer)

12. At node υ_n, the node-voltage equation gives:

$$\frac{\upsilon_n}{R_a} + \frac{\upsilon_n - \upsilon_o}{R_f} = 0 \qquad \text{(Eqn. 12.1)}$$

At node υ_p, the node-voltage equation gives:

$$\frac{\upsilon_1 - \upsilon_p}{R} + \frac{\upsilon_2 - \upsilon_p}{10R} = 0 \qquad \text{(Eqn. 12.2)}$$

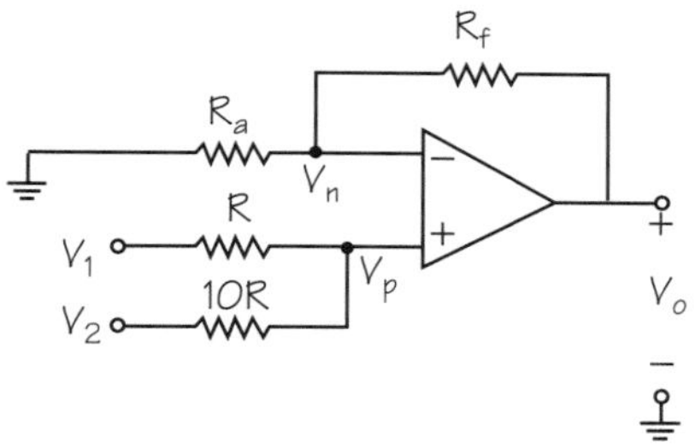

Fig. S8.12

If we solve equation 12.1 for υ_n, then:

$$\upsilon_n = \frac{\upsilon_o}{1 + \frac{R_f}{R_a}} \qquad \text{(Eqn. 12.3)}$$

Since $\upsilon_n = \upsilon_p$ (for ideal op-amp) (Eqn. 12.4)

Thus $$\upsilon_p = \frac{\upsilon_o}{1 + \frac{R_f}{R_a}} \qquad \text{(Eqn. 12.5)}$$

Equations 12.2 and 12.5 give:

$$\frac{\upsilon_1 - \frac{\upsilon_o}{1 + (R_f/R_a)}}{R} + \frac{\upsilon_2 - \frac{\upsilon_o}{1 + (R_f/R_a)}}{10R} = 0 \qquad \text{(Eqn. 12.6)}$$

Solving equation 12.6 for υ_o, results in:

$$\upsilon_o = (10\upsilon_1 + \upsilon_2)\left(1 + \frac{R_f}{R_a}\right)\left(\frac{1}{11}\right)$$

(Weighted summer)

13. At node υ_n, the node-voltage equation is:

$$\frac{\upsilon_n}{R_1} + \frac{\upsilon_n - \upsilon_o}{R_1} = 0 \qquad \text{(Eqn. 13.1)}$$

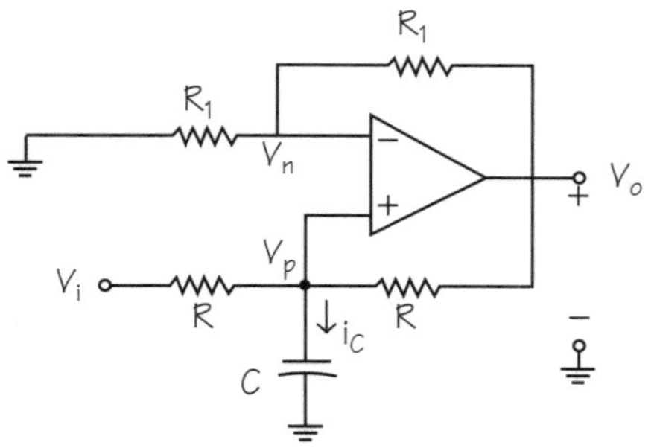

Fig. S8.13

From equation 13.1:

$$\upsilon_n = \frac{\upsilon_o}{2} \qquad \text{(Eqn. 13.2)}$$

At node υ_p, the current balance gives:

$$i_C = \frac{\upsilon_i - \upsilon_p}{R} - \frac{\upsilon_p - \upsilon_o}{R} = \frac{\upsilon_i - 2\upsilon_p + \upsilon_o}{R} \qquad \text{(Eqn. 13.3)}$$

Since $\upsilon_n = \upsilon_p = \dfrac{\upsilon_o}{2}$ (Eqn. 13.4)

Thus, the combination of equations 13.3 and 13.4 gives:

$$i_C = \frac{\upsilon_i}{R} \qquad \text{(Eqn. 13.5)}$$

For the capacitor:

$$i_C = C\frac{d\upsilon_C}{dt} = C\frac{d\upsilon_p}{dt} = C\frac{d\left(\frac{\upsilon_o}{2}\right)}{dt} \qquad \text{(Eqn. 13.6)}$$

Equation 13.6 gives:

$$\frac{d\upsilon_o}{dt} = \frac{2i_C}{C} \qquad \text{(Eqn. 13.7)}$$

Equations 13.5 and 13.7 will give:

$$\frac{d\upsilon_o}{dt} = \frac{2\upsilon_i}{RC}dt \qquad \text{(Eqn. 13.8)}$$

By integrating equation 13.8 we have:

$$\upsilon_o = \frac{2}{RC}\int_o^t \upsilon_i(\tau)\, d\tau$$

(Non-inverting integrator)

14. The node-voltage equation at node υ_n gives us:

$$\frac{V_n - V_i}{X_C} + \frac{V_n - V_o}{R} = 0 \quad \text{[phasor domain]} \qquad \text{(Eqn. 14.1)}$$

where X_C is the capacitor reactance.

$$X_C = \frac{1}{\omega C} \qquad \text{(Eqn. 14.2)}$$

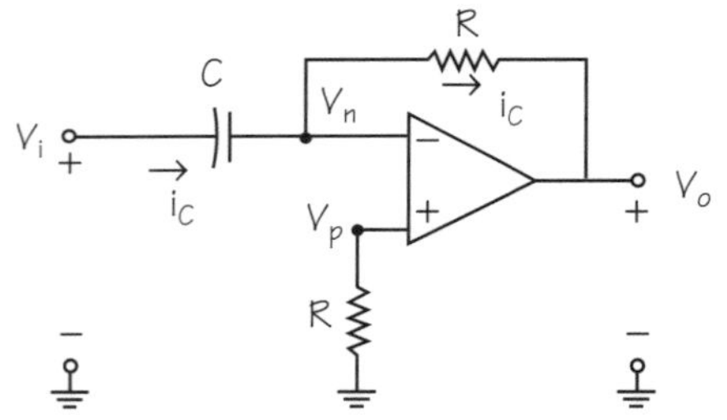

Fig. S8.14

Since $V_n = V_p$ and $V_p = 0$ in this case, since there is no current entering the terminal υ_p, then equation 14.1 gives:

$$V_o = -V_i\frac{R}{X_C} = -V_i R\omega C \qquad \text{(Eqn. 14.3)}$$

In time domain, equation 14.3 is written as:

$$\upsilon_o = -RC\frac{d\upsilon_i(t)}{dt}$$

$$= -RC\frac{d}{dt}(\upsilon_m \sin \omega t)$$

$$\upsilon_o = -\omega RCV_m \cos \omega t$$

Note: This problem can be solved directly in time domain as follows:
Since at node υ_n,

$$i_C + i_R = 0$$

Then $i_C = -i_R$

But $i_C = C\frac{d\upsilon_i}{dt}$

and $i_R = \frac{\upsilon_o}{R}$

Thus $C\frac{d\upsilon_i}{dt} = -\frac{\upsilon_o}{R}$

or $\upsilon_o = -RC\frac{d\upsilon_i}{dt}$

$$= -RC\frac{d}{dt}(V_m \sin \omega t)$$

$\therefore$ $\upsilon_o = -\omega RCV_m \cos \omega t$

(The differentiator)

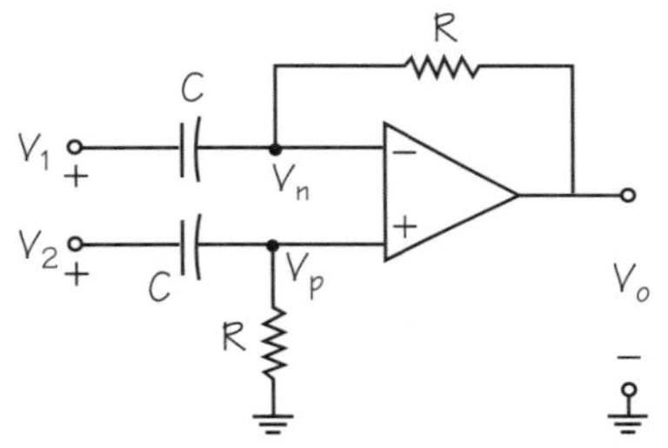

Fig. S8.15

15. The node equation—in phasor domain—at node υ_n gives:

$$\frac{V_n - V_1}{X_C} + \frac{V_n - V_o}{R} = 0 \quad \text{(Eqn. 15.1)}$$

Solving equation 15.1 for V_n results in:

$$V_n = \frac{V_1 R}{R + X_C} + \frac{V_o X_C}{R + X_C} \quad \text{(Eqn. 15.2)}$$

At node V_P, voltage divider will give us:

$$V_P = \frac{V_2 R}{R + X_C}$$

Since for ideal op-amp, $V_P = V_n$ (Eqn. 15.3)

Then, by equating equations 15.2 and 15.3:

$$\frac{V_2 R}{R + X_C} = \frac{V_1 R}{R + X_C} + \frac{V_o X_C}{R + X_C} \quad \text{(Eqn. 15.4)}$$

and $V_o = \frac{R}{X_C}(V_2 - V_1)$

since $X_C = \frac{1}{\omega C}$

$$V_o = \omega RC(V_2 - V_1) \quad \text{phasor domain} \quad \text{(Eqn. 15.5)}$$

In time domain, Eqn. 15.5 takes the form:

$$\upsilon_o = RC\frac{d}{dt}(\upsilon_2(t) - \upsilon_i(t))$$

(The differencing differentiator)

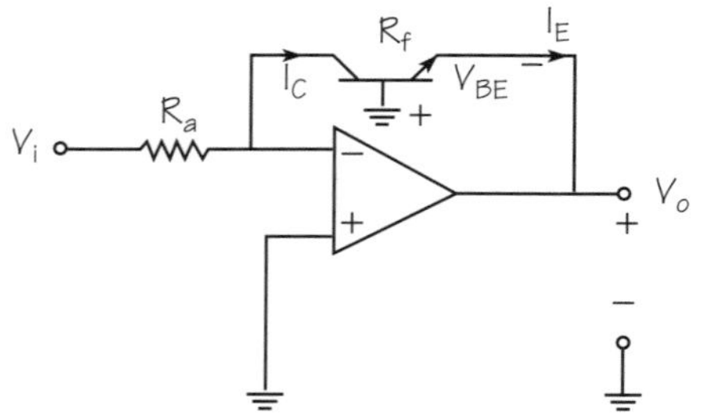

Fig. S8.16

16. Clearly, from Fig. S8.16, we see that

$$\upsilon_o = -V_{BE} \quad \text{(Eqn. 16.1)}$$

and $$I_C = \frac{\upsilon_i}{R} \quad \text{(Eqn. 16.2)}$$

For a diode or a p–n junction, the current is given by:

$$I = I_S\left[\exp\left(\frac{V}{V_T}\right) - 1\right] \quad \text{(Eqn. 16.3)}$$

where V is the applied voltage (V_{BE} in this case), $V_T = kT/q$. (Here k is Boltzmann constant, T is the temperature in K°, and q is the electron charge.) I_S is the reverse saturation current. In equation 16.3, $\exp(V/V_T) >> 1$ in the forward-bias configuration, then equation 16.3 can be approximated as:

$$I \approx I_s \exp\left(\frac{V}{V_T}\right) \quad \text{(Eqn. 16.4)}$$

Since for the transistor, $I_C = I_E$ (Eqn. 16.5)

Then equations 16.1, 16.2, 16.4 and 16.5 give:

$$I_C = I_S \exp\left(\frac{V_{BE}}{V_T}\right) = \frac{V_i}{R}$$

or

$$\exp\left(\frac{V_{BE}}{V_T}\right) = \frac{V_i}{I_S R}$$

Thus $$V_{BE} = V_T \ln\frac{V_i}{I_S R} \quad \text{(Eqn. 16.6)}$$

Equations 16.1 and 16.6 give:

$$V_o = -V_T \ln\frac{V_i}{I_S R}$$

(The logarithmic amplifier)

17. From the solution of P8.16:

$$I_C \approx I_E \approx I_S \exp\left(\frac{qV_{BE}}{kT}\right)$$

since the node υ_n is virtually grounded, then:

$$\upsilon_o = -RI_C = -RI_S \exp\left(\frac{qV_{BE}}{kT}\right)$$

Clearly, from Fig. S8.17 that $V_i = V_{BE}$.

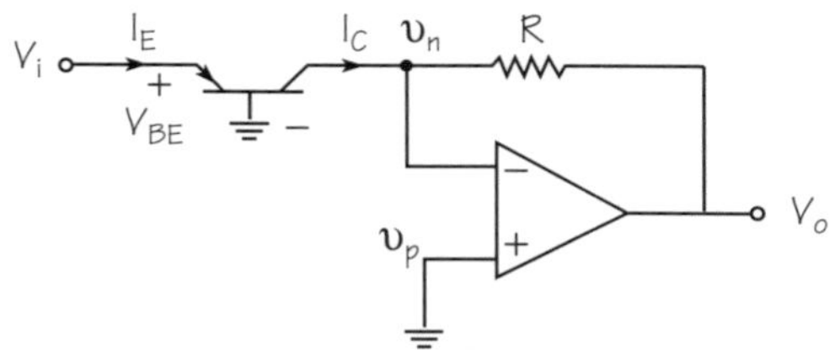

Fig. S8.17

Thus $\upsilon_o = -RI_S \exp\left(\frac{qV_{BE}}{kT}\right)$

(The exponentiator)

18. a) $\upsilon_n = \upsilon_p = 0$ since node V_P is grounded

$\therefore \quad i_C = i_i = C\frac{d\upsilon_o}{dt}$

$\therefore \quad \frac{d\upsilon_o}{dt} = \frac{i_C}{C}$

b) $i_i = G_m\upsilon_i$

in phasor domain

$$I_i = G_mV_i = I_C = \frac{V_o}{X_C} = \frac{V_o}{\frac{1}{\omega C}}$$

$\therefore \quad \frac{V_o}{V_i} = \frac{G_m}{\omega C}$

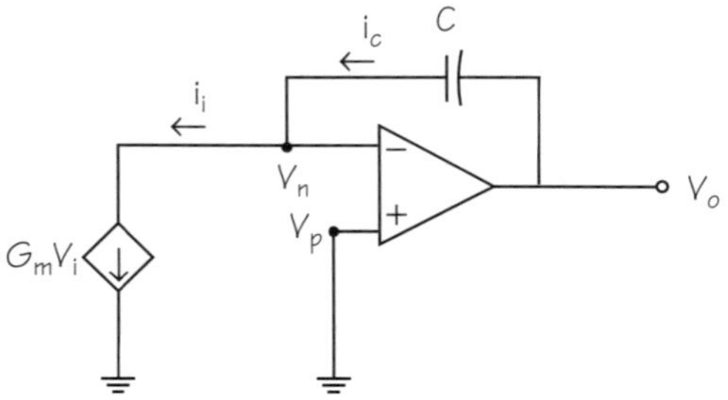

Fig. S8.18

By the definition of the voltage gain, A_V

$$A_V = \frac{V_o}{V_i} = 1 \quad \text{by the statement of the problem}$$

$\therefore \quad \frac{G_m}{\omega C} = 1$

$$\omega = \frac{G_m}{C}$$

or $\quad 2\pi f = \frac{G_m}{C}$

and $\quad f = \frac{G_m}{2\pi C}$

(Slew rate)

19. Assuming ideal op-amp, then I = 0. Thus:

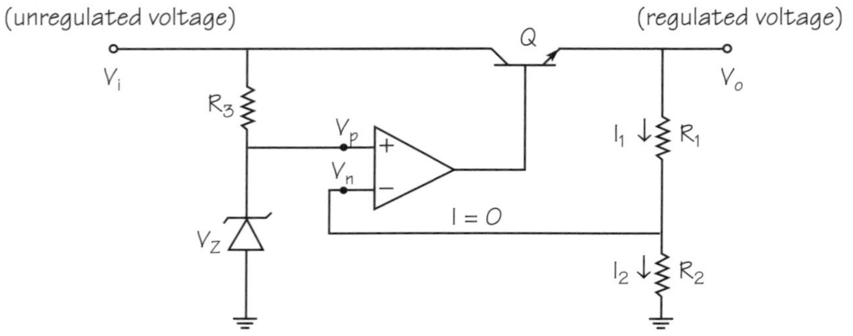

Fig. S8.19

$I_1 = I_2$, and $V_p = V_n = V_z$ (Eqn. 19.1)

$$I_1 = \frac{V_o - V_n}{R_1} = \frac{V_0 - V_z}{R_1} \quad \text{(Eqn. 19.2)}$$

and $$I_2 = \frac{V_n}{R_2} = \frac{V_z}{R_2} \quad \text{(Eqn. 19.3)}$$

Since $I_1 = I_2$, then from equations 19.2 and 19.3:

$$\frac{V_z}{R_2} = \frac{V_o - V_2}{R_1} \quad \text{(Eqn. 19.4)}$$

Solving equation 19.4 for V_o results in:

$$V_o = V_z\left(1 + \frac{R_1}{R_2}\right)$$

(Voltage regulator operational amplifiers)

20. Assume that the op-amp is ideal; thus:

$V_n = V_p = 0$ (Eqn. 20.1)

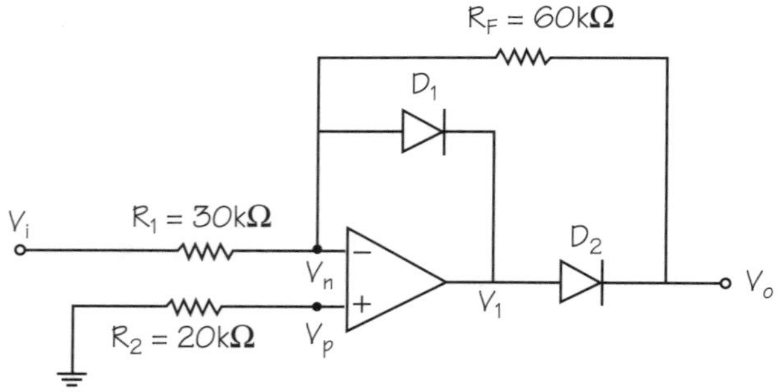

Fig. S8.20

i) For $V_1 \geq 0.7V$, D_1 conducts, then the voltage V_1 is given by:

$V_1 = V_n - 0.7 = -0.7V$

Since V_1 is negative, the diode D_2 is nonconducting and acts as an open circuit. Therefore, $V_o = 0$.

ii) For $V_1 < 0.7V$, V_i becomes positive and diode D_2 conducts when $V_1 \geq 0.7V$. Diode D_1 is nonconducting. The circuit in this case can be redrawn, as shown in Fig. S8.20b.

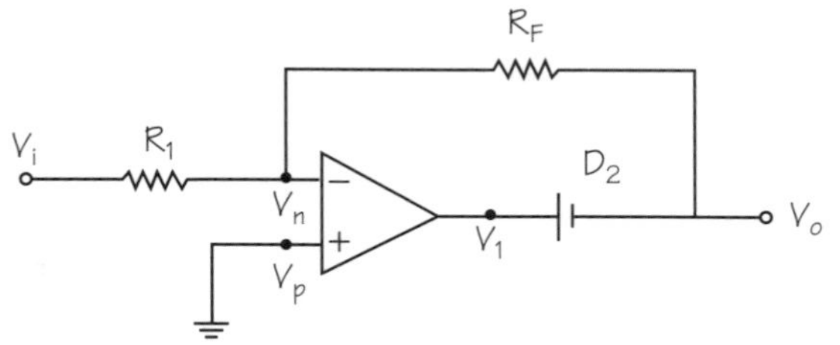

Fig. S8.20b

The node equation at V_n gives:

$$\frac{V_n - V_i}{R_1} + \frac{V_n - V_o}{R_F} = 0$$

Since $V_n = V_p = 0$

Then $V_o = -\frac{R_f}{R_1}V_i$

$$V_o = -\frac{60}{30}V_i = -2V_i$$

The results of V_o are summarized below:

$$V_o = \begin{Bmatrix} 0 & \text{for } V_i \geq 0.7V \\ -2V_i & \text{for } V_i < 0.7V \end{Bmatrix}$$

Notice that the built-in voltage for the diodes does not appear in the results of V_o.

(Inverting half-wave rectifier operational amplifiers)

21. a) Notice that in Fig. S8.21, we replace C by its equivalent impedance. That is:

$$Z_C = \frac{1}{j\omega C} = \frac{1}{sC}, \quad \text{where } s = j\omega.$$

It is easier to analyze the circuit by using Fig. S8.21b.

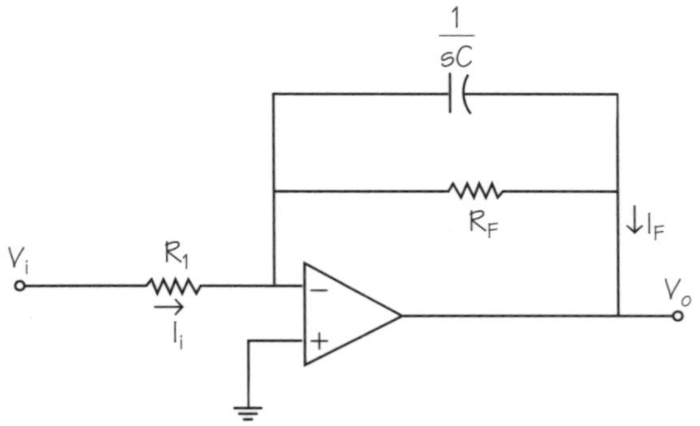

Fig. S8.21

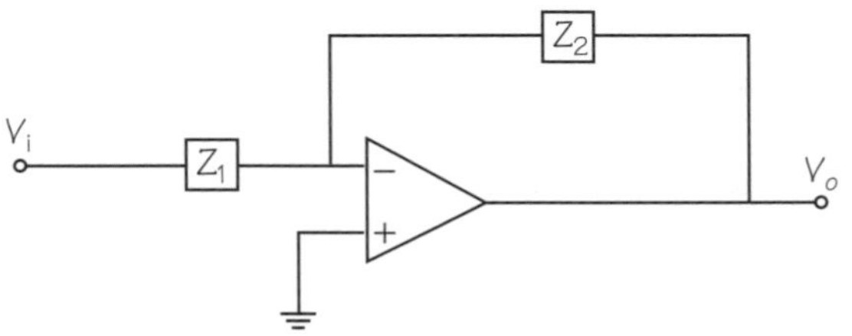

Fig. S8.21b

Here, $Z_1 = R_1$

and $Z_2 = R_F // \frac{1}{sC}$

Fig. S8.21b is nothing but inverting op. amp. with a feedback impedance of Z_2.
Thus, and as shown in previous similar problems, that:

$$V_o = -\frac{Z_F}{Z_i}V_i$$

or $\frac{V_o}{V_i}$ = Transfer function $= -\frac{Z_F}{Z_i}$

$$\frac{V_o}{V_i} = \frac{-R_F // \frac{1}{sC}}{R_1} = \frac{\frac{R_F}{R_1}}{1 + sRC}$$

b) From the transfer function, the corner frequency

$$\omega_C = \frac{1}{RC}$$

At frequency range $0 \le \omega < \omega_c$, the transfer function value

$$\left|\frac{V_o}{V_i}\right| \approx \frac{R_F}{R_1}.$$

At $\omega = \omega_c$, $\left|\frac{V_o}{V_i}\right| = \frac{1}{\sqrt{2}}\frac{R_F}{R_1}$

which corresponds to 20 $\log\frac{R_F}{R_1}$ (in dB)

As the frequency increases beyond ω_c, the gain is attenuated by 20 dB/decade. The plot is shown in Fig. S8.21c.

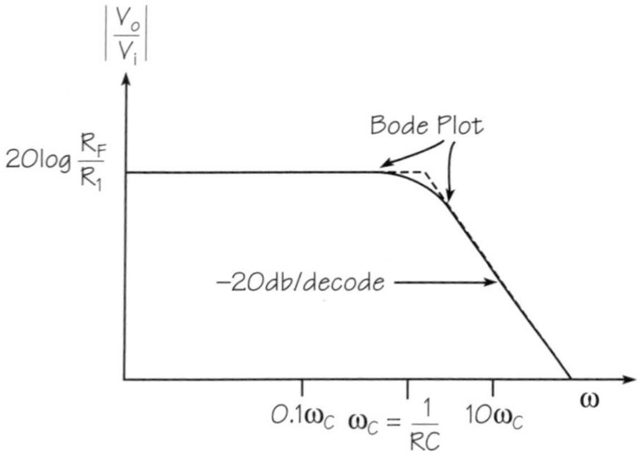

Fig. S8.21c

(Low-pass filter)

22. As you notice in the problem, there are four unknowns and three equations available for the solution, which are:

i) The corner frequency, ω_C

$$\omega_c = 2\pi f_c = \frac{1}{RC} \qquad \text{(Eqn. 22.1)}$$

ii) Given that $R = R_F // R_1$ (Eqn. 22.2)

iii) Since at high frequency the impedance of the capacitor is small, then the capacitor can be replaced with a short-circuit approximation. Thus the voltage gain is that for a non-interverting op. amp., which has been shown to be given by:

$$A_V = 1 + \frac{R_F}{R_1} = 10$$

As a designer electrical engineer, you are free to choose one element value, at will, to complete your design. For example, choose a reasonable value of the capacitor, C, that is available in your laboratory, such as C = 0.1μf.

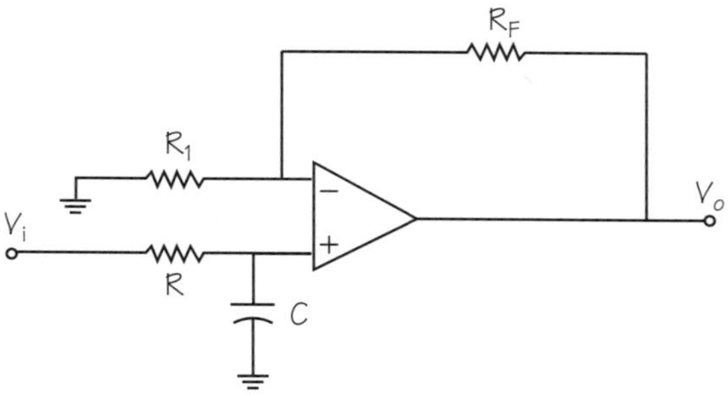

Fig. S8.22

From equation 22.1

$$\omega_c = 2\pi f_c = \frac{1}{RC}$$

$$2\pi \times 1000 = \frac{1}{R \times 0.1 \times 10^{-6}}$$

from which R = 1.59 kΩ.

By solving equations 22.2 and 22.3, simultaneously,

$$1.59 = \frac{R_F R_1}{R_F + R_1}, \text{ and}$$

$$10 = 1 + \frac{R_F}{R_1}$$

we obtain

$$R_1 = 1.78 \text{ k}\Omega$$
$$R_F = 16 \text{ k}\Omega$$

end of the design.

(First-order active low-pass filter)

23. a) To show that the circuit of Fig. S8.23a is a high-pass filter, we find the transfer function V_o/V_i. The node equation at the inverting terminal, V_n, gives:

$$\frac{V_n}{R_1} + \frac{V_n - V_o}{R_F} = 0 \qquad \text{(Eqn. 23.1)}$$

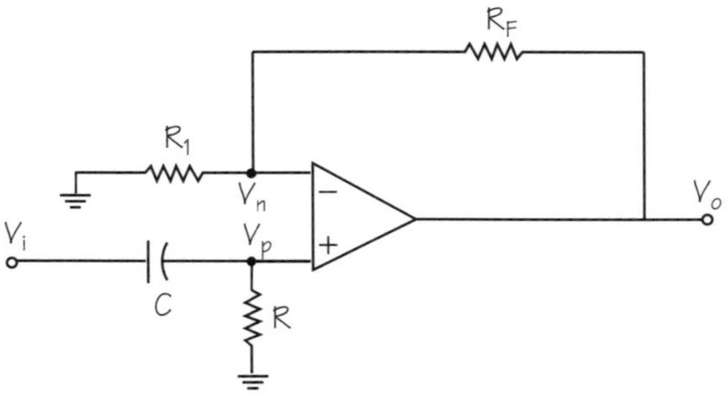

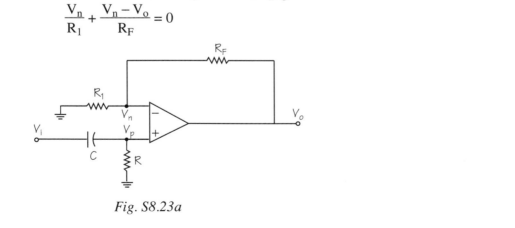

Fig. S8.23a

Solving equation 23.1 for V_n:

$$V_n = \frac{V_o}{1 + \frac{R_F}{R_1}} \qquad \text{(Eqn. 23. 2)}$$

At the non-inverting terminal, V_p, by using a voltage divider, we get:

$$V_p = \frac{V_i R}{R + \frac{1}{sC}} = \frac{V_i(sRC)}{1 + sRC} \qquad \text{(Eqn. 23.3)}$$

Since $V_n = V_p$ (assuming ideal op. amp.), thus:

$$\frac{V_o}{1 + \frac{R_F}{R_1}} = V_i \frac{sRC}{1 + sRC}$$

The transfer function V_o/V_i is therefore:

$$\frac{V_o}{V_i} = \frac{sRC}{1 + sRC}\left[1 + \frac{R_F}{R_1}\right] \qquad \text{(Eqn. 23.4)}$$

From equation 23.4, we notice:

i) At $\omega = 0$, the frequency response is zero.

ii) At high frequency the gain $\approx (1 + R_F/R_1)$. Since $|sRC| >> 1$.

The gain is almost constant. This indicates that the filter passes high frequencies and attenuates low frequencies, so it is a high-pass filter circuit.

b) $\omega_c = 2\pi f_c = \frac{1}{RC}$

$$2\pi \times 1000 = \frac{1}{R \times 0.01 \times 10^{-6}}$$

$$R = 15.9\ k\Omega$$

Since

$$R_1 \mathbin{//} R_F = 15.9$$

and $1 + \frac{R_F}{R_1} = 10$

Then $R_1 = 17.7\ k\Omega$

and $R_F = 159\ k\Omega$.

c)

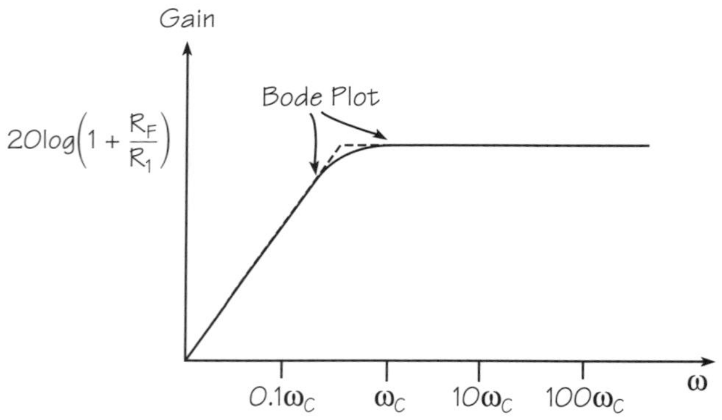

Fig. S8.23b

(High-pass filter)

24. It can be easier to redraw the circuit of Fig. P8.24. The new figure is shown in Fig. S8.24, where the common ground is separated into two ground points.

For the calculations of the dc gain, the capacitor acts as an open circuit. Since the input voltage is applied to the non-inverting terminal, the dc voltage is then given by:

$$A_V = 1 + \frac{R_F}{R_1}$$

$$A_V = 1 + \frac{100}{10} = 11$$

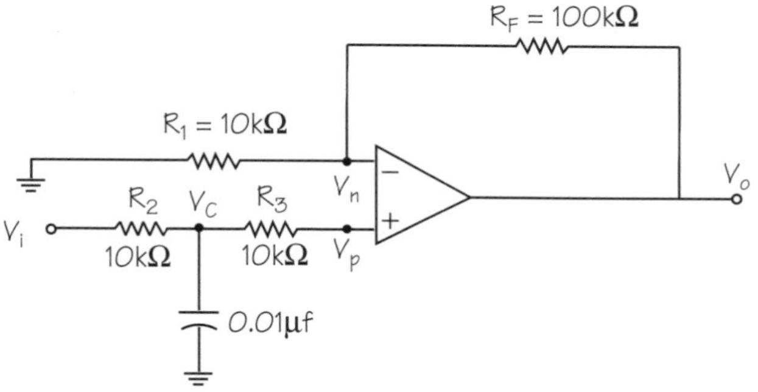

Fig. S8.24

The corner frequency $\omega_c = \dfrac{1}{R_2C}$

$$\omega_c = \frac{1}{\qquad\qquad} = 10^4 \text{ rad/sec.}$$

To determine the type of the filter, we solve for the transfer function V_o/V_i.
We assume an ideal op. amp.; thus:

$$V_n = V_P$$

Note that $V_P = V_C$ since the current entering the positive terminal of the op. amp. is zero.
At the inverting terminal:

$$V_n = \frac{V_o}{1 + \dfrac{R_F}{R_1}} \quad \text{(see Fig. S8.23)}$$

At the non-inverting terminal:

$$V_P = V_C = \frac{V_i \dfrac{1}{sC}}{R_2 + \dfrac{1}{sC}} \qquad \left\{\begin{matrix}\text{voltage}\\ \text{divider}\end{matrix}\right\}$$

Since $V_n = V_p$, then:

$$\frac{V_o}{1 + \dfrac{R_F}{R_1}} = \frac{V_i}{1 + sCR_2}$$

Thus the transfer function:

$$\frac{V_o}{V_i} = \frac{1 + \dfrac{R_F}{R_1}}{1 + sCR_2}$$

From this equation, we conclude that:

i) As $\omega \to 0$

$$\left|\frac{V_o}{V_i}\right| = 1 + \frac{R_F}{R_1}$$

ii) As $\omega \to \infty$

$$\left|\frac{V_o}{V_i}\right| = 0$$

Therefore, the circuit is a low-pass filter.

(Low-pass filter)

25. Z_F and Z_1, which are endorsed in the break lines rectangular of Fig. S8.25, are, respectively, the feedback impedance and the impedance of the circuit at the inverting terminal.

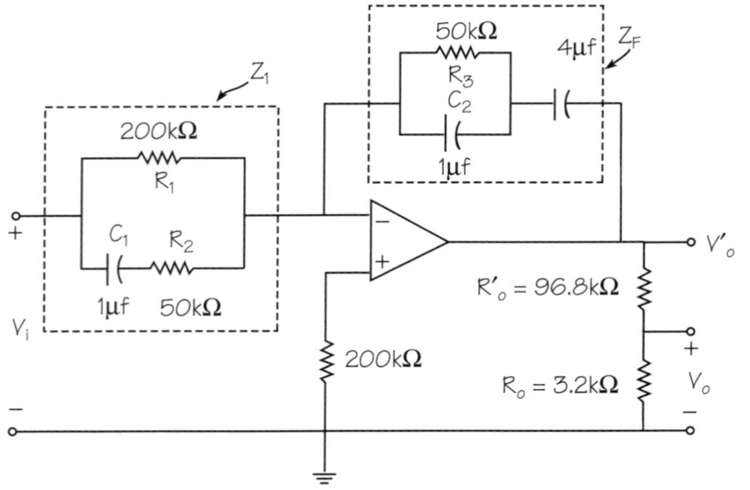

Fig. S8.25

$$Z_1 = \left(\frac{1}{sC_1} + R_2\right) // R_1$$

$$Z_1 = \frac{(sC_1R_2 + 1)R_1}{sC_1R_2 + sC_1R_1 + 1}$$

$$Z_1 = \frac{(s \times 1 \times 10^{-6} \times 50 \times 10^3 + 1) \times 200 \times 10^3}{s \times 1 \times 10^{-6} \times 200 \times 10^3 + S \times 10^{-6} \times 50 \times 10^3 + 1}$$

$$Z_1 = \frac{(0.05s + 1) \times 2 \times 10^5}{0.25s + 1} \Omega$$

$$Z_f = \left(R_3 // \frac{1}{sC_2}\right) + \frac{1}{sC_3}$$

$$Z_F = \frac{sR_3C_2 + sR_3C_3 + 1}{sC_3[sRC_2 + 1]}$$

$$Z_F = \frac{s \times 50 \times 10^3 \times 10^{-6} + s \times 50 \times 10^3 + 4 \times 10^{-6} + 1}{s \times 4 \times 10^{-6}\ [s \times 50 \times 10^3 \times 10^{-6} \times 1]}$$

$$Z_F = \frac{0.25s + 1}{} \Omega$$

The voltage gain with respect to V'_o

$$\frac{V_o}{V_i} = -\frac{Z_F}{Z_1}$$

By using voltage divider at the series connection of R'_o and R_o

$$V_o = \frac{V'_o R_o}{R_o + R'_o}$$

Thus, the voltage gain

$$\frac{V_o}{V_i} = \frac{V'_o R_o}{V_i(R_o + R'_o)}$$

$$\frac{V_o}{V_i} = -\frac{Z_F}{Z_1} \frac{R_o}{R_o + R'_o}$$

$$\frac{V_o}{V_i} = \frac{-(0.25s + 1)^2}{0.8s(0.05s + 1)^2} \times \frac{3.2}{3.2 + 96.8}$$

$$\frac{V_o}{V_i} = \frac{-\left(\frac{1}{4}s + 1\right)^2}{s\left(\frac{1}{20}s + 1\right)^2} = \frac{-(s + 4)^2}{s(s + 20)^2}$$

(Transfer function)

Grade Yourself

Circle the numbers of the questions you missed. Then fill in the total incorrect for each topic. If you answered more than three questions incorrectly, you need to focus on that topic. If a topic has less than three questions and you had at least one wrong, we suggest you study that topic also. Read your textbook, a review book, or ask your teacher for help.

Subject: Operational Amplifiers

Topic	Question Numbers	Number Incorrect
Inverting operational amplifiers	1	
Non-inverting operational amplifiers with feedback	2	
Dual-input operational amplifiers	3	
Weighted-differencing operational amplifiers	4	
Sign-switcher operational amplifiers	5	
Non-ideal inverting operational amplifiers	6	
A buffer-non-ideal operational amplifier	7	
Non-ideal operational amplifiers	8	
Non-inverting operational amplifiers with shorted feedback	9	
Input resistance for non-ideal operational amplifiers	10	
Dual-inverted weighted summer	11	
Weighted summer	12	
Non-inverting integrator	13	
The differentiator	14	
The differencing differentiator	15	
The logarithmic amplifier	16	
The exponentiator	17	
Slew rate	18	
Voltage regulator operational amplifiers	19	
Inverting half-wave rectifier operational amplifiers	20	
Low-pass filter	21, 24	
First-order active low-pass filter	22	
High-pass filter	23	
Transfer function	25	